C000181137

THE
ANARCHY

THE DARKEST DAYS OF MEDIEVAL ENGLAND

THE
ANARCHY

THE DARKEST DAYS OF MEDIEVAL ENGLAND

TERESA COLE

AMBERLEY

First published 2019

Amberley Publishing
The Hill, Stroud
Gloucestershire, GL5 4EP

www.amberley-books.com

British Library Cataloguing in Publication Data.
A catalogue record for this book is available from the British Library.

ISBN 978 1 4456 7849 8 (hardback)
ISBN 978 1 4456 7850 4 (ebook)

Typesetting by Aura Technology and Software Services, India.
Printed in the UK.

Contents

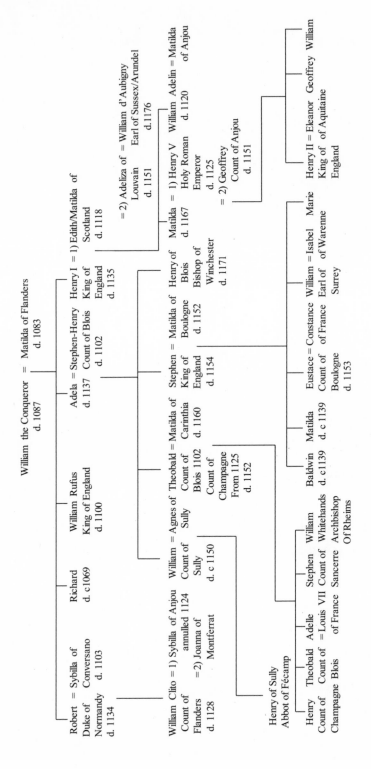

Fig. 1 Selected Members of the Family of William the Conqueror

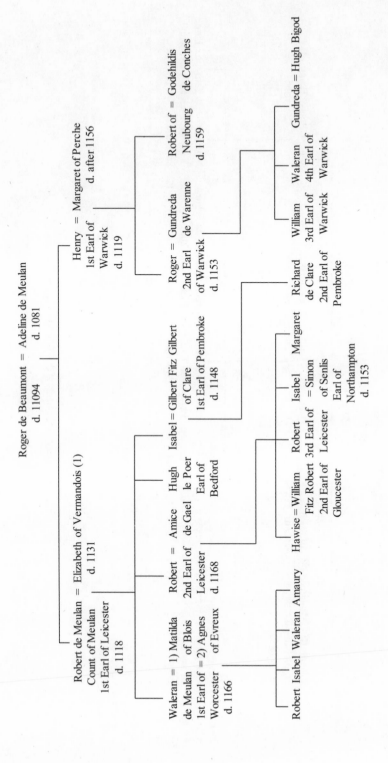

Fig. 2 Selected Members of the Beaumont Family

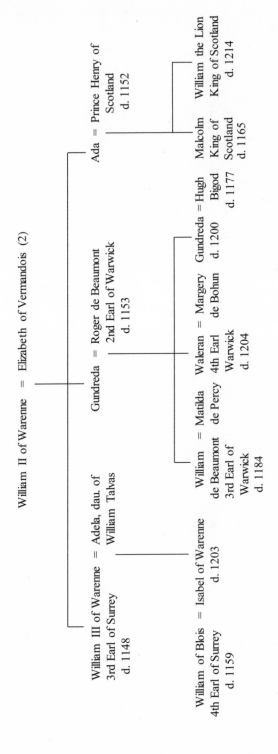

Fig. 3 Selected Members of the Warenne Family

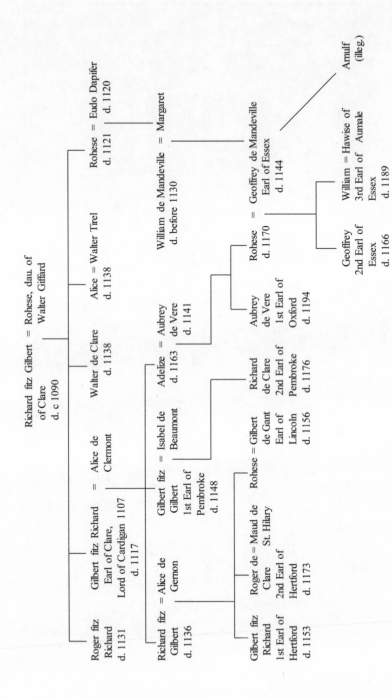

Fig. 4 Selected members of the Clare Family

THE WEST OF EUROPE

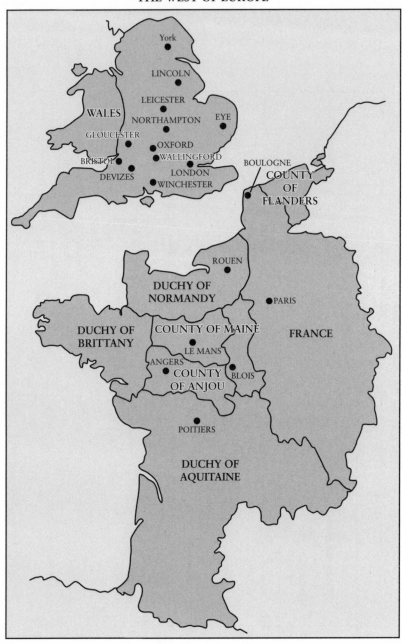

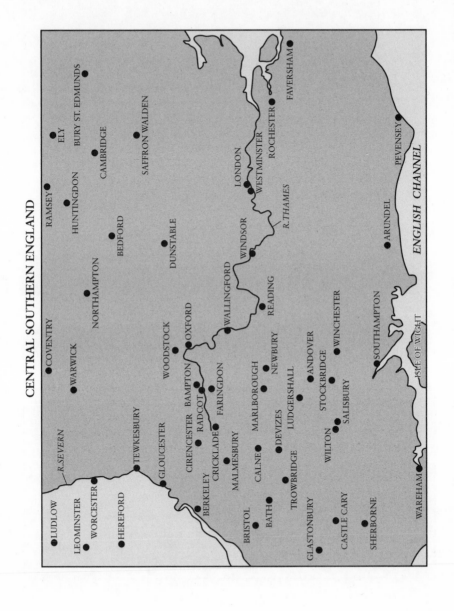

CENTRAL SOUTHERN ENGLAND

NORTHERN ENGLAND

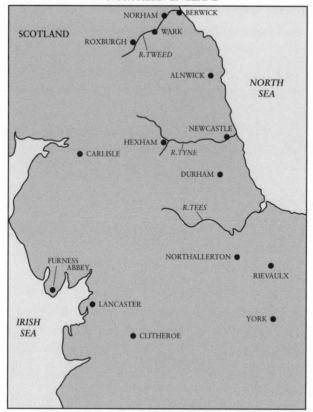

12TH CENTURY NORMANDY

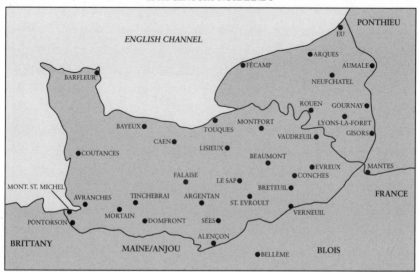

1

The Royal Cousins

Of all the large, unruly brood produced by William the Conqueror and his wife Matilda, only two can be said to have had a long and happy relationship with each other. Clearly there was no love lost between the three sons who survived to adulthood: Robert, William and Henry. For nearly twenty years they fought over the Conqueror's legacy, and there is some persuasive evidence that Henry, the ultimate victor, was involved in the death of one brother. He certainly kept the other one in fairly comfortable imprisonment for the last twenty-eight years of his life.

It was the two youngest children, Adela and Henry, who formed a lasting bond of friendship. They had a lot in common. Close in age, and some years younger than the other children, they seem to have been similar in ability and temperament and had the distinction of being children of a crowned king of England, rather than just a duke of Normandy. Adela was the elder. Though her birth date is not known precisely, it is likely to have been in 1067, probably before April in that year. Adela was born in Normandy but her younger brother Henry was born in England itself, at Selby in Yorkshire. The generally accepted date for his birth is September 1068. Although we have no details of their early upbringing, in all probability the royal siblings would have spent at least some years together, before being parted to undergo the different forms of education appropriate to the son and daughter of a king. Adela's would have prepared her for being a wife and mother, and for running an extensive household appropriate to her rank. In addition, she would have learnt her letters since William and Matilda believed in educating all their children, male and female. Henry might originally have been intended for the church. We know he received some of his education in England in the household of Osmund, Bishop of Salisbury. Such a plan would have been abandoned in the mid-1070s, when the death of one brother, and the rebellion of another, moved him several rungs up the ladder in terms of possible inheritance.

At the age of fourteen or fifteen Adela was married to Stephen-Henry, eldest son and heir to Count Theobald III of Blois. Stephen-Henry was some twenty years older than his bride, but, as was usual at the time, this would have been a political marriage arranged by the parents of each, the alliance of Blois with Normandy, its northern neighbour, bringing advantages to both sides. By the time he inherited Blois-Chartres in 1089, Stephen-Henry and Adela had at least one and possibly two sons, William, born around 1085, and Theobald, around 1088. More sons followed, the short-lived Odo around 1090, and then Stephen, variously described as being born in either 1092 or 1096. There were daughters, too, including Lucia-Mahaut, Agnes and Eleanor.

Whichever birth date is correct for Stephen, he would have had little opportunity to know his father, for in 1095 the count became swept up in the tide of religious fervour that followed Pope Urban's call for a crusade to the Holy Land. Jerusalem, so the Pope said, had been occupied by a people wholly opposed to Christianity, and he appealed to the Franks, 'men of exemplary courage and intrepidity', to go to the aid of their fellow Christians in the East. This appeal followed a plea for help from the Byzantine Emperor, Alexius Comnenus, who had merely asked for help in driving the Seljuk Turks from lands he had previously ruled in modern-day Turkey. Nevertheless, the Pope's translation of this into a crusade to reclaim the Holy Land carried far more popular appeal, and in the end no fewer than four armies made their way to Constantinople en route for Jerusalem.

Stephen-Henry was one of the leaders of the Norman-French army, which also contained his brother-in-law Robert Curthose of Normandy. Slow to set off, they over-wintered in southern

Italy and did not reach Constantinople until the spring of 1097. In the meantime, his lands and children in Blois were being cared for and very capably managed by his young wife. It says a lot for the confidence Stephen-Henry had in Adela that he seems to have had no qualms about appointing her regent in his absence, and the terms in which he wrote to her – apparently regularly – throughout his travels, suggest that theirs was a more loving partnership than many arranged marriages at the time. From Nicea in the summer of 1097, he addresses her as 'Adela, sweetest love, wife, and whatever the mind is better able to imagine' and is clearly awe-struck by the riches he has seen at the Byzantine court. He boasts to his wife that there is no one in the whole army that the Emperor trusts or favours more than he, and that he and his followers have been showered with precious gifts. The army was about to move on to Antioch, and in his letter he declares they would be in Jerusalem in five weeks unless Antioch prevented them. Antioch duly did.

Initially all went well, as they took part in the Battle of Dorylaeum and shared in the great riches plundered from the Turks following their victory. At Antioch, however, they found a well-prepared, well-defended city. Stephen-Henry himself describes it as 'fortified with incredible strength and almost impregnable'.

The Siege of Antioch began at the end of 1097, and was barely halfway through when the count again wrote to his wife in March 1098. In this letter the general impression given is one of confidence, by the end, though, there is a sober recognition that this might not end well. He charges Adela to do her duty, and to govern her lands, children and vassals well and with honour. The implication is that this may be a farewell letter, though he reassures her that he will return as soon as he possibly can.

In fact, that return was to be sooner than either of them might have imagined, and the shadow of it probably hung over the family for decades to come. According to Orderic Vitalis, a monk-chronicler of the time, when Antioch finally fell on 3 June 1098, 'Stephen ... was absent, being, as he said, detained by severe illness at Alexandretta whither he had gone for the recovery of his health.' It is highly possible that the count had fallen ill in the months since his letter, when he had assured his wife he was well and unharmed. There is, however, much more to the story than that. Immediately before the fall of Antioch it was clear that a large army was on its way to relieve the city. When the crusaders finally got inside they failed to take the citadel, and were almost at once themselves besieged by this relieving army.

Orderic Vitalis gives possibly the most acceptable version of Stephen-Henry's absence, although even he uses the phrase, 'as he said', as if not entirely believing it. There were, however, a number of others. One suggestion is that the count deserted his friends as late as 2 June, having seen, or at least heard of, the size of the army moving against them. Another says he was one of the 'funambuli', the deserters who escaped from Antioch by night, letting themselves down from the walls on ropes. Even if he had been ill at Alexandretta, a fortified town relatively close by, there would have been an expectation that once the crusaders themselves became besieged he would have gathered his forces, stated as being some 4,000 men, and come to their rescue. Instead, Stephen-Henry decided the cause was hopelessly lost and ran away.

Fleeing to the city of Tarsus, he was probably not aware that Antioch had initially been taken. Later, however, deserters would have told him of the true situation, and even then he stuck to his idea that all was lost. Worse than this, when the Emperor Alexius sent a force to aid the trapped crusaders, Stephen-Henry persuaded them that it was far too late to help them and sent them away. Henry of Huntingdon, another chronicler of the time, says he 'induced him to retire by telling him with tears that all the Franks had perished'.

Taking the riches he had accumulated, the count made his way home, only to learn that, far from being a hopeless cause, the crusaders had fought their way out of Antioch and even taken Jerusalem itself. Vitalis describes the 'shame and confusion attached to the base deserters of the crusade in the sight of all men'.

Nor was that the end of the matter. The crusaders had taken an oath to get to Jerusalem. Labelled now as cowards and oath-breakers, even the Pope declared the deserters must go back and complete what they had promised or face excommunication. No doubt the shame was felt by the whole family, maybe even the whole county. Certainly Stephen-Henry found no peace at home.

Adela, too, was constantly telling him he must return to the East, 'reminding him of it even amidst the endearments of conjugal caresses', so Vitalis claims, though how a monk would know this is hard to guess. The conjugal caresses may have resulted in another son, Henry, whose birth dates have been variously given as 1096, 1099 or even as late as 1101. If the latter, then by this time his father had already bowed to pressure and returned to the Holy Land, with many of the other deserters, in what became known as the 'Crusade of the Fainthearted'.

This thoroughly disorganised affair, suffering repeated attacks and massacres at the hands of the Turks, eventually reached Jerusalem, whereupon many of the crusaders immediately returned home. Stephen-Henry, though, stayed on, possibly hoping to overturn his reputation for cowardice by helping King Baldwin of Jerusalem fend off an invasion of Egyptian Fatimid warriors. In May 1102, seriously underestimating the numbers of the enemy in the area, they made an expedition to Ramla, a town between Jerusalem and the sea. There, facing overwhelming forces, they became cut off in a tower. Baldwin managed to escape, eventually making his way back to Jerusalem. For the others, including Stephen-Henry, however, there was nothing for it but an almost suicidal attempt to break out, and he met his death there in Ramla on 19 May 1102.

At the age of thirty-five, Adela, who had once again been left as regent in Blois, found herself a widow with a family of children ranging in age from seventeen down to a baby of maybe two years old. William, the eldest, had already been recognised and acknowledged as heir before his father's final departure. He was still too young, however, to take on the role and responsibilities of Count of Blois formally, so Adela's regency continued.

In the absence of a father figure – and Adela showed no inclination to marry again – the education of the younger children would now be solely in her hands, as would the direction of their future careers. As such, a great deal would depend on her own character. She is known to have been pious, devout and a strong supporter of the church. Bishop Ivo of Chartres, and Anselm, Archbishop of Canterbury, were counted among her friends and correspondents, and she is regarded as a saint by the Catholic Church. This is not to say, however, that she was in any way unworldly. Scholars, poets, artists and musicians were attached to her household, and she showed a shrewd intelligence in managing both her estates and her children. Orderic Vitalis was clearly a fan, devoting an entire chapter to this 'illustrious mother and her prosperous children'.

We don't know what contact Adela had had with her brothers up to this point. Their father's death in 1087 had left Robert as Duke of Normandy, while William Rufus had contrived to become King of England. Henry was left no land but £5,000 in silver, and for the next few years his existence was precarious, at one time lord of the Cotentin peninsular in Normandy, then forced into exile by both brothers uniting against him. By the time Robert set off for the Holy Land with Stephen-Henry, however, Henry had firmly attached himself to the court of William Rufus.

He was a member of the king's hunting party in the New Forest on that fateful day in August 1100 when William Rufus met his death. Henry of Huntingdon tells us simply that 'Walter Tirel unintentionally shot the king with an arrow aimed at a stag,' but it is fairly sure Henry was close to his brother at the time. It is the incredibly opportune timing of the accident and the actions of Henry afterwards that have raised the question as to whether or not he had plotted the death of his brother – the third member of the family to die while hunting in the New Forest – although no suspicion seemed to attach to him at the time.

Involved or not, Henry certainly acted swiftly to take advantage of the king's death. Leaving his brother's body for others to deal with, he immediately rode to nearby Winchester and, after a brief argument, took possession of the royal treasury. Then, with the consent of the few available nobility, he had himself declared king, and within three days was crowned and anointed as such at Westminster Abbey.

We have no clue as to how Adela viewed these events, or indeed her feelings towards her elder brothers in general, but it is more than likely that the tale of how Henry acted swiftly to take the crown soon became a staple of family history. Only weeks later Robert returned from the Holy Land, but given the circumstances of their parting before Antioch it seems unlikely he would have sought the company or the support of his brother-in-law in Blois, and by the time he launched his own unsuccessful invasion of England, Stephen-Henry was already committed to return to Jerusalem.

In the autumn of 1100, Henry gained not only a crown but also a wife. He married Edith, the daughter of Malcolm, King of Scotland, who then changed her name to the more acceptably Norman 'Matilda'. Her mother, the saintly Margaret, was descended from the old Saxon royal line, so this marriage united the old royal dynasty with the new. This apparently fulfilled a deathbed prophecy of Edward the Confessor and no doubt there was eager anticipation to see what fruit would be produced by the union. It may have caused some disappointment, then, when the first child turned out to be a girl. There is no specific record of the date of her birth but all the indications point to it occurring early in February 1102, and she was christened Matilda, after her mother and grandmother.

Henry may have been particularly disappointed in that he already had at least two and probably three illegitimate sons among the numerous children produced by his many mistresses before the date of his marriage. It would have been a further blow when his brother Robert, who also married in 1100, was presented with a son and heir in October 1102. Soon after this, however, Edith/Matilda was pregnant again, and in August 1103 Henry had a legitimate male heir of his own. Both these boys were christened William, no doubt emphasising their descent from the mighty Conqueror. Henry's son was given the suffix 'Atheling' or 'Adelin', the old Saxon term traditionally attached to the acknowledged heir, meaning 'throne-worthy.' The Norman equivalent, 'Clito', was attached to the name of Robert's son.

Neither brother produced any further legitimate children. Robert's wife, Sybilla of Conversano, died six months after giving birth, and it may well have been that Henry, with his own dysfunctional family in mind, decided that one legitimate heir, with no potential challengers in the family, was quite enough. At the time, young Matilda was no doubt seen as quite irrelevant to the succession to the throne. She was a girl so her only function was to be married off to obtain the best possible advantage for her country, wherever and whenever that might be. Her early years were almost certainly passed within her mother's household, and about this time, according to William of Malmesbury, Edith/ Matilda began to retire from the bustle of the travelling court and establish herself in her own court at Westminster. It is tempting to see this withdrawal as the queen wanting to be close to her children during their early years, but she is also clearly indulging her own tastes, and Malmesbury declares there was 'no part of royal magnificence wanting to her' in her 'superb dwelling'.

Henry was becoming increasingly involved in Norman affairs. In the summer of 1104 he made a provocative expedition through Normandy to the castle of Domfront, which had been given to him a dozen years before and which he had retained ever since. Unchallenged on his journey, he then summoned his brother to meet him and lectured him on his incompetence in ruling the duchy. The following year Henry was back, this time with a full-scale invasion force, ostensibly to rescue the churches of Normandy from the ravages of the robber barons that Robert was unable or unwilling to deal with. Here, though, he met a check that was none of his brother's doing; and this is when we find the first real involvement of Adela in her younger brother's affairs.

The Investiture Controversy was a dispute raging at the time between the pope and monarchs in Western Europe. These monarchs had traditionally selected their own bishops and archbishops, who were also major landowners and advisors. They had 'invested' them with ring and crozier, the symbols of their religious authority, and received homage from them for their 'temporalities', the lands attached to the office. Now the pope demanded that 'lay persons' such as monarchs, should not be involved in selecting or investing these higher clergy, since that was solely the business of the church.

When Henry came to the throne in 1100, his Archbishop of Canterbury was Anselm, a former monk of the prestigious monastery of Bec in Normandy. Anselm had been appointed, with reluctance on both sides, by William Rufus, but at that time was in exile at Lyons following serious disagreements with the king. Before settling at Lyons he had attended the pope in Rome and been present at the Easter Council in 1098. There Pope Urban in no uncertain terms had condemned the appointing and investing of clergy by lay persons, and fixed excommunication – cutting a person off from the church community and its services – as the penalty for a bishop so appointed, the person appointing him and anyone else consecrating a bishop so appointed. Anselm took the message to heart.

Immediately after his coronation Henry wrote to Anselm in terms of friendship, earnestly inviting him to return to England. He was welcomed with great joy, but when the king wanted to re-invest him with ring and crozier and receive his homage, Anselm instantly refused. The waters were considerably muddied in England by the fact that the Conqueror, with the connivance of his archbishop and friend, Lanfranc, had managed to fudge the issue for his lifetime. Henry claimed he was only seeking to do what the pope had permitted his father to do. In any case, there was a new pope since Urban had laid down his rules at the Easter Council, and the king no doubt hoped that Paschal II would have a new approach to the matter. Eventually it was suggested Anselm himself should visit Paschal, and when it became clear the position remained unchanged, Henry's own envoy dropped heavy hints that the archbishop might as well stay away from England. Once more Anselm settled down at Lyons, and that was how matters stood at the beginning of 1105.

At this point the pope began to lose patience. In March 1105 he excommunicated the bishops Henry had appointed, as well as the king's chief advisor, Robert de Meulan. This last was clearly seen as a warning that, if Henry did not mend his ways, he too would be excommunicated – not a happy position for a man at that time leading armies across Normandy with the avowed aim of protecting the church.

It is here that we first find evidence that Adela, Countess of Blois, was inclined to favour her younger brother over her elder, and to use her influence in his favour. By May 1105 Henry's allies were starting to drift away. Helias of Maine withdrew his men from the siege of Falaise and others followed his example. Adela had been particularly supportive of Anselm in his exile, and when she now apparently fell seriously ill, it seemed natural for Anselm to visit her. We don't know if the illness was real or feigned, or whether Adela specifically requested Anselm's visit. It may well be that she was among those who knew he had left Lyons to travel north, in order to deliver to Henry personally the news that the pope had approved his excommunication. Whatever brought about their meeting, it was a fortuitous one for Henry.

Adela, making a remarkable recovery from her illness, now used all her influence to set up a meeting between Anselm and Henry at L'Aigle. There, with their earlier friendship renewed and goodwill on all sides, a compromise on investitures was worked out. Henry would give up the right to invest with ring and crozier, but homage would still be paid for the 'temporalities', the lands that went with the office. In addition, although appointments would be formally nominated by the king, he would do so only on the advice of the clergy. After a short delay the pope's approval was received, albeit suggesting he regarded this as a temporary concession, and Henry could now be regarded as fully reconciled with the church.

This was in the spring of 1106 and soon afterwards the king was in Normandy, again at the head of an army. On 28 September of that year, Robert's rash decision to offer his brother a battle led to his own crushing defeat, the loss of his duchy and his imprisonment in England for the rest of his life. Thanks to Adela's timely intervention Henry was utterly triumphant, and was now clearly a major power in Western Europe.

The Battle of Tinchebrai in September 1106 was, in fact, a turning point in many lives, not least those of Adela's sons. She had been managing their futures for a number of years and, possibly with the disastrous example of her brothers before her, had clearly decided there should be no such competition among her own children. The youngest, Henry, had already been dealt with, being dedicated to the church as a child oblate at the age of two or three years. By 1106 he was receiving his education at the famous monastery of Cluny.

The destiny of the eldest, William, might also be thought settled since he had been designated and accepted as heir before his father's death. Yet again, however, Adela had shown her strength and decisiveness. William had in some way failed to achieve her approval as Count of Blois. He has been designated 'William the Simple' with the suggestion that he was lacking in mental ability. However, other stories tell of a violent temper and an assault and threat to murder a bishop. In 1104 he was married to Agnes of Sully, an heiress and member of Adela's household. Subsequently, for whatever reason and however Adela managed it, William was shunted aside to become Count of Sully, and from 1107 onwards it was the second son, Theobald, who would be designated Count of Blois.

Like his brother before him, Theobald was still under age so Adela's regency continued. This was not merely a ploy to keep her in power, however, since she clearly had a different plan for her third son, Stephen, who at that time would have been at most fourteen years old and was probably younger. He had been brought up to expect a future as a knight, and from now on Adela seems to have steered him firmly in the direction of her brother Henry. One account suggests Stephen joined Henry's court as early as 1106, but this decisive move could have occurred up to half-a-dozen years later. His first visit to England was not before 1113, and he would therefore have been too late to meet his young cousin Matilda, who by this time had already left her native land.

Henry's growing wealth, power and prestige had been noted by others besides Adela, in particular by the King of the Germans, Henry V. This Henry had rebelled against and overthrown his own father, ostensibly backing the pope on the issue of investitures. Having achieved his throne in 1105, however, he found himself equally reluctant to give up that right. His position was more complicated, though, than that of the English Henry. At that time Germany was made up of a collection of states – principally Saxony, Lotharingia, Franconia, Swabia and Bavaria – but for centuries, the German kings had claimed to be the heirs of Charlemagne, ruling lands far beyond these boundaries – in northern Italy, Bohemia, Austria and Burgundy – under the title Holy Roman Emperor. To hold together and govern so many disparate and competitive entities was no easy matter and many years before the tactic had emerged of vesting considerable administrative power in the church leaders, the bishops, abbots and particularly archbishops spread throughout the land. As William of Malmesbury expressed it, 'to keep in check the ferocity of these nations (the emperors) had conferred almost all the country on the church; most wisely considering that the clergy would not so soon cast off their fidelity to their lord as the laity.' To make this work, however, there needed to be close co-operation between the German king and the church, something that had not been a problem when the Holy Roman Emperor had been seen as protector of the pope. Indeed, for some considerable time he had been a decisive influence on who would be appointed to that office. Even Pope Paschal conceded, in a controversial 'Privilege' addressed to Henry V: 'Divine providence has so ordered that there is a singular union between your kingdom and the holy Roman church.'

When this relationship began to break down, however, as it did in the latter part of the eleventh century, it left the monarch in an extremely vulnerable position. Given a choice between backing the pope or the emperor, there was no knowing which the clergy would prefer and any split could be eagerly seized on by potential rebels within the empire – as, indeed, Henry himself had done in order to depose his father. It was an additional complication that, in theory at least, the emperor was an elected monarch rather than in an hereditary post, a position which the German states were keen to emphasise, despite the fact that Henry V was the fourth of his Salian line to be elected.

Born around 1086, he had become King of the Germans in 1099 when his father crowned him as such. He added to this the title 'King of the Romans' in 1101 when his brother Conrad died. It was, however, for the pope alone to anoint and crown him as Holy Roman Emperor, and this Pope Paschal refused to do as long as Henry clung to the right to invest his bishops with the symbols of their authority, the ring and crozier. Without such a coronation, Henry's position at home in the German lands was considerably weakened. Having restored these lands to order within a few years of his father's death, he was now seeking for a way to put pressure on the pope. An impressive show of strength might do it, with a tightening of his control over the lands of northern Italy. In order to achieve this, he needed money, and casting around for a potential source of sufficient funds his eye fell on the wealthiest state in Western Europe, England.

King Henry of England had wealth. Furthermore, he had the potential for greater wealth due to the efficiency of the tax system established by the Anglo-Saxons and taken over wholesale by their Norman conquerors. He also had a daughter, albeit one who was only six years old, while the German king had not yet taken a wife. The potential for a deal was obvious. First contact was made when the English king Henry was in Normandy in 1108, and the representatives of the two states quickly thrashed out the details. One of the channels used to advance the German suit seems to have been Queen Edith/Matilda, at this time acting as a most competent regent in England for her husband. The emperor was later to write and thank her for her support.

The deal was, of course, a business deal, as were all marriages of the nobility at the time. There were clear advantages for both monarchs. For the English Henry, an alliance with the mighty Holy Roman Emperor would strengthen his hand in dealings with the new King Louis of France. Nor would his prestige be at all harmed by having the emperor as a son-in-law. In return for this connection he was prepared to find a dowry of 10,000 silver marks to go with his daughter. For the German Henry, there were other benefits besides the money. He would obtain a wife and the potential mother of sons to carry on his line. True, there would be some delay in this, but the youth of his bride meant that she could be carefully trained for the part she was to play as empress, whereas an older partner might be less amenable. He may also have had in mind that his future father-in-law had just managed to settle his own problems with investitures, and might be able to help find a solution to suit the German king and ease his way to the coronation he so badly needed.

By Easter of 1109 when the English king returned to his realm, the deal was done. Matilda, of course, had no say in the matter. Child as she was, however, she would already have been well aware that it was her duty to make an appropriate marriage for the benefit of her country; it was maybe just a little sooner than she had expected.

The Whitsun court that year was a splendid affair. Robert of Torigny, a chronicler writing in Normandy a little later, but with excellent sources, declares that the envoys sent from Germany were 'conspicuous by their personal appearance and the splendour of their appointments', and it is certain that the English did not want to be outshone. The terms of the agreement were confirmed and oaths of betrothal were sworn in the name of the emperor. Then the king set about raising the money for his daughter's dowry.

Geld was a form of taxation based on landholding. It had been originally established as a way of raising money to pay off marauding Vikings – the Danegeld – but having been established, it had been continued ever since as a most useful source of finance, first for Anglo-Saxon kings, and latterly for the Normans. Land was reckoned in hides, a variable acreage depending on the quality and productiveness of the land involved. A typical geld was charged at the rate of a shilling per hide. Many of the chronicles of the time made very little of Matilda's marriage beyond saying that the king 'gave her to the emperor', but the raising of the dowry called for comment. 'The king taxed every hide of land in England three shillings for his daughter's marriage,' reported Henry of Huntingdon, while the long-running Anglo-Saxon Chronicle, kept for centuries by monks in different abbeys, declared that 1110 was 'a year of much distress from the taxes raised for his daughter's dowry'. It did add, though, that the weather was bad 'by which the crops were greatly injured and nearly all the fruit on the trees destroyed throughout the country,' which loss can hardly be put down to the king.

Even with the efficiency of the system, it took some time to assemble 10,000 silver marks and it was not until February 1110, about the time of her eighth birthday, that envoys came again from the German lands to escort the child to her future husband. She left accompanied by 'manifold treasure', and also, according to Vitalis, a crowd of young men hoping to find positions, wealth and honour at the emperor's court. In fact, that was not at all part of his plan, and he gave them all rich presents and sent them home. Apart from a few chaplains and, no doubt, a personal servant or two, Matilda was to grow up surrounded by the people she was to rule.

Travelling via Boulogne she first met her future husband at Liège. She was eight years old and he about twenty-four. Nevertheless, she was received with all the honour due to a future queen. The royal court moved on to Utrecht, where, at Easter, on 10 April 1110, the formal betrothal took place, each now speaking their promises in person. Over the next few months a progress down the Rhine visited Cologne, Speyer and Worms before returning in July to Mainz. Matilda was too young to be married but not too young to be crowned as Queen of the Germans and Romans, and her coronation was planned for 25 July, the Feast of St James. This was a significant date for the empire since, among the treasures held by the Holy Roman Emperor, was the hand of the apostle James, the provenance of which could be traced back at least as far as the sixth century.

Traditionally the coronation would have been performed by the Archbishop of Mainz, the most senior cleric in the kingdom. The previous incumbent had died the year before, however, and the vacancy not yet filled, so it was Frederick, Archbishop of Cologne, who performed the anointing and crowning. To ease the ceremony for the child in her formal coronation robes, she was carried by Bruno, Archbishop of Trier, and when all was done it was the same Archbishop Bruno who was given charge of the new queen, to take her away to his cathedral city on the river Moselle where she would spend the next few years learning the language, laws, culture and customs of her new country.

In the meantime the German king was not slow in putting in place the plans for his expedition to Rome. Almost immediately after Matilda's coronation, he set off with an army that some estimates put at 30,000 men. Crossing into northern Italy he opened negotiations with Pope Paschal, the result of which was an apparent agreement. Abbot Suger, a French chronicler contemporary with these events, declares, however, that Henry was only pretending when he said he would give up investitures and that he promised this and other things with the sole intention of securing entry to Rome. Indeed, when he and his followers arrived at Rome in February 1111, the agreement at once broke down. Paschal refused to crown Henry, whereupon the infuriated emperor cast caution to the wind and seized the pope, along with sixteen cardinals, and carried them off to imprisonment. 'Never,' says Suger, 'have Christians heard of such a deed by a Christian.' Nor was the imprisonment in any way gentle. According to Suger, who was well placed to know, Henry treated the cardinals disgracefully, seized the pope's mitre and insignia, and didn't hold back from manhandling the pontiff himself, injuring him in the process. For two months the pope held out against this treatment before giving in and allowing Henry what he wanted. In a so-called 'Privilege' granted to the emperor, he agreed that Henry would be allowed to invest with ring and crozier. Furthermore, he swore he would take no action against the emperor for the injuries he had suffered at his hands, and that he would crown him according to the prescribed ritual without delay.

On 13 April 1111 Henry finally achieved his ambition, being anointed and crowned as Holy Roman Emperor by Pope Paschal in St Peter's Basilica in Rome. At the same time, he was given a further confirmation by the pope of his right to appoint and invest bishops and archbishops, this being dressed up as a special concession due to the close relationship between the empire and the church. Well satisfied, Henry set out for home, rewarding one of his 'negotiators', Adalbert, with the Archbishopric of Mainz.

Adalbert had taken over from Archbishop Bruno of Trier as Henry's chief advisor, and had worked closely with the emperor up to this point. Within a year, however, the relationship had soured and the former friend had been seized and thrown into prison. Henry accused Adalbert of inciting rebellion, seizing castles and plotting against his life. The archbishop claimed he was simply being punished for siding with the reform movement within the church. This may well have amounted to the same thing, for by now the 'Privilege' granted to Henry, and particularly the way in which it had been obtained, was causing outrage throughout Western Europe. A council of clergy, led by Guy, Archbishop of Vienne, had demanded that Henry be excommunicated and the privilege so obtained be declared void. Mindful of his oath to take no revenge, Paschal held back from excommunication, but he confirmed the findings of a Lateran synod in March 1112 that the grant of privilege was indeed invalid. As so often before in this long-running dispute, church leaders within the empire once again had to decide whether to follow their emperor or their pope.

In the midst of all this, and possibly to provide a unifying distraction, the young Queen Matilda was married. She was still a month short of her twelfth birthday when, in a magnificent ceremony at Worms on 6 January 1114, she became the wife of the Holy Roman Emperor. No one, according to the chroniclers, could remember such a mighty assembly of clergy and nobility – five archbishops, thirty bishops, five dukes and countless numbers of abbots and lower nobles. No expense was spared in celebrating the union of Henry and Matilda, despite the disparity of their ages, but this great gathering also provided a perfect opportunity for exchanging views, gathering supporters and plotting plots.

Almost immediately afterwards vague unrest broke out into open rebellion. The citizens of Mainz rose up in favour of their archbishop, while Saxony and Rhineland followed the pattern set by Henry himself a decade before in taking up arms against their emperor on behalf of the pope. The defection of Frederick, Archbishop of Cologne, to the papal party must have been a mighty boost for the rebels, especially when he finally pronounced on German soil the sentence of excommunication of the emperor that the pope had sanctioned two years earlier. It was becoming difficult to see how a Holy Roman Emperor could hold his empire together if he was no longer seen as 'holy'. Two defeats for the imperial army in quick succession made negotiations vital and the services of, among others, Bruno, Archbishop of Trier, brought about at least a temporary truce. Archbishop Adalbert was released – more dead than alive, as he claimed – and was formally reconciled to the emperor, but it was clear that some kind of settlement with the pope was needed to lay the basis for a lasting peace.

A reason to return to Italy was provided by the death in July 1115 of Matilda of Tuscany. This formidable lady, who had seen off two husbands and led her own army into battle, held a great swathe of land across northern Italy, partly as fiefs of the empire and partly as her own freehold land. She had been closely involved in supporting papal reforms, and at one point had willed her lands to the pope, but Henry had won her over on his visit to the area in 1111 and it now appeared he was to have all her lands. To secure them, however, it was important he should return to the area quickly – and that would also provide an opportunity for further discussions with Pope Paschal.

Accordingly, in the depths of winter, Henry and Matilda travelled south to Augsburg, and in March 1116 crossed the Brenner Pass into Italy. The forces that accompanied them were considerably smaller than on the emperor's previous visit, but this time his aim was to conciliate and to strengthen his position in the north of Italy before turning his attention to Rome. After the severe rule of the old Matilda, the cities of Emilia, Tuscany and Lombardy were won over by a generous bestowal of privileges (which would eventually lead to the establishment of the city-states of the region), while at Canossa, the base and stronghold of Matilda of Tuscany, the new young Matilda was welcomed as a happy replacement.

It was a year later, in March 1117, that Henry and his wife set off southwards to Rome. In the meantime, Abbot Pontius of Cluny had been sent ahead to begin negotiations with the pope while the emperor had also been gathering forces from the now-supportive lands of the north. Pope Paschal had had one taste of Henry's 'negotiations', however, and had no appetite for more. As the royal couple approached, he paused only long enough to publish the emperor's excommunication, before fleeing south to the safety of the monastery of Monte Cassino. From there he dispatched Maurice Bourdin, Archbishop of Braga, to act as his representative in the coming discussions.

It was Easter time as Henry approached Rome. Traditionally he should have been welcomed into the city and ceremonially crowned by the pope in St Peter's Basilica. There was no pope in Rome, however, no cardinal would crown him, and the way to St Peter's across the River Tiber was guarded by Paschal's supporters in the fortress of Castel Sant'Angelo. Yet for an emperor with money and favours to bestow, anything was possible. Crowds duly cheered his entrance to Rome – though a chronicler sourly noted that every cheer was paid for – the Tiber was crossed by boat, and Henry and Matilda were duly crowned by Archbishop Maurice Bourdin, shifting his allegiance from pope to emperor in one smooth step.

According to some accounts the crowning was repeated a few weeks later at Pentecost, but these were the only times Matilda was crowned as empress, and many declare they were merely 'crown-wearings' rather than coronations. In neither case was she crowned by a pope, though she might have claimed Maurice Bourdin was a papal legate and that was good enough. Nor was she ever anointed. Nevertheless, she would always insist that she was a crowned empress, rather than merely the wife of the emperor, and she clung to the title for the rest of her life.

When Henry and Matilda withdrew to their lands in northern Italy, Pope Paschal returned to Rome and the Archbishop of Braga was duly excommunicated for his part in the emperor's triumph. Henry had still not achieved the settlement he needed, however, and before further negotiations could take place, Paschal died on 21 January 1118. Within a few days a successor, Gelasius II, was unanimously elected, but he flatly refused to negotiate and in a matter of weeks Henry had driven him from Rome, setting up instead his own tame candidate, Maurice Bourdin, as Antipope Gregory VIII. The response of Gelasius was to excommunicate the pair of them.

By now the situation in the German states was becoming serious, whipped up by the unforgiving Adalbert. More church leaders were abandoning the emperor and encouraging others to do the same, and rebellions were breaking out in a number of places. Henry was forced to return northwards in order to regain control, but he left Matilda behind as his regent in Italy. She was then sixteen years old.

She had been playing the part of a queen for some time now, interceding with her husband on behalf of petitioners, witnessing charters, and generally helping in the work of government according to a tradition long established in the empire. Now, although she had a chancellor to assist her, for at least a year – and possibly as much as eighteen months – the full weight of government fell on her shoulders. She appears to have managed very well. Courts were held and decisions given by Matilda, with no whisper of dissent or dissatisfaction. If she had had her theoretical training from Archbishop Bruno, this now was her practical, on-the-job training, and she certainly appears to have been equal to the task. By the time she rejoined her husband in the north at some point in 1119, events had moved on again. Pope Gelasius had died in January of that year and while the election of Guy of Vienne as Pope Calixtus II initially appeared to be a setback for the imperial cause, in fact he proved to be as anxious as Henry to find a permanent settlement to the long-running and damaging dispute. The emperor received a papal embassy at Strasbourg, and enough progress was made for him to withdraw his support from his hapless Antipope Gregory VIII, who all this time had been holding out in Rome for his imperial master. Even now Gregory had enough support from influential Roman families to maintain his position, but he must have known his days were numbered.

A meeting between emperor and pope was arranged for autumn that year at Chateau de Mousson near Rheims, where Calixtus had called a great council to deal with a number of outstanding church matters. With goodwill on each side the investiture dilemma might have been resolved there and then, but the meeting never took place. Orderic Vitalis, whose report is so detailed he must have been present at the council, gives us the fullest account of what happened. He describes how the pope and his retinue set out for the meeting place, only to find that Henry was putting on another show of strength. 'In fact we found that the emperor had come to the place of meeting with a great army, and, as if he was about to fight a battle, was at the head of nearly 30,000 men.' The pope was immediately sheltered in a nearby castle, but when his representatives went on to try to speak with Henry, they found it impossible to do so since he was always surrounded by followers who 'brandished their swords and lances and caused us great alarm'.

It was a serious misjudgement on the part of the emperor, immediately bringing to mind his earlier use of force against Paschal. Calixtus was not going to wait around to be kidnapped. Returning to the council at Rheims, he confirmed the church's refusal to allow lay investitures, and for good measure, 'pronounced with grief the sentence of excommunication against ... the emperor, and the Enemy of god, Bourdin'.

Each side blamed the other for the failure of the meeting, but still the aim of both was to bridge the gap between them. Meanwhile each secured his own position, Henry putting down opposition at home, and Calixtus marching on Rome and ousting his rival, Gregory. By the end of 1120 it must have been clear to all that it was only a matter of time before the whole sad situation would be resolved, but nearly two years were to pass before the final steps were taken to end the impasse.

While Matilda was being acknowledged as empress over a large part of Western Europe, the career of her cousin Stephen of Blois was developing quite nicely. Certainly by 1120 he was doing well enough for a younger son, but his achievements were considerably more modest than Matilda's.

The year 1111 marked a decisive change of policy in the County of Blois. It was in that year that the young Count Theobald (no doubt prompted by his mother, Adela) turned against his overlord, the French king Louis VI. Ostensibly the dispute was over the construction of a castle, but from that time onward Theobald was a staunch supporter of his uncle, King Henry of England, who was in the middle of his own dispute with Louis. That, too, was theoretically about a castle. At base, though, it concerned Henry's reluctance to pay homage to the new French king for Normandy, as required by the feudal laws, a situation complicated by the fact that if he did not do so Louis might accept homage from Robert's son, William Clito, and recognise him as rightful duke of Normandy instead. Theobald's intervention proved a timely distraction, particularly as he raised other men in rebellion so that Louis was forced to turn his attention to problems at home rather than attacking Normandy. Henry himself crossed the Channel to support Theobald, and it seems reasonable to suppose that this might be the time when young Stephen of Blois joined his uncle's court. He would then have been around fifteen years old.

At that time Stephen was not the only young man seeking his fortune there. Probably the oldest of the group would have been David of Scotland, younger brother of the Scots king Alexander, and brother-in-law to Henry. In theory he should have been sharing rule in Scotland with Alexander but this had not happened, and no doubt he was looking to Henry to bolster his position. As well as David, a pair of illegitimate sons some half-a-dozen years younger were also being brought up at Henry's court. One was Robert of Caen, the king's own son, and the other Brian Fitz Count, illegitimate son of the king's brother-in-law, Alan of Brittany. Younger again, and probably of an age with Stephen, was another of Henry's illegitimate sons, Richard of Lincoln, along with Richard, Earl of Chester, who had been in Henry's care since his father died in 1101.

While these young men would become increasingly useful to the English king in his conflicts with Louis of France, they also served another purpose. There were large estates in England and in Normandy that had fallen into Henry's hands on the defeat of those who had rebelled against him or shared the fate of his brother Robert at Tinchebrai. As late as 1112 he finally captured and imprisoned a long-time enemy, Robert de Bellême, bringing the last of the Montgomery lands in southern Normandy under his control. It was Henry's intention that all these estates should be held by people wholly indebted to him for their advancement, and therefore totally loyal to him. Who better to advance than these young men, all of whom were, in one way or another, 'family'?

We are fairly sure that Stephen was knighted by Henry in 1112, and it may have been soon after this that the landless younger son was given the title Count of Mortain, and with it the Norman lands that had been confiscated from William of Mortain after Tinchebrai, and held in the interim by Robert de Vitry. Giving them to Stephen brought these prosperous lands on the southern border of Normandy back into the family of the Norman dukes and provided an incentive for Stephen and his older brother, Count Theobald, to defend them against Fulk of Anjou, whose lands lay to the south.

Stephen was with Henry when the court visited the Abbey of St Evroult, home of Orderic Vitalis, in 1113, and it is fairly certain that he accompanied the king to England in the summer of that year, following the settlement of the conflict with Louis. This was a time when many of the titles and estates that had fallen into

Henry's hands over the years were redistributed, and his new 'family' followers were rewarded and set in positions where both they and the crown could benefit. In many cases this was achieved by marrying a young man to an heiress or wealthy widow. Robert of Caen, for instance, had already obtained the extensive estates of the Honour of Gloucester and the Lordship of Abergavenny by marrying Mabel FitzHamon, the daughter and heiress of Robert FitzHamon, the king's friend and supporter who had died in 1107. Now David of Scotland was married to Matilda, the widow of Simon of Senlis who brought with her the Honour of Huntingdon, spread over three counties in the east midlands.

In Stephen's case the gift of lands came without marriage, first the Honour of Eye, one of the largest in England with estates in a number of eastern counties, and then, a little later, the Honour of Lancaster in north-west England, reaching from the Mersey up as far as Carlisle, though the northernmost area was disputed with Scotland. Together these made for a very substantial landholding, and it has been suggested that this marked out Stephen as a special favourite of the king. There is a danger of reading too much into this, however. Stephen was still a very young man and relatively untried, and there was certainly no suggestion at the time that Henry saw him as a possible future heir. He may have been charmed by the generous and open nature of one who, outside his immediate family, was his closest blood relation in England, but he had his own heir in William Adelin, now about eleven years old. Early in 1115 Stephen was likely to have sworn the oath of allegiance to William that was taken at that time by all the major landholders in Normandy. This oath was then repeated the following year by the English magnates.

When hostilities broke out again in Normandy in 1116, Blois was, for a time, the only ally Henry had against the forces of France, Flanders and Anjou. During his *annus horribilis*, 1118, many in Normandy were deserting the king in favour of William Clito and Henry declared he could trust no one. At that time the loyalty of Theobald and Stephen was most important. On one occasion outside the castle of L'Aigle, when Theobald fell into the hands of the king's enemies, it took a spirited action on the part of Henry and Stephen to rescue him, and certainly the young man seemed most capable in military matters. It was when he was entrusted with the hostile town of Alençon, however, that his limitations were first exposed.

The town and surrounding lands had belonged to the Montgomery family, the family of Robert de Bellême, and though the castle was garrisoned with Henry's men no doubt he felt the loyalty of the area could not be relied on. With his hands full elsewhere, Henry initially transferred the lands to Theobald, who then, with the king's permission, passed them on to his brother. According to Orderic Vitalis, it was Stephen's youth and inexperience that was to blame for what happened then. He 'had not the regard for the burgesses which he ought, nor did he treat them with respect'. Like many a young, insecure commander, he saw defiance everywhere, and thought harsh measures were called for when a different approach might have been more useful.

'At last,' says Vitalis, 'he summoned a general assembly and required them to deliver to him their sons as hostages for their good behaviour.' Not only sons, but wives too seem to have been demanded, and when they were handed over, he 'did not give them honourable treatment'. The specific complaint that Vitalis records concerns the wife of a 'worthy townsman', who was imprisoned in the citadel, 'where, much to her sorrow, she was in the hands of debauched guards.' She was apparently not the only one as he goes on to say that her husband 'made a secret association with several others who had similar causes of complaint'.

They clearly had no faith in Stephen for redress – he was almost certainly absent at the time – or indeed King Henry, thinking he 'would turn a deaf ear to their charges against his nephew'. Instead they contacted Arnulf de Montgomery, brother of Robert de Bellême, who recommended turning to Fulk of Anjou, at that time allied with Louis of France against the English king. Fulk was delighted to accept their invitation. Admitted to the town by night, his forces set up a siege around the citadel, and when Henry, with Stephen and Theobald, tried to relieve the garrison and retake the town, they were thoroughly routed – the only time, in fact, that Henry was defeated in battle.

Stephen had held Alençon for a matter of weeks, and Vitalis is not the only one to blame the loss of the town on his mismanagement. It was a serious loss to the king, though, and although Henry was able, by good luck, diplomacy and military might, to turn his fortunes around in the following year, we don't find Stephen's name among those involved in the Battle of Brémule in the summer of 1119, or in the extensive diplomacy that followed a meeting with Pope Calixtus in the autumn of that year. The latter was perhaps the more pointed snub, as both his brother Theobald and his mother were heavily involved in bringing about the settlement that was finally achieved with King Louis in the autumn of 1120.

By this time the young William Adelin was married to the daughter of Fulk of Anjou, thereby securing his friendship towards England and Blois, and Louis had accepted some form of homage from William, not only acknowledging him as Henry's lawful heir but tacitly accepting Henry's own position as de facto Duke of Normandy. In fact, the next time we find Stephen particularly mentioned, it is as part of a large and rowdy party of young men on board a ship in Barfleur harbour on the evening of 25 November 1120.

2

Changing Plans

(November 1120 – December 1135)

In the autumn of 1120 King Henry of England was coming home in triumph. In the words of John of Worcester, he had 'successfully accomplished all his designs', and he and his court were returning. There must have been a huge number of them, lords, knights and household officials, along with their wives and children and, more especially, Henry's son and heir, William Adelin and his young wife Matilda of Anjou. A fleet of ships was assembled to carry them across the Channel, and the court was divided among them. One in particular, *la Blanche-Nef* or *White Ship*, was assigned to the seventeen-year-old William. The ship's owner had begged for the privilege of carrying the king, since, he said, his father had piloted the ship carrying Henry's father on his expedition to conquer England. Henry had declined the honour but, perhaps as a sop to the man's feelings, had said he could carry Henry's son – in fact two sons, as the illegitimate Richard of Lincoln would be travelling with William. 'I entrust you with my sons,' Vitalis has him say, 'whom I love as myself.'

Many of the younger lords and a great crowd of household officers and servants were also assigned to this ship, though William's young bride travelled with Henry. Vitalis estimates some 300 embarked altogether, including fifty experienced rowers and a force of armed marines. Before they set sail, however, a great drunken party seems to have taken place on board. The crew, puffed up, no doubt, by the honour of carrying the king's heir, asked him to give them something to drink. He, equally exuberant to find himself in charge, had three great casks of wine broached, and everyone seems to have joined together to get roaring drunk.

Stephen, Count of Mortain, had also been assigned to the *Blanche-Nef*, along with many of the lesser nobles of that county, but it appears he was not in a party mood. Suffering from a stomach disorder, he decided that the ship was overcrowded with rowdy, headstrong youths and disembarked before it sailed, accompanied by two men-at-arms. That stomach disorder was to save their lives and alter the course of English history.

The writers of the time describe the extraordinary calmness of the weather, and how, when the king's ship set off just before twilight, it was wafted to England on light breezes. When the *Blanche-Nef* put out to sea some time later, it was not the weather but the drunkenness of its crew and passengers that doomed it. With a crazy idea of overtaking King Henry in the dark, freezing night, the rowers pulled on their oars with all their might, but 'the luckless pilot steered at random.'

On a treacherous coast filled with hazards the end was inevitable. The *Blanche-Nef* shattered her starboard planks on a submerged rock and the efforts of the crew to free her only let the water in more quickly. A boat was launched to try and save the life of William Adelin, but the cries of his half-sister, the Countess of Perche, brought him back dangerously close to the stricken vessel, whereupon all those on board tried to jump to safety and swamped the little craft. Within a matter of minutes, as John of Worcester recounts, 'all on board were swallowed up by the waves, except for one churl, who ... was not worthy of being named.' (He was, in fact, Berold, a butcher from Rouen who, wearing thicker clothes, survived by clinging to the mast until rescued early the next morning.)

The sinking of the *Blanche-Nef* was a catastrophe for Henry. Not only did he lose two sons, a daughter and a niece, but all his plans for the peaceful succession of an acknowledged heir were also sunk on that dark November night. When they finally plucked up courage to give him the news two days later, he collapsed and had to be helped to his private chamber. As soon as he had recovered, however, he began to consider what alternatives remained in the way of a suitable succession.

Henry's wife, Edith/Matilda, had died in 1118 and he had already thought of remarrying. Now it became a matter of some urgency. His chosen bride was Adeliza of Louvain, the 'fair maid of Brabant', seventeen years old, intelligent and descended from Charlemagne. They married on 29 January 1121 and Adeliza was crowned as queen the following day. Until recently the king had been regularly begetting bastard children and he probably hoped that his new young wife would produce a legitimate male heir.

He was more than fifty years old, however. This was a good age for the time he lived in, but he had to expect that even if a son was born quickly, he might not be around to see him grow up. It was probably for this reason that in 1121 or 1122 the king's eldest illegitimate son, Robert, was made Earl of Gloucester.

Robert was by then in his early thirties, married and with children of his own. Among the estates he had inherited through his wife were the castles at Bristol and Cardiff, and he was one of the greatest landowners in England. There were estates, too, in Normandy, and Robert had already ably supported his father there, notably at the recent Battle of Brémule. Some have seen Robert's elevation to an earldom as a sign that Henry was lining him up as a fall-back candidate in case he should fail to produce the necessary legitimate heir. There is no evidence, though, that the king ever saw his natural son as a possible successor. Although rules of inheritance were still fairly fluid, recent church reforms that had stigmatised illegitimacy made it unlikely that an illegitimate candidate would be easily accepted when there were other legitimate claimants. It is more probable that the strengthening of Robert's position in England was intended to establish him as a firm and totally trustworthy support for any son that might be born to Henry and his new wife.

As far as legitimate claimants were concerned, there were several to choose from, all nephews of the king and grandsons of William the Conqueror. In the eyes of many, pre-eminent among these would be William Clito, son of Henry's older brother Robert Curthose, who was still imprisoned at Devizes Castle in England.

Under no circumstances, however, would Henry acknowledge that Clito had any legitimate claim, either to Normandy or to England. To do so would be to raise questions as to the legitimacy of his own rule in the duchy, if not in the kingdom itself, and he would spend a large part of the next eight years undermining Clito and fighting off any challenge made on his behalf. Nevertheless, as long as the boy lived there would be a substantial number of Norman lords who would be happy to support him as having the greater right, at least to the duchy.

The other possible candidates for the succession would be Adela's sons, William, Theobald, Stephen and Henry. They would all be seen as having roughly the same claim as William Clito, although drawn through the female, rather than male, line of descent. Of these, two could be immediately discounted. William had already been found unsuitable and put aside, while Henry was now a monk at Cluny Abbey. Theobald, Count of Blois, however, was now ruling on his own, his mother having finally retired from the world to the Cluniac convent of Marcigny, while Stephen had already been generously established by Henry with lands and honours in Normandy and England. Both had been firm supporters of Henry in his Norman wars, with Theobald probably the more successful.

At no point, however, does the English king ever hint at either of these as possible successors. Stephen was later to claim he was Henry's favourite nephew, but the king's generosity to him may simply have been to help his widowed sister Adela by making provision for her sons when she was not able to do so herself. This view is supported by the fact that the monk, Henry of Blois, was also given substantial support by Henry, while no great favours were bestowed on Theobald, though his service to the king had been considerably greater than that of his brothers. Theobald already had his future secured in his own lands.

Neither Theobald nor Stephen was married at this time. Though Adela had been careful to arrange matches for William and for her daughters, her younger sons seem to have been left to fend for themselves. Possibly she was again looking to Henry to provide something. In fact, Theobald was the first to wed in 1123, apparently without Henry's intervention. It was not until some time later, however, that a wife was found for Stephen, and though most say this was arranged by Henry, it was not directly within the king's gift.

Stephen's bride was another Matilda, heiress of Eustace, Count of Boulogne, who not only held a strategically placed French county on the Continent, but also large estates in England. Eustace had led an eventful life, supporting Robert Curthose in his attempt in 1088 to wrest the English crown from William Rufus, then joining the First Crusade to Jerusalem where his brother, Baldwin, became king. He had recently nearly become king of Jerusalem himself. When Baldwin died in 1118, the title was offered to Eustace who initially turned it down. Then, changing his mind, he had travelled as far as Apulia in southern Italy before discovering that a distant relative, another Baldwin, had accepted the honour and already been crowned. Possibly a certain amount of disgruntlement had something to do with his decision in the early 1120s that he wished to abdicate and spend the rest of his life peacefully in a monastery.

On his return from the First Crusade he had married Mary of Scotland, the sister of the English queen Edith/Matilda, who had almost certainly had some influence in arranging the match. They had produced only one child, a daughter, Matilda, and Eustace now wanted to find a suitable husband for her before he handed over his earthly possessions and duties and retired from the world. As a grandson of William the Conqueror, Stephen was certainly suitable, and his estates in England and Normandy gave him the wealth to support his status. Again, we don't know exactly how much influence Henry brought to bear on his brother-in-law, but the match would have been of considerable importance to him.

Boulogne lay a short channel crossing away from the south-east coast of England. It was an important route for the wool trade, connecting the English wool producers with the skilled cloth makers in Flemish cities such as Bruges and Ghent. Strategically, it also lay to the north of Ponthieu, ruled by William Talvas, son of Robert de Bellême, and a confirmed enemy of the English king. A firm ally in Boulogne would hold Talvas between that county in the north and Normandy in the south, leaving him vulnerable on both sides if he chose to try to reclaim his father's lost lands in southern Normandy.

All round, the match between Stephen and Matilda was a good one, and it duly took place in 1125. Eustace immediately abdicated – in fact he would die later that year – and Stephen took over as Count of Boulogne, ruling jointly with his wife, the Countess Matilda. Many have seen this marriage as proof that Henry favoured Stephen as a successor in England. It is pointed out that it united, as did Henry's own marriage, the old English royal family represented by Matilda's mother Mary, and the new, represented by the Conqueror's grandson Stephen. It would fulfil the conditions of Edward the Confessor's prophecy as Henry's marriage had done, while the joining of Stephen's Honour of Eye and Matilda's Honour of Boulogne made them dominant landowners in south-east England. It is possible that Stephen himself viewed the match in the same light, but a different interpretation is equally plausible.

Important though it might be as an ally, the little county of Boulogne was not England, and it is clear from charters issued that Stephen and Matilda ruled jointly. Henry had had ample opportunity to weigh up the qualities of his nephew over a number of years, and while he no doubt valued the family connections and the man's reputed good humour, piety and honesty, he may well have found him lacking the necessary grit and intelligence that makes a good king. It is likely that Henry approved the match with the heiress of Boulogne precisely because he felt that this was about the right level for the young man's abilities. Anything less would have been an insult to his royal blood; anything more might stretch his talents too thinly. It is noticeable that the count and countess spent significantly more time in Boulogne than they did in England, and that their first sons were named Baldwin and Eustace, names traditionally associated with the county. Only the third son was named William, referring to his royal great-grandfather. By contrast, Theobald of Blois named his first son Henry. If the king himself was not considering him as a successor, Theobald may well have calculated that he was next in line, should William Clito be discounted.

Henry, though, was looking for an heir of his own. Nephews were all very well, but probably like the majority of men he wanted his own line to continue and if he had no new child himself, he could still look to his daughter to produce a grandson. In the early 1120s he probably had no thought of Matilda herself inheriting the crown. For one thing, she was already queen of a far distant country and by most reckonings an empress to boot. For another, he had not seen her since she was a child of ten. This situation, however, was about to change.

In 1122 the Emperor Henry V finally achieved a settlement of the lay investiture question with Pope Calixtus in a compromise very similar to that achieved in England nearly two decades before. With this most pressing matter out of the way, the emperor could now turn his mind to other things and he too may have been considering the possibility that a son of his might one day be able to add England to the already extensive lands of his empire. Certainly there seems to be a subtle policy shift towards England and its allies around this time. When the daughter of his supporter Engelbert of Carinthia married the English ally, Theobald of Blois, it is likely Henry gave his approval. Similarly when in 1124 the English king was hard-pressed in Normandy by an uprising of nobles, an imperial army threatening France prevented the French king Louis from adding to his difficulties. There were clearly regular communications between the imperial court and the English. Empress Matilda is believed to have assisted in arranging her father's remarriage to a daughter of the emperor's vassal, Geoffrey of Louvain, while Matilda herself tried to visit her father in 1122, only to be refused permission to cross Flanders by Count Charles. It was, perhaps, in an effort to open a direct route from his own lands to England that the emperor undertook what was to be his last action, early in 1125, against the city of Utrecht.

Despite the hopes and wishes of both sides, however, no son had been born to the imperial couple, and now never would be. It became apparent that Henry was suffering from a devastating illness. As it has since been persuasively identified as cancer, it is possible he had been suffering from it for some time, and it is equally possible the English king had been aware of this even as he gave his approval to the marriage of his nephew Stephen to Matilda of Boulogne.

The Holy Roman Emperor Henry V died at Utrecht on 23 May 1125, and though he had passed the imperial insignia to his wife before he died, it was soon clear that there would be no role for the young widow in the German empire. She had been a queen for nearly fifteen years, and, in some eyes at least, an empress for eight, but now, at twenty-four years old, the only options open to her seemed to be to remarry to a German prince, or to enter a convent.

In England, however, King Henry had other plans in mind. Robert of Torigny claims the people of the German states wanted to keep 'Good Queen Matilda' but her father refused to consent to that. According to William of Newburgh 'he recalled his daughter,' while William of Malmesbury says: 'The empress returned with reluctance as she had become habituated to the country and had large possessions there.' She left them all behind, bringing with her only her jewels, two crowns and 'the hand of St James the Apostle'. This latter had been part of the imperial treasury for more than fifty years and Matilda probably had no right to it at all. Nevertheless it ended up in Reading Abbey, which had recently been founded and generously endowed by King Henry.

In September 1126 Matilda arrived back in England, accompanied by her father with whom she had spent some time in Normandy. We don't know to what extent he had let her into his own plans by then, but she is given credit for advising him on a movement of prisoners at the time. Some of these were captives from Henry's recent successes in Normandy. In particular, Waleran de Meulan, who had already spent two years in prison in Rouen, was now to be incarcerated first at Bridgnorth and then at Wallingford. It would be another three years before Henry forgave him sufficiently to release him and reinstate him in the position he had previously held in England and Normandy. The other long-term prisoner to be moved was Robert Curthose. Until then he had been held at Roger of Salisbury's castle at Devizes but now he was moved to Bristol Castle under the control of the king's son, Robert of Gloucester.

It was in January 1127 that Henry finally made his intentions known as regards the succession. Until then (and possibly for some time after) he had held firm to the idea that he would have another legitimate son. Now, however, he put in place an alternative. His Christmas court that year had been more than usually full of magnates and clergy from around England and beyond. David of Scotland was there, the first time he had attended since succeeding his brother as king the previous year, but he was more likely needed as holder of the Honour of Huntingdon in England, than as the Scottish representative. It is possible he had been part of the 'long continued deliberation' that Malmesbury reports concerning the succession, but it is equally possible Henry had deliberated only with himself. According to the Anglo-Saxon Chronicle, before the court broke up in January the king held a council where he 'caused the archbishops, bishops, abbots, earls and all the thanes who were present to swear to place England and Normandy, after his death, in the hands of his daughter.' More detail is added to this bald statement by other chroniclers of the time, in particular by William of Malmesbury and John of Worcester.

Malmesbury, for instance, makes the oath in some ways more precise, but also conditional. In his version, those assembled were 'compelled … to make oath that, if he should die without male issue, they would, without delay or hesitation, accept his daughter Matilda, the late empress, as their sovereign.' Then he recites in some detail the lineage that justified requiring them to accept Matilda, 'to whom alone the legitimate succession belonged' and lists the order of their swearing to do so. This began with William Corbeil, Archbishop of Canterbury, and proceeded through the various bishops and abbots, before the laity in turn were asked to swear.

First of these was David of Scotland, ranked before the others as he was a king. After him, though, issues of precedence were not quite so clear. Did a legitimate nephew rank ahead of an illegitimate son, or vice versa? 'There was a singular dispute,' says Malmesbury, 'between Robert (of Gloucester) and Stephen (of Boulogne), contending with rival virtue which of them should take the oath first; one alleging the privilege of a son, the other the dignity of a nephew.' In the end Stephen took the oath first, followed by Robert, but Malmesbury makes it sound as though they were contending for an honour, each claiming precedence over the other. John of Worcester, though, has a different view of the matter.

There are, in fact, a number of discrepancies in John's account. First, he places the council at Easter, rather than Christmas, but it is clear he is writing about the same event. Then he suggests that there was a discussion of many matters at the council, only one of which was 'who would succeed when the king died if he was lacking an heir.' In John's version it was 'the king's wish that his daughter ... should receive the English kingdom ... with her lawful husband, if she had one,' and that all present should swear an oath to ensure this, in fact, took place. After the matter had been discussed, says John, all agreed to this.

As regards the actual oath-swearing, more than anything John seems offended that the abbots were not given their rightful precedence after the bishops, but were made to wait until last to swear the oath. The abbot of Bury St Edmunds complained to the king about this, he says, and was told what was done was done, and to get on with the matter. He does, however, record a completely different version of the dispute between Robert of Gloucester and Stephen of Boulogne.

In his account King David was the first of the laity to swear, followed by Queen Adeliza. Then Robert, the king's son was approached. He was sitting to the left of the king, with Stephen of Boulogne on Henry's right. 'Get up, get up,' Robert was instructed, 'and swear the oath as the king desires.' Robert, however, declared that Stephen should go first. 'Stephen, Count of Boulogne was born before me and should do this first, he who is sitting at the king's right hand,' and this was done. This certainly puts a different complexion on the matter, and it is hard to know exactly what we should read into it. Was Robert simply annoyed that Stephen had the favoured seat at the right hand of the king? Was he acknowledging that Stephen ranked ahead of him, not because he was born first (he probably wasn't), but because he was legitimate? Whatever else, it seems clear that there was no competition to be first in the oath-taking, and probably that each was equally reluctant to do what the king wanted.

Which version of the dispute is true? It is unlikely we will never know. Each of the chroniclers, however, offers a comment on the likely intentions of those who had just sworn to uphold Matilda's right to the crown. Malmesbury writes, 'all declared, prophetically, as it were, that, after (Henry's) death they would break their plighted oath,' while John of Worcester, clearly writing after they had done so, declares that all the oath-takers were perjurers.

Only John of Worcester mentions the possibility that Matilda might have a husband by the time she came to inherit the throne, but the possibility must have been in everyone's mind. Women did not rule, or if they did, they did not rule alone and on their own behalf. With the notable exception of the redoubtable Matilda of Tuscany, those who had wielded power before had been regents acting for absent husbands or infant sons. Adela of Blois might have done an excellent job, but she did it in the name of Stephen-Henry and later of her son Theobald.

Yes, it was clear that Matilda must have a new husband, but who was he to be? The course of events over the next few months indicates that Henry already had a plan, but he seems to have revealed nothing at this stage. It is only with the benefit of hindsight that William of Malmesbury could declare that Henry recalled Matilda to England, 'designing by the marriage of his daughter to procure peace between himself and the earl of Anjou.'

Henry and Fulk of Anjou had had an up-and-down kind of relationship over a number of years. Initially siding with his overlord the French king, Louis, Fulk had inflicted a serious defeat on the English king at Alençon. Then, enticed away by money and promises, he had married his daughter Matilda to Henry's son, and had helped him achieve peace with France.

Following the *White Ship* disaster, relations had soured again when Henry failed to return the dowry of the widowed child bride, and a low point was reached with the marriage of Fulk's other daughter, Sybilla, to William Clito. It had taken time and money for Henry to persuade Pope Honorious that this marriage should be annulled as the parties were too closely related – something that had not troubled him when his own son was the bridegroom – and

Fulk had been so furious that he had locked up the papal legate who brought him the news.

Anjou was an important part of Henry's plans, however. A traditional enemy to the south of Normandy, it was essential to engage it as an ally in order to ensure peace in the region and, more especially, to prevent it making alliances with those within and without Normandy who were hostile to the English king. Twice already a line-up of Flanders, France and Anjou had threatened him on all sides, and Fulk had been more than ready to help William Clito when he had tried to organise opposition to Henry's rule.

It might be thought Henry had set himself an impossible task in mending the latest breach, but circumstances had already changed in his favour. The enticements that had previously won over Fulk still existed, in particular a prospect that his grandson would be king of England. Now, of course, that honour might be held by his own son as well. In addition, it is possible he was already thinking of a return to the Holy Land. Whispers may have reached him that his visit to Jerusalem some years before had borne unexpected fruit. King Baldwin, ageing and with no male heir, wanted a suitably powerful husband for his daughter Melisande, who was already assisting his rule, and who he intended to go on ruling after his death. Fulk had already impressed him as a suitable candidate, and his name had been put forward by Louis of France when asked for a recommendation, possibly with the aim of removing a powerful and potentially troublemaking subordinate from his dominions. Negotiations began in 1127, initially suggesting Fulk might simply be a consort, then accepting him as co-ruler with Melisande. First, however, he had to settle his affairs in Anjou.

In early 1127 his eldest son, Geoffrey, was thirteen years old. The boy's mother had died a few months before, so there was no possibility of a regency. With a strong backer such as King Henry of England, however, there should be no real difficulty if Fulk was to abdicate and proclaim his son Count of Anjou in due course, when the appropriate arrangements had been made. In fairness to the boy it is recorded that Henry had heard good reports of his talents and abilities, though, as he was thirteen, this must surely have been a matter of promise rather than achievement. Negotiations with Fulk were proceeding nicely, therefore, when other events introduced rather more urgency into the situation.

While Henry had waited in hope for a new heir in the years since his son had died, the French king Louis had shown little active interest in the affairs of William Clito. Possibly he had thought there was a chance the young man might even be considered as a possible successor, at least to Normandy, which was Louis's main concern, if not to England itself. When in January 1127 it became clear this would not happen, he immediately took up his cause with renewed vigour. A marriage was arranged between Clito and Joanna de Montferrat, half-sister of Louis's own Queen Adelaide, and the French king granted him lands in an area most likely to annoy Henry – Pontoise, Chaumont, Mantes and 'all the Vexin', a disputed border area – where Clito immediately set about making his claim a reality. An opportunity would soon arise, however, for Louis to do far more for his protégé.

On 2 March 1127 Charles the Good of Flanders was assassinated while at prayer in the Church of St Donatian in Bruges. With no heir and a number of potential claimants, civil war was a likely result and, as overlord of Flanders, Louis took immediate steps to prevent this. William of Ypres and Thierry of Alsace were both grandsons of an earlier count, Robert I, but the one was illegitimate and the other was claiming through the female line. Overriding the claims of both of these, the preferred candidate of the French king was William Clito, the great-grandson of a yet earlier count, Baldwin V. By a combination of bribes, promises and a show of force, William Clito was duly installed as Count of Flanders before the end of March.

Within days the news was reported to Henry at his Easter court at Woodstock, and according to Robert of Torigny, he was 'distressed at this intelligence'. Of course, any improvement in William's fortunes was a cause of distress to the English king, but this was worse than most. Flanders was a rich country, mainly through its prowess in textiles, but it was also famous for the quality of its mercenary soldiers. Henry himself had often used them. It was likely with such resources at his back that William Clito would regard Flanders as merely a stepping stone on the way to achieving his main goal in life, the recovery of the Duchy of Normandy. Furthermore, situated as it was on the northern borders of Normandy, Flanders would easily attract all those disaffected Norman lords who had already supported Clito as their rightful duke. In fact Orderic Vitalis notes a little later that: 'Numbers flocked to his standard out of Normandy, for there were many whose attachment to him was so great … that they abandoned their native country with their natural lords and their kindred to serve under him.'

At all costs Henry had to prevent Clito establishing himself in the county, and as a first step he seems to have offered financial support to all the other candidates. William of Ypres, however, after using Henry's funds to hire soldiers and persuading the town of Ypres to accept him as count, was quickly taken prisoner when that town was besieged by Louis and Clito and weapons were needed so now Henry turned to Stephen of Boulogne.

What role he had in mind for Stephen is not entirely clear. In theory Stephen's claim to Flanders would have been nearly as good as William's. They were first cousins, both of them descended through their grandmother, Matilda, from Baldwin V. In fact Henry himself could have made a better claim, being a grandson of Baldwin, but it seems unlikely either of these rights were ever asserted.

Some accounts say Henry sent Stephen to make war on William, but Vitalis puts this the other way about. 'In the month of August,' he says, William 'marched an army against Stephen, Count of Boulogne, and in order to reduce him to submission, laid waste his territories with fire and sword in the most cruel manner.' Whether or not this was a pre-emptive strike, we don't know.

It is recorded elsewhere that Stephen met with William and Louis towards the end of April. It may be that, at that time, they had demanded homage from Stephen, which he had refused. In theory the counts of Boulogne were subordinate to the counts of Flanders, though in the past a fair amount of independence had frequently been demanded and tolerated. By August, however, Louis had returned home, so this campaign seems to be William's own enterprise.

Another reason for the invasion might have involved further weapons of agitation on Henry's part. While still, like all Western European countries, an agricultural economy, in Flanders the towns had assumed an increasing importance as centres of the cloth trade. Places such as Bruges, Ghent, Ypres, Lille and St Omer had attracted skilled spinners, weavers and fullers from the surrounding areas, and it was on them that the county's prosperity was built. For some time they had been major importers of English wool, prized for its high quality, much of which was imported through Boulogne. William Clito had largely come to power by promising privileges to these towns, but Henry now acted to cut off these imports altogether. He banned the export of wool to Flanders, and was likely backed up by Stephen in refusing to allow free access for the wool traders through his lands.

Whatever the reason for Clito's attacks, we don't hear much about Stephen's response. No doubt he defended his territory but Vitalis seems to suggest there was no decisive confrontation, and that the devastation was widespread. Nowhere is there a suggestion that Stephen drove off his opponent, or brought him to beg for a negotiated end to the violence. In fact it was a change in outside events that led to a truce.

By mid-September the threat to their prosperity from Henry's embargo had led a number of Flemish towns to rethink their support for their new count. In addition, William's enthusiasm in hunting down those allegedly responsible for the death of his predecessor had alienated another powerful group. 'He condemned about 111 of them to perish by being cast down headlong, or by other cruel deaths,' says Vitalis. In fact, those cast from the high church tower were probably the lucky ones, since the French chronicler Suger, who was close to the court of Louis, describes a number of truly grisly deaths inflicted on some of those blamed for the assassination. Suger ascribes these to Louis, but no doubt William was at least a passive bystander and, since he was the count, he would undoubtedly have carried a share of the condemnation attached to this by those connected to the men tortured to death.

These relatives and friends of the dead men were now looking for revenge and according to Vitalis, it was they who now urged

Thierry of Alsace to challenge William's rule. They 'reproached him for suffering his hereditary rights to be sacrificed by his neglect and silence, and promised that if he asserted his claims they and others would support him.' Among the others, of course, was Henry of England, and Robert of Torigny in fact declares that Thierry 'laid claim to Flanders at the suggestion of King Henry'. Both versions are combined by Henry of Huntingdon, who, never a great fan of Henry, adds his own spin to the tale. 'And now,' he says, 'by the king's intrigues, a certain duke ... came from out of Germany, having with him some Flemish nobles, and set up false pretensions to the possession of Flanders.'

Once again with solid financial backing from the English king, Thierry now marched into action, winning over a succession of key towns between September 1127 and March 1128, and it was this, rather than any action of Stephen's, that led to a withdrawal of Clito's troops from Boulogne and the agreement of a three-year truce. Thierry was making the same sort of promises as William and Louis had made earlier, only this time backed up with Henry's money and Henry's assurances of access to English wool.

By April 1128 William Clito was again forced to turn to Louis for support, and he had no illusions about the cause of his predicament. Henry, he wrote to Louis, was a powerful and malignant enemy with innumerable knights and vast amounts of money at his disposal. Grieved at William's success, he was using these out of pure spite to lure away men who should have been loyal to their count, and as a result of his bribes, William was facing serious opposition. Louis responded by arriving in person with an army, but his stay was very short. By the end of May he was gone again, called back to France by power struggles within his court, and by Henry's only personal intervention in the affairs of Flanders.

The English king, says Henry of Huntingdon, 'made a hostile incursion into France because the French king supported his nephew and enemy.' In fact Henry spent eight days at the castle of Épernon, to the south-west of Paris, close enough to threaten the French capital without any significant risk to himself. There he stayed, 'as securely as if he had been in his own dominions,' says Huntingdon, adding that he spent his time enquiring into the origins of the Franks.

These were recited to him in some detail, beginning, rather fancifully, with the Trojans, and continuing down to the present King Louis. 'And if he trod in the footsteps of his warlike ancestors, you, O king, would not now be so safe within his dominions.'

Henry's purpose was as a decoy, however, not an invader. As soon as he had drawn Louis away from William Clito he returned to his own lands. There he had a more important role to play. While all this had been going on in Flanders, he had not taken his eye off his main objective, the marriage of Matilda to Geoffrey of Anjou. Agreement had been swiftly reached with the young man's father, but it is possible Henry had had more resistance from his own daughter. Letters exist, though they cannot be precisely dated to this time, suggesting Matilda was distressing her father with threatened disobedience to his wishes, and it is easy to see her point of view. For many years she had been queen and empress over a mighty territory, and now she was being asked to marry the son of a count, a son, moreover, who had not yet reached his fourteenth birthday. In the end, though, by persuasion or by coercion, Henry had his way. On 22 May 1127 Matilda set off for Normandy, escorted by her half-brother Robert and Brian FitzCount. These two men, both now in their thirties, were clearly the most trusted of the many who had grown up in Henry's court and owed their prosperity to him. Indeed, Roger of Salisbury was later to complain that they were the only two in the kingdom who had been let into the secret of Matilda's forthcoming wedding.

A formal betrothal to Geoffrey now took place, either immediately after Matilda's arrival or shortly after her father joined her at the end of August, depending on which account is read. The wedding itself was delayed for a year, possibly to enable Fulk to finalise his plans for his own marriage in Jerusalem, and possibly to add another year to the meagre tally of the bridegroom. When Henry returned from his foray into France in time to knight him on 10 June 1128, however, the young man was still a few months short of his fifteenth birthday. His bride was twenty-six. The disparity was not as great as in some contemporary marriages, but still enough to chill the dignity of a former empress. On 17 June, in the cathedral at Le Mans, Geoffrey and Matilda were made man and wife. Both fathers were present, with the Bishop of Le Mans presiding, assisted by Henry's right-hand man in Normandy, Bishop John of Lisieux. As far as they were concerned it was a job well done. Henry could again look forward to a grandson to inherit his lands, while Fulk of Anjou immediately began involving his son in the running of Anjou. Elsewhere, things were not going so smoothly.

In Flanders more and more towns were declaring for Thierry of Alsace, but William Clito was not giving up without a fight. Louis himself had gone, but Clito still had French troops, along with the Normans who had flocked to him and some loyal Flemings. On 21 June 1128, just a few days after Matilda's wedding, he joined in battle with Thierry at Axspoele, just outside Bruges. 'The conflict was a sharp one,' Robert of Torigny records, while Huntingdon declares 'Earl William supplied his inferiority in numbers by his irresistible valour. His armour all stained with the enemy's blood, his flaming sword hewed down the hostile ranks, and unable to withstand the terrible force of his youthful arm, they fled in consternation.' It was a mighty victory, but it was not the end of the conflict.

Thierry's castle at Aalst was Clito's next target. A siege was established, but within a matter of weeks, in the course of an assault on the castle, the young count received the wound that would end his life. It didn't appear to be serious, a cut on the hand and arm from a lance, but it was enough. Within days, his arm had turned black up to the shoulder and Clito died, a few months short of his twenty-sixth birthday. Before he died he sent a letter to Henry asking forgiveness for all the harm he'd done him. Henry, with a major weight lifted from his mind, was no doubt happy to comply.

There was now only one feasible candidate to be Count of Flanders, and Thierry of Alsace was quickly recognised as such, both by Henry and, probably reluctantly, by Louis of France. The traditional treaty between England and Flanders was renewed and, according to Vitalis at least, Henry made sure that Stephen did homage to Thierry as overlord of Boulogne. Stephen's place in the order of things was thus confirmed. He may have been a mighty landowner in England, but outside of that country he was joint ruler of a fairly small county, subordinate to both France and to his neighbour the Count of Flanders. He was a useful ally for Henry, holding open a route to the Continent and guarding the northern borders of Normandy, but it is hard to see from the king's own actions that he ever regarded him as anything more.

It was around this time that Henry took steps to secure the future for the final son of Adela not yet provided for. By the mid-1120s Henry of Blois was a monk at Cluny Abbey, and the English king had already generously contributed towards the rebuilding of the abbey church and its upkeep. In 1126 he appointed Henry as the abbot of Glastonbury at the tender age of, at most, thirty years. Glastonbury is usually referred to as one of the richest abbeys in England, and so it had been some years before. By this time, however, it had gone through a period of decline, and the king's selection of an energetic young abbot may have been a shrewd choice. Certainly, the younger Henry immediately set about revitalising the abbey, restoring its fortunes and status, and embarking on an extensive building programme of cloisters, chapter house and dormitory. He even commissioned William of Malmesbury to write a history of Glastonbury, though it has been commented that this work was not up to his usual standard of accuracy, so maybe his heart was not in it. When in 1129, again with his uncle's backing, Henry was promoted to become Bishop of Winchester, he did not give up his abbacy, continuing to work to improve everything about a place he clearly loved, and since his efforts were producing so much in the way of good results no one seemed to comment on this most unusual – and generally frowned upon – dual role.

For some time, maybe even amounting to a period of years, Stephen seemed to be largely absent from the court of the English king. With two counties, Mortain and Boulogne, to keep him occupied, he was no doubt busy enough, and family life was probably centred on the latter. His first son may have been a boy called Baldwin, about whom we know very little. A tentative birthdate of around 1126 has been suggested but the boy died young, certainly before his tenth birthday and possibly earlier.

The eldest to survive was a son called Eustace, probably born between 1127 and 1129, followed by a daughter, Matilda, around 1133. She too was to die young, probably at some time in her fourth year. Politically, dynastically and probably personally, however, Stephen's marriage was going well. Not so that of his cousin Matilda.

It seems clear that from the start the only persons happy with Matilda's marriage were Henry and Fulk. The couple themselves appeared to dislike each other, and when the news of the union became general, the Anglo-Saxon Chronicle notes that it 'displeased all the French and the English'. Included among them was probably Theobald of Blois. For nearly twenty years he had loyally supported Henry, fighting at times both Louis on one side of his county and Fulk of Anjou on the other. Now, if Henry's wishes were to be carried out, he would be replaced in importance by young Geoffrey, while still disputing with him the county of Touraine, which lay between the two of them. If he had ever seen himself as a potential heir (and the naming of his son Henry suggests he might have) he could possibly have swallowed being replaced by Henry's own daughter, but this marriage must have seemed scant reward for all his loyalty. He had not even been consulted about it.

For some time after the wedding the newly-weds remained at Angers while Geoffrey became more and more involved in the administration of Anjou along with his father. This was a role he had been training for almost from birth. His name first appears as a witness to charters when he was only three years old, and he had regularly attended court gatherings. His mother, Eremburga, had also played a full part in the administration, acting as regent when Fulk was absent, and regularly witnessing charters with her husband. Both parents were determined their children would be well prepared for their roles in life, and it is notable that when Sybilla of Anjou later married Thierry of Alsace she proved as capable as her mother. If Geoffrey expected that his wife would play a similar part he was to be sadly disappointed.

Matilda seemed to take little interest in her new domain, rarely witnessing charters and loath even to use the title of 'countess'. And when, in February 1129, Fulk departed for the

Holy Land – probably scheduling his journey to arrive in time for Easter – shortly afterwards Matilda also quit Anjou. We don't know why she left, or even who instigated the split. Matilda is usually blamed, the implication being that she stormed off in a huff, unable to stand her young husband a moment longer. It is offered as an example of the arrogant, overbearing personality she is said to have displayed later. Robert of Torigny, however, who is more likely to have actually met the lady, says, 'She was truly a woman of excellent disposition, kind to all.' In fact, there could be many other explanations for her sudden departure.

It may have been Geoffrey that sent her away, and if so, there could again have been a number of different reasons. Perhaps she *was* overbearing, the difference in age and former status being hard to overcome. More likely there may have been problems with the business side of the deal. Geoffrey's own status had never been clearly defined and even after the marriage disputes could have arisen as to whether he was intended to become a joint-ruler or simply a consort when Matilda entered into her inheritance. It is clear, too, from later conflicts that Matilda's dowry had never been handed over. This consisted of a string of castles in southern Normandy, all of which were still held by King Henry's men. There is even a small chance Matilda might have been sent away for her own safety, the departure of Fulk triggering a rash of rebellions across Anjou and Maine, testing the mettle of the new young count. For a number of years he had his hands full, besieging castles and leading armies, possibly with the sprig of broom in his cap – the *planta genista* – from which he derived his nickname, 'Plantagenet'.

What is almost certainly well wide of the mark is the one unreliable account that suggested Henry withdrew his daughter because of disputes with Geoffrey. By 1128 the English king was far too desperate for an heir to have considered such an action. For whatever reason, Matilda spent more than two years in Normandy before accompanying her father back to England in June 1131. For part of this time Henry, too, had been in Normandy, even entertaining the pope at Rouen in May 1131, where there was a mighty gathering of nobles and clergy including, apparently, Suger himself in his role as the abbot of St Denis. Whether the pope's advice was sought on Matilda's marriage we don't know. The sole reference made to this visit by Orderic Vitalis is a rather sour comment: 'During the whole of that year the pope travelled from place to place in France, causing most burdensome expenses to the churches in that country.' Henry had, in fact, already met him – and knelt at his feet – in Chartres.

In June 1131 the royal party returned to England, and whatever had been discussed at Rouen, the topic of Matilda's marriage was now once again a matter for national debate. Robert of Torigny tells us that in September 1131 'there was a large and deliberative assembly held at Northampton in which all the chief men in England took part.' William of Malmesbury confirms this, but there is an important difference in the accounts of what happened at this meeting. Torigny says only that a decision was taken that Matilda must return to Anjou, 'her husband having claimed her'. Malmesbury, on the other hand, declares that at this meeting the previous oath of fidelity to Matilda was repeated. This is significant since many would later claim they had not been bound by oaths taken before the unpopular Angevin wedding. If Malmesbury's reporting is accurate they could have no such excuse. 'The oath of fidelity to her,' he says, 'was renewed by such as had already sworn, and also taken by such as hitherto had not.' He is the only chronicler to note this, and it must be remembered that he dedicated his work to Robert of Gloucester, Matilda's most faithful supporter. On the other hand, he claimed to be writing only of things that he could himself authenticate, so it is equally possible that the oath he describes did occur, but that he was the only one to underline the full significance of it.

Geoffrey, now an older and probably wiser eighteen-year-old, had not only requested the return of his wife but provided a suitably impressive escort for her and she duly returned to Anjou, though still taking a lesser role in the county than earlier countesses had done. Nevertheless, the marriage was revived, at least to the extent that the longed-for grandson for King Henry arrived on 5 March 1133. Some accounts say that Henry was present at his christening in the cathedral of St Julian at Le Mans, though the boy's own father was not. If so, then the christening must have been somewhat delayed, as the king did not leave England until August of that year – accompanied by earthquakes, eclipses and other significant omens. Needless to say, the boy was christened Henry, a rather blunt indication of where the power and prospects of the family lay.

By the end of the year Matilda was pregnant again, and she left Anjou for Rouen once more. It has been suggested that at this time Henry was instructing her in how to rule in England and Normandy, but troubles had broken out again in Anjou and it could be that she moved to Normandy for greater safety. Her second son, christened Geoffrey, was born on 3 July 1134; yet again Henry's carefully laid plans were put in jeopardy, as the birth was a difficult one and Matilda nearly died. By the time she had recovered, the relationship with her father seems to have taken a turn for the worse.

There were clearly disputes between Henry and Geoffrey of Anjou that had never been settled satisfactorily – Geoffrey's status after Henry's death, and the castles promised as Matilda's dowry, for instance – but Henry of Huntingdon appears to put the blame for the sudden revival of these issues squarely on the shoulders of Matilda. The problems, he says, were 'fomented by the arts of his daughter'. We don't know exactly what Matilda is supposed to have done, but certainly at this time Geoffrey is believed to have demanded that Henry hand over a number of castles in Normandy. Robert of Torigny and Vitalis both suggest that he wanted Henry to do fealty for them, and that in this he was backed by his wife.

Insecurity is probably the reason for such a demand. It may well have become clear to both Geoffrey and Matilda that there was strong opposition in England and in Normandy to the arrangements for their succession that Henry had made. With no stronghold in either place, their position would have been weak in the extreme if even a few of the more powerful barons decided to flout the king's wishes.

Geoffrey, in particular, had already seen how hard it was to oppose semi-independent lords who were prepared to defy a weak successor, even when that succession had been fully endorsed and established by a strong predecessor.

Henry, however, saw things differently. He had spent most of his life establishing a firm rule in both England and Normandy, and, like his father before him, had no intention of resigning any of his power, still less offering fealty to an upstart count. Matilda returned to Anjou, to her husband's side, and through the whole of 1135 tensions simmered between the opposing camps. The English king, who had wanted to return to England to deal with unrest in Wales, instead spent the summer prowling from castle to castle along the southern borders of Normandy like an ageing lion preparing to fight off all challenges. His own castles were improved and their defences strengthened, while in at least one case a lord suspected of divided loyalties had his castle taken from him and garrisoned with the king's men. Geoffrey, meanwhile, attacked and burnt the town and castle belonging to Henry's son-in-law Roscelin de Beaumont, and gave encouragement to any Norman lord who might be prepared to oppose the king. 'These disputes,' says Henry of Huntingdon with masterly understatement, 'irritated the king and roused an ill feeling.' However, he also suggests that the stress of all this may have contributed to Henry's sudden and unexpected death.

Taking time out for a hunting trip late in the autumn of 1135, the king partook of a meal of lampreys, an eel-like fish of which he was very fond, and which almost always disagreed with him. Acute food poisoning was the result. Over the course of a few days the king rapidly weakened and on 1 December 1135 he died. After more than thirty-five years of strong, decisive rule, King Henry was dead. Who could possibly replace him?

3

Long Live the King

(December 1135 – May 1136)

We have no way of knowing exactly when the thought occurred to
Stephen that he could become king of England. The *Gesta Stephani*,
that anonymous account of the *Acts of King Stephen*, describes him
as 'instantly conceiving a great design' when he heard the news
of King Henry's death, but this seems as fanciful as the account
preserved at Ely that describes Henry bequeathing his kingdom to
Stephen on his deathbed. The fact that Stephen was not present at
that deathbed gives the lie to both these accounts.

Henry took exactly a week to die and the certainty of his death
was apparent several days in advance. Time enough for most of
the leading nobles of England and Normandy to gather, and for
the Archbishop of Rouen to be summoned to hear his confession
and give him absolution and the last rites. Robert of Gloucester
was there, along with William of Warenne, Rotrou of Perche, and
the Beaumont twins, Waleran de Meulan and Robert of Leicester.
Stephen, though, was in Boulogne – not an insuperable distance
away – and he seems to have made no attempt to set out for the
castle at Lyons-la-Forêt where his uncle lay.

It is possible, of course, that the news of the illness was slow
in reaching him, though the news of the death met no such
delay. In the absence of such certain knowledge, however, we
can surmise that if he had at that time any expectation at all
that Henry might abruptly reverse his policy of the last decade
and name him his successor, surely Stephen would have moved

heaven and earth to get there and be publicly acknowledged. But he remained in Boulogne.

Boulogne, of course, was very handy for England, and the fact that Stephen remained there waiting for news of Henry's death very strongly suggests that he was already thinking in terms of the crown. He would probably have been brought up with the story of how Henry himself had taken advantage of his brother's sudden death – and the absence of the leading magnates – to seize the throne of England. Circumstances in 1135 were not so very different. True, the death was not as sudden and Stephen was farther away than Henry had been, but the absence of leading magnates from England and the fact that the other possible claimant was even farther away must have suggested a parallel opportunity – enough, at least, for Stephen to keep his powder dry and remain in Boulogne until he could see his way clear. When the other magnates decided they would remain with the old king's body until it could be transported to England for interment, as he had wished, the opportunity must have seemed like a gold-plated invitation.

Whether Stephen had shared his ambitious thoughts with anyone else is, again, very doubtful. He may possibly have consulted his wife and co-ruler, Matilda, but we don't have any evidence of her reaction to events as they unfolded. In later years she would often prove the wiser and steadier of the two, and on this occasion Stephen may have valued her opinion as to his chances of success. At the time of King Henry's death, however, she was in the later stages of pregnancy and may have been unavailable for such a consultation.

If Matilda knew, it seems clear that none of the other magnates shared the secret. A suggestion has been made that Stephen's coup was the result of a plan hatched between the Blois brothers to undermine the growing power of their less than friendly neighbour in Anjou. As regards Henry of Blois, Bishop of Winchester, this might be plausible, but it is clear from Count Theobald's reaction that the event was as much a surprise to him as it was to everyone else. It seems, therefore, that the scheme was entirely Stephen's own, and certainly in the initial stages he went about it very circumspectly, no doubt prepared to withdraw and deny any thoughts of the crown if circumstances went against him.

Thus, he did not cross the Channel as an invader with a mighty force at his back. Instead, the *Gesta* tells us, he 'landed in England with a small retinue'. Other sources fill in the details that he attempted to land at Dover but was turned away and, far from welcoming him with open arms, the people of Canterbury shut their gates against him. Since both these places were garrisoned by men loyal to Robert of Gloucester, it seems likely that the purpose of Stephen's sudden arrival was not hard to guess. It also suggests there was suspicion and hostility between the two men even at this early stage.

The speed of his actions was probably the giveaway. While other magnates were still gathered at Rouen, paying tribute to dead King Henry, Stephen was already in England. It is estimated he had landed by Thursday 5 December, a matter of four days after Henry's death, and a few days after that he was safely at his house in London. This timetable, however, hardly allows for all the 'trouble and confusion' in the whole kingdom, described so vividly in the *Gesta* in the pages before Stephen's arrival. There it is declared that 'people, long clothed in the garments of peace, clamoured and became frantic for war. Seized with a new fury, they began to riot against each other … and men, giving the reins to all iniquity, plunged without hesitation into whatever crimes their inclinations prompted.' Even the wildlife was affected, according to this account, when 'myriads of wild animals … suddenly disappeared … a single bird was a rare sight, and a stag nowhere to be seen.' Wildlife apart, the scenes described seem far more representative of later events, but the *Gesta* is determined to see Stephen as the one who rescued the nation from this apocalypse, insisting that it was 'while the English were in this state of turbulence and trouble', that Stephen arrived. His arrival was not without its omen, according to William of Malmesbury, though this supporter of Robert of Gloucester seems to have been the only one to record it. 'It is well known,' he says, 'that on the day when Stephen disembarked in England, there was, very early in the morning, contrary to the nature of winter in these countries, a terrible peal of thunder, with most dreadful lightning, so that the world seemed well-nigh about to be dissolved.'

It was in London that Stephen met with the first encouragement for his scheme, and we must be clear that here we are referring to the city of London, not Westminster – at that time a place some miles away, upstream on the Thames. The division is important. The city represented commerce, while Westminster was concerned with royalty and politics, and at this point commerce would be far more favourably inclined towards Stephen. The merchants in London traded in many things, but particularly in wool and especially with the major cloth towns of Flanders, accessed most conveniently through Boulogne. There may have been Flemish merchants present in the city who could speak up for Stephen and the English merchants themselves may have travelled through his territories. They would certainly be in favour of anything and anyone who could guarantee such a free passage for themselves and their goods in the future.

Another consideration might be the status of the Flemish towns themselves. During the troubled times after the death of Count Charles the Good, these towns had played a vital role in helping or hindering the progress of the various claimants to the county. It was their support, first for William Clito and then for Thierry of Alsace, that had proved decisive and, in return, many had received recognition as 'communes', that is, towns permitted to elect their own officials and, within limits, to govern themselves. No doubt the Londoners felt if they could play a similar 'king-making' role, they might win similar privileges for their own city. Thus, says the *Gesta*, when Stephen arrived, 'the city which had been in mourning for the death of King Henry, came out to meet him with shouts of joy, and received him in triumph, regaining in Stephen what they had lost in their protector Henry.' It goes on to describe how the Londoners now assembled in council 'men of rank and experience' who 'claimed it ... as their undoubted right and especial privilege, when the throne was vacant by the king's death, to provide that another should take his place.' They may well have done so, but there seems to be no justification in law or in precedent for such a claim. Certainly before 1066 there was a right for a council known as the Witanagemot to select a king from a recognised number of 'throne-worthy' candidates, but this procedure had died at the Conquest. In any case, the Witanagemot was made up of the leading landowners and clerics in the country, not a group of self-appointed London merchants.

Notwithstanding such small matters, the council proceeded to debate the merits and claims of Stephen and 'no one openly controverting them, the assembly came to the resolution of offering the crown to Stephen, and he was chosen by common consent.' A good beginning, then, for the would-be monarch, but Stephen himself would have known he needed far more than this to make such a title a reality. He would need the backing of the clergy, and in particular the Archbishop of Canterbury, whose role it was to crown and consecrate kings. He would also need the backing of the administrators of the sophisticated system Henry had established for the smooth running of his realm during his frequent absences. Stephen no doubt remembered that Henry's first aim in claiming the crown had been to secure the royal treasury, situated at Winchester. It was still at Winchester, as was the centre of the administration, therefore to Winchester Stephen must go.

Once again speed was essential, and it is likely he reached this ancient city at the latest by 12 December. There, according to the *Gesta*, he was met by his brother Henry, who was, most usefully, the Bishop of Winchester. All that followed can be put down to the diplomatic skill – what that source calls the 'persuasive eloquence' – of Henry. It may well be that Stephen himself recognised his need for such skills. He is described as hurrying to join Henry, 'on whom his chief reliance was placed', and even at this first meeting the bishop had brought along the chief citizens of Winchester who were quickly won to his cause. William of Malmesbury puts it even more categorically when he declares, 'not to conceal the truth from posterity, all his attempts would have been vain, had not his brother Henry, Bishop of Winchester ... granted him his entire support.'

One who seemed to need little persuasion to endorse the election of Stephen was William Pont de l'Arche, whom the *Gesta* describes as 'the trusty treasurer of King Henry'. He had apparently had some dealings with Bishop Henry in the past, refusing to allow him to take over the king's castle and treasury. Now, however, 'as soon … as he heard of the king's coming, whether through love or fear of him I know not, he presented himself before him with a cheerful aspect, and made him master of King Henry's treasure … together with the castle.' Roger, Bishop of Salisbury, was another whom it was essential to win over for Stephen's cause, and again he came quite willingly. He had long been King Henry's chief administrator and right-hand man in England. As is pointed out in several chronicles, he had not only taken the oath of loyalty to Matilda but had administered it to everyone else. Malmesbury, however, makes clear that certainly after Matilda's marriage, he had severe reservations about the matter. In particular, Roger claimed he had only sworn the oath on condition that Henry would not marry his daughter to anyone outside the kingdom without his consent and that of the English nobility. Not only had they not consented, they had not even been consulted and no doubt this, as much as anything else, had prejudiced the bishop against the marriage. Certainly he now seemed to have no qualms about breaking his word and Henry of Huntingdon says he 'contributed all in his power to raise Stephen to the throne'. There is also a suggestion that the price demanded for his support was that his son, also called Roger, should become the new king's chancellor.

By this time the claimant's cause had achieved a certain momentum. The *Gesta* describes how he was now 'joyfully acknowledged by numbers, those especially who were before in friendly relations with himself and his brothers.' Among them was listed William Corbeil, Archbishop of Canterbury, who nevertheless seems to have had some reservations about going against his sworn oath. Again it is the *Gesta* that gives the fullest description of the discussion that followed and the arguments put forward by Bishop Henry to overcome the archbishop's scruples. First of all, William, when urged to anoint and consecrate the new king, replies that this 'ought not to be done lightly or suddenly, but should be first maturely considered, and careful inquiry made whether it was wise and expedient.' He then reminded them that they were all bound 'by a most solemn oath' not to accept any monarch but

Matilda, who not only had her father's blessing but had also been favoured by God in having a male heir. 'Therefore there was great presumption in endeavouring to set aside this engagement.'

The counter argument was firstly that Henry had 'compelled, rather than persuaded the great men of the kingdom to take the oath of fealty' and that he himself had known it would therefore not be binding. Furthermore: 'We willingly admit that this thing was agreeable to him while he lived, but we say that he would not have been satisfied that it should be unalterable after his death.' This seems a truly bizarre argument, for when else would an oath to accept a successor be expected to apply, except after the death of the incumbent? However, the clinching argument seemed to be that in the end, Henry himself had changed his mind, 'for those who stood round him when he was at the last extremity, and listened to his true confession of his sins, heard him plainly express his repentance for the oath which he had enforced on his barons.' This is a rather ambiguous statement. It is not clear whether the claim is merely that Henry regretted forcing them to take the oath, or whether he regretted the content of the oath. Nor does it anywhere suggest that the king had nominated an alternative successor.

For that we have to look at another source, the *Liber Eliensis*, a chronicle written in the mid-twelfth century by monks at Ely. Here we find a detailed story, which, whether or not influential at the time of his succession, certainly formed part of Stephen's later defence of his actions. According to this account, in King Henry's last hours, he assembled a great number of noble and powerful men around his deathbed and, in answer to their concern about the succession, presented to them 'the most worthy knight, my most dear kinsman, Stephen,' to be king after him by right of inheritance, adding, 'and you will all be witnesses of this.'

Strange to say, if this did really happen, none of the noble and powerful men did come forward as witnesses, not even those who were happy to accept Stephen as king. The only name we have of someone prepared to swear to the truth of the story is Hugh Bigod, a royal steward and constable of Norwich Castle, who was supported by two unnamed household knights. The *Liber* declares that Hugh swore on the holy gospels that he had been present at the king's deathbed, and states that immediately after he made his pronouncement, King Henry died. Again, these statements cannot be reconciled. While almost certainly present at some point during the week the king took to die, it seems clear that Hugh was not one of those around the deathbed at the end. John of Salisbury, a later writer, records the Bishop of Angers refuting his claims, saying that neither Stephen nor Hugh could possibly have direct knowledge of Henry's last dispositions, 'because neither of you was there.'

The story in the *Liber* is also directly contradicted by William of Malmesbury's account of Henry's deathbed pronouncement. He too describes the nobility gathering at the king's bedside, and continues: 'Being interrogated by these persons as to his successor, he awarded all his territories, on either side of the sea, to his daughter, in legitimate and perpetual succession.' Furthermore, Henry seems to clarify the position of Geoffrey of Anjou, since Malmesbury adds to this statement that the king was 'somewhat displeased with her husband, as he had irritated him both by threats and by certain injuries.' The intention clearly is that Matilda is to be sole ruler, rather than ruling jointly with her husband.

Which of these accounts, if any, should we believe? For although attempts have been made to reconcile them, it seems impossible to do so. William of Malmesbury is clearly on the side of the empress, dedicating his work to her most faithful supporter. On the other hand, he maintains that he puts nothing of contemporary matters into his work unless he could corroborate it by a reliable source. Indeed, just a little earlier, he skips over King Henry's time in Normandy as he says he has no detailed knowledge of what was done there. He was obviously not present himself at the deathbed, but he would have been well placed to hear from those who were. He also quotes a letter written immediately afterwards from the Archbishop of Rouen to the pope. In this the archbishop recounts the events of the last days of the king, even giving details of his directions as to the distribution of his wealth and his intended almsgiving. He adds, 'I wish they who held, and do hold, his treasure had done this.' Nowhere, though, does he mention any startling change of successor, even though this would have been a matter of supreme importance, and he must have known of Henry's settled plans up to that point.

We don't know where the story contained in the *Liber* originates, but the Bishop of Ely at the time was Nigel, a nephew of Roger of Salisbury, who was, of course, firmly backing Stephen. This would not in itself make the account suspicious, but it is odd that none of the other chroniclers mention such an important piece of evidence. If Hugh Bigod's testimony was not given at the time, which seems possible, one has to wonder why not, and in particular why the *Gesta*, which is solidly behind Stephen, does not add this further concrete nomination to its story of Henry's change of heart about the oath. It may well have been one of the 'other considerations, which for brevity I omit,' but its significance, if true, raises a suggestion that although the testimony was believed by many, the anonymous writer of the *Gesta* was not one of them.

The *Gesta* implies that with or without the testimony of Hugh Bigod, these arguments convinced Archbishop William that he could safely bestow the crown on Stephen. William of Malmesbury, however, indicates that like many others he had a price which had to be met first, albeit one intended to benefit the church rather than himself personally. 'Stephen was bound,' he says, 'by the rigorous oath which William, Archbishop of Canterbury required from him, concerning restoring and preserving the liberty of the church,' and, in relation to this, 'the Bishop of Winchester became his pledge and security.' This suggests that while the archbishop was prepared to crown the king, he wanted to be sure that Henry of Blois would take a share in the responsibility.

This flurry of diplomacy, persuasion and possibly bribery was compressed into a very short time. If Stephen arrived in Winchester on 12 December, he was back at Westminster a week later. Orderic Vitalis puts the coronation at 15 December, but this is surely too early. Most chroniclers have it as either 20 or 22 December. It was not a very lavish ceremony. Despite the *Gesta* describing a 'large attendance of clergy,' William of Malmesbury declares that 'Stephen, therefore, was crowned king of England on ... the twenty-second day after the decease of his uncle ... in the presence of three bishops, that is the archbishop and those of Winchester and Salisbury; but there were no abbots and scarcely any of the nobility.' Most of the important nobility, of course, were still in Normandy, awaiting favourable weather to bring the late king's body back across the Channel to England. The attendance didn't matter, though. It was the actual ceremony that was important. Even the crowning, though significant, was not the heart of the matter. That lay in the anointing of the king with holy oils and the words of consecration spoken by the archbishop, from which point onwards, whatever his shaky credentials, Stephen could claim to be God's anointed King of England.

King he was, and as the *Gesta* says, 'the report spreading throughout England, almost all the great men of the kingdom willingly and reverently gave their adhesion.' In the eyes of the majority of the chroniclers, however, possibly with the benefit of hindsight, this in no way legitimated Stephen's claim to the throne. Henry of Huntingdon writes of him 'seizing the crown of England with the boldness and effrontery belonging to his character', and indeed the word 'seized' crops up regularly. For William of Newburgh, 'Stephen, violating the oath which he had sworn to King Henry's daughter of preserving his fidelity, seized upon the kingdom,' while Robert of Torigny declares, 'although he had promised the kingdom of England to the daughter of King Henry by an oath of fealty, nevertheless, in his audacity, he laid hands upon the crown.'

An oath at the time was a sacred undertaking, and it is this breach of faith that sticks in the throats of most of the writers. Society was built on the premise that a person would keep his sworn oath. Homage and fealty, the glue that held the system together, was based on just such an assumption. If a man could break his word in such a way with no adverse consequences, the whole basis of Western civilisation might be put at risk. There had to be consequences and again with the benefit of hindsight, these writers could spell out what they were. William of Newburgh puts the case against Stephen most succinctly. He was, he says, 'elevated to the throne equally against right both human and divine – transgressing the one by not being the legitimate heir, and the other by his perfidy.' In order to achieve the throne he had promised everything that clergy and nobles had demanded, but the consequences were that nothing good came from even the best of his promises, 'for by the judgement of God, that good, for the attainment of which these wise and powerful men had resolved on the commission of such an atrocious crime, was not permitted to take effect.'

Those who had helped Stephen to the throne, in particular Archbishop William Corbeil and Roger of Salisbury, also came in for a good kicking in the chronicles of these writers, and again the consequences are spelled out. William of Newburgh points out that the archbishop had been the very first to take the oath of loyalty to Matilda, while Roger of Salisbury had been the second. The consequences for these two are made quite plain by Robert of Torigny: 'William, Archbishop of Canterbury, who himself had already made oath to the king's daughter, consecrated (Stephen) as king; after which he did not survive a whole year.' To be fair, the archbishop was probably in his sixties at the time, so this may not have been particularly surprising. For Roger of Salisbury, however, who had sworn the oath twice, divine judgement was more specific. 'Roger, the great Bishop of Salisbury, who did this same thing a second time, and exhorted all others to do the like, gave (Stephen) the crown and aided him to the utmost of his power. But the just sentence of God decreed that this very person whom he had created king, should cause him to be imprisoned, tormented and at last come to a wretched death.'

All this was for the future, however. In December 1135 a rather sparse coronation was immediately followed by an equally meagre Christmas court held at Westminster. It is possible that at the time Stephen was bracing himself for whatever might happen when a change in the winds and tides would bring back to England not only the body of his dead uncle, but also all those magnates and their followers who had spent this time together in Normandy. On the other hand, if messages had already reached him from Normandy, he might have known that he would not have to face furious supporters of the empress, for there, too, the majority at least had shown a very relaxed attitude to the oaths they had sworn.

'Meanwhile,' says Vitalis, 'the Normans holding a counsel at Neubourg, inclined to place themselves under the government of Theobald.' Robert of Torigny backs this up with some slight variations. 'Upon the death of the king ... the nobles of Normandy lost no time in sending for earl Theobald to come and take possession thereof.' It is not absolutely clear from Torigny's version whether they were offering the count the throne of England, or simply the Duchy of Normandy. Either way it was a logical move. If they were resolved to abandon the empress, Theobald was clearly the next in line. Theobald himself seemed happy to go along with this, quickly travelling to meet them. Reading between the lines of Torigny's account, it may be that Robert of Gloucester was not quite in line with his fellow magnates on this matter. Torigny describes Theobald going initially to Rouen and then on to Lisieux, where he was actually in conference with Robert of Gloucester when news from England reached them. A monk sent as an envoy from Stephen announced to those assembled in one version that Stephen had received the submission of the English and was about to become king, and in another that he had already been made king. On hearing this news, the magnates, with or without Robert of Gloucester, 'unanimously resolved, with Theobald's consent, to serve under one lord, on account of the fiefs which the barons held in both countries'. This was the old, old problem that had existed since the time of the Conquest. Twice in the past, lords with estates on both sides of the Channel had been forced to try to please two different and hostile masters, and both times they had been required to choose which side to back when it came inevitably to fighting. They were not prepared to be put in that position again. Stephen had achieved a fait accompli in England, so Stephen got their support, whatever they might individually think of the way he had achieved his coup.

Vitalis and Torigny also give us insights into the reactions of two of the players in this game. Vitalis tells us that Theobald was 'indignant at not being called to the throne, although he was the elder brother' and that he 'departed in haste to transact important affairs which urged his attention in France.' It may very well be that the sudden change of circumstances called for a rapid diplomatic exchange with Louis of France, but Theobald's huff seems to have gone further than that. There had already been trouble on the borders of Normandy, which, in King Henry's day, Theobald would have been swift to deal with. Now, according to Vitalis, 'his negligence allowed Normandy to be oppressed for a long time.' Stephen may have become king and duke in one swift move, but he was going to have to work a little to obtain the active support of his brother in the difficulties that lay ahead. In the meantime, while Stephen was occupied in England, the Duchy of Normandy was effectively without a ruler.

Robert of Gloucester's reaction is recorded by Torigny, who tells us that on hearing of Stephen's success, he immediately surrendered the castle at Falaise, having first removed from it King Henry's treasure. He does not specify to whom it was surrendered or why, but clearly Robert was not going to hold it for Stephen. In the past it had been a major base and stronghold for the English king, and the place in which the money needed for his Norman enterprises was held – a function equivalent to the English treasury at Winchester. Now, it seemed, Robert was handing over the responsibility for this to Stephen himself.

Even during the Christmas season Stephen and his supporters were taking steps to add some measure of legitimacy to his seizure of the crown. The way to do this, of course, was by appealing to the acknowledged leader of the Western world, the pope. Letters were prepared, setting out Stephen's case, probably along the lines of that recorded in the *Gesta*. We don't have the actual letters, but since Stephen widely circulated the pope's reply and at least one copy of this still exists, we can reconstruct the likely points of the argument from that. It appears, in fact, that a whole dossier was sent, not only Stephen's letter but supporting letters from a number of English bishops. The whole is likely to have been orchestrated by Bishop Henry of Winchester, who might with some justice be described as the brains behind the regime, certainly in its early stages.

It almost certainly helped Stephen's case that the pope himself was in need of support at that time. Pope Innocent II, formerly Gregorio Papareschi, had been elected pope by a group of eight cardinals immediately following the death of Pope Honorius in February 1130 and had been consecrated on 14 February of that year. However, another larger group of cardinals claimed that this election was not valid under canon law and they elected a rival, Pietro Pierleoni, as Pope Anacletus II. The rivalry reflected splits between powerful Roman families, and since the supporters of Anacletus were in the majority, Innocent was forced to flee Rome, while Anacletus took possession of St Peter's Basilica. The hugely influential monk Bernard of Clairvaux persuaded the French clergy to accept Innocent as the true pope, however, and he was also accepted by Lothair III, whom he subsequently crowned as Holy Roman Emperor. King Henry of England had also accepted him, entertaining him at Rouen in 1130, and the saying got about that 'Peter possesses Rome, but Gregory has the whole world.'

At the time of Henry's death in 1135, Anacletus still possessed Rome, while Pope Innocent was based at Pisa. The rivalry was still ongoing, and it might have been apparent to Innocent that if he failed to recognise Stephen's kingship, the appeal might then be sent to Anacletus, and he might lose the support of the English realm. It would have helped that the messengers from England pursued a rather circuitous route to Pisa, apparently picking up letters of support for Stephen from Louis in Paris and Theobald in Blois on the way. Both of these would, of course, have supported anything rather than an increase in power for Geoffrey of Anjou.

We have no evidence of any similar appeal to either pope made by Matilda at this time. Bishop Ulger of Angers was in Pisa when Stephen's dossier would have been delivered, but he was there on business to do with his own diocese and several years would pass before he was briefed to make an appeal on behalf of his countess. It may well be that he had left Anjou before news of Stephen's coup arrived there.

While Stephen's dossier was on its way to Pisa, the king himself played a full part in the funeral of King Henry when, early in January 1136, the body was finally brought back to England. 'The king went to meet it,' John of Worcester records, 'attended by a large body of nobles, and for the love he bore his uncle, he supported the bier on his royal shoulders, assisted by his barons, and thus brought the corpse to Reading.' In modern terms this would be seen as a wonderful photo opportunity, and in medieval times the imagery would not be lost on the assembled clergy and nobility. Here was the king humbling himself to show how close he was to his deceased kinsman, and acting in co-operation with the other lords bearing the precious coffin. Nothing was spared in either the funeral ceremonies or in the associated almsgiving – Stephen had, after all, the royal treasury amassed by his predecessor to draw on – and Henry was finally laid to rest before the high altar in the abbey church that was his own foundation.

By this time it seems that almost all the English nobility had accepted Stephen on his own terms. A challenge by David of Scotland was swiftly dealt with, and the crown was even more firmly settled on Stephen's head when the pope's response to his dossier was received in time for Easter. The first few words of the letter would have removed any remaining fears, as Pope Innocent sent his greeting to 'Stephen, illustrious king of England'. He referred especially to Stephen's promise of obedience to the church and his close relationship to his predecessor, and speaking of the integrity and love of peace and justice shown by Henry, he urged Stephen to live up to this. Clearly he had accepted the story of the breakdown of society in England, and the good character given to Stephen by all those who had sent letters on his behalf. It was God, he declared, moved to pity by the prayers of holy men, who had prompted the nobles, commoners and clergy of England to choose Stephen as king, and he quoted a verse from the Book of Daniel in the Bible to the effect that God ruled over the kingdoms of men, and could give them to whomever he chose. Presumably it was diplomacy (or possibly a subtle papal joke) that caused him to leave off the end of this verse, 'Even to the basest of men'.

Buoyed by this clearest indication of papal approval, Stephen's Easter court at Westminster was a confident display of royal splendour. By this time his wife Matilda had joined him in England after giving birth to her fourth child. She now had a formal coronation, probably on Easter day, 22 March, and the king and queen wore their crowns at a court gathering attended by almost all the nobility and higher clergy. Three archbishops were there, those of Canterbury, York and Rouen, together with almost every bishop of England and Normandy. The only Norman absentees were John of Lisieux – whose position at the head of Norman administration was comparable to that of Roger of Salisbury in England – and Richard of Bayeux, the illegitimate son of Robert of Gloucester. Of the seven English earls, four were present, and another may have been represented by his twin brother, Waleran de Meulan, himself Count of Meulan in Normandy. As well as these, a considerable number of royal officials are named as attending this important court. The constables included Miles of Gloucester, Robert d'Oilly and Brian FitzCount, respectively castellans of Gloucester, Oxford and Wallingford castles, while the named stewards included Hugh Bigod, who, if he had expected a reward for his prompt support of the new king, had not received one. A large number of barons from around the country are also listed, some of whose loyalty would not stand the test of time.

The most notable absentee from this impressive list is Robert of Gloucester, who presumably had accompanied his father's body to its burial place, but apparently had not obeyed a subsequent summons to court. William of Malmesbury, in fact, seems to suggest Robert was not in England at this time and that he only returned after Easter, having considered his position in Normandy. It is inconceivable, however, that he would not have been at his father's funeral, and if he returned to Normandy immediately afterwards, this must have appeared as a very substantial snub to the newly crowned king. Robert, though, was a very large fish to land, and Stephen showed admirable patience in waiting for him to finish his deliberations. The only step he took in the meantime was to make Miles of Gloucester answerable directly to himself, rather than to Robert, for the safekeeping of Gloucester castle.

Robert's dilemma is neatly summed up by William of Malmesbury: 'If he became subject to Stephen, it seemed contrary to the oath he had sworn to his sister; if he opposed him, he saw that he could nothing benefit her or his nephews, though he must grievously injure himself.' At the time it seemed that Stephen held all the aces. With the vast treasures amassed by Henry at his disposal, he would not even need to depend on the loyalty of the English to defend his position. As Malmesbury put it: 'A man possessed of such boundless treasures could not want supporters, more especially as he was profuse and ... even prodigal.' Stephen was prepared to pay well for his security and the use of large numbers of mercenaries from Brittany, and especially Flanders, would be a feature of his reign.

Nor was it only superior force that Robert would have to face if he opposed the new king. Stephen apparently had charm by the bucketful, and even those chroniclers who generally disapproved of him had to concede his easy manners, his readiness with a joke and his ability to sit and 'regale' even with lowly persons. 'So kind and gentle was his demeanour,' the *Gesta* tells us, 'that, forgetful of his royal dignity, on many occasions ... he put himself on an equality with, and sometimes even seemed to be inferior to his subjects.' This was quite a refreshing change from the forceful, domineering personality of his immediate predecessor. In later times, when push came to shove, this easiness would be seen as a weakness in the king, but certainly in the early days it made him a popular figure with nobility and commoners alike.

An anointed king with power behind him and the popular touch would be very hard to dislodge and this seems to have been the conclusion reached by Robert of Gloucester when he finally made his appearance at Stephen's court sometime after Easter in 1136. We need to be careful here with Malmesbury's account. Writing for Robert, he is likely to be putting the best possible face on things but, at the same time, he would have been well placed to receive inside information. According to him, the earl's motive for seeming to capitulate was to get close to his fellow nobles who had already done so and 'to convince them of their misconduct and recall them to wiser sentiments'. Again implying that he had still been in Normandy before this time, he declares Robert 'had not the liberty of coming to England' unless appearing to support Stephen, and therefore 'he dissembled for a time his secret intentions.'

No one else mentions these secret intentions, or the fact recorded by Malmesbury that Robert's homage given to Stephen at this time was conditional. 'He did homage to the king,' we are told, 'under a certain condition; namely, so long as he (Stephen) should preserve his (Robert's) rank entire, and maintain his engagements to him.'

Thus, if Stephen should treat the earl in any way that did not befit his rank, Robert could regard himself as freed from his fealty.

The reason for this, again according to Malmesbury, was that Robert, 'having long since scrutinised Stephen's disposition … foresaw the instability of his faith.' What Robert hoped to get from this is fairly clear, but it is debatable whether the two men interpreted 'rank entire' in the same way. All his life Robert had been treated as a king's son, and in later years he had been Henry's right-hand man, totally trusted and highly influential. Had his sister inherited the crown, especially if Geoffrey of Anjou had contented himself with a major role in Normandy, Robert would have had every prospect of continuing in such a position. Stephen, however, would be likely to pick his own inner circle, and, considering the pre-existing tensions between the men and this inauspicious beginning, Robert was unlikely to be among them.

Why Stephen would have agreed to such a conditional homage is harder to understand unless he still feared the earl could mount a substantial challenge to his new status. The clue may lie in the *Gesta*'s description of Robert's return. 'After being frequently summoned by messages and letters from the king to attend his court, at last he came, and was received with extraordinary favour, everything he required being granted on his doing homage.' It would certainly be an extraordinary favour to be accepted on his own terms, but the *Gesta* goes on to state, 'His submission, at length gained, was followed by that of almost all the rest of England.' From the names on the list of those present at the Westminster court, it might have appeared that most of the nobility had already submitted to Stephen, but, of course, doing so involved breaking a sworn oath. The king may have feared that such a submission and homage might be just as easily cast off if Robert had shown a continued and principled resistance. The earl's capitulation may well have led to a general feeling that what was good enough for King Henry's son was good enough for all, and Stephen may well have breathed easier for bringing him into line, whatever the cost. A pithy comment from John of Worcester seems to sum up the situation. 'If I were not afraid that the royal majesty would harm John's head, I would assert that all oath-takers are guilty of perjury.'

It was not at the royal court at Westminster that Robert of Gloucester finally made his appearance, but at some point in the days that followed when the court was making a leisurely progress along the Thames Valley to Oxford. Wallingford Castle would be a likely spot. With his close friend Brian FitzCount as castellan, he would be sure of some support if things turned sour. In the event, however, everything went smoothly and the earl travelled on with the court to Oxford.

With the last substantial magnate safely on side, it was at Oxford that Stephen issued what became known as the *Oxford Charter*, or sometimes the *Oxford Charter of Liberties* for the church. This began by reciting his credentials as king and continued by repeating and expanding on the promises made in his brief coronation charter, in particular those promises relating to the church which had, to a large extent, contributed to his successful seizure of power. The church was to be free. The bishops were to have jurisdiction over all clergy and persons in orders and their property. The king would not sell or permit others to sell church offices (the sin of simony). The king would not hold the property of vacant sees pending the appointment of a new bishop. Bishops and abbots might reasonably dispose of their personal property before death. (In the past the king had simply seized such property and added it to the royal treasury.) Finally, the king guaranteed to the church all lands, privileges and customs it had held at the time of the death of his grandfather, the Conqueror, and confirmed all later gifts.

Most of these were not exactly new promises. They had been around since the Abbey of Cluny had obtained its decisive influence over the church in the previous century. King Henry had made very similar promises in his own coronation charter, though his performance had not always lived up to the promise. What they amounted to in the eyes of the bishops, however, was a triumph of Cluniac policy, a free church, answerable only to its own bishops and ultimately to the pope. These were the terms exacted by Bishop Henry of Blois, himself a Cluniac monk, for his support for his brother's coup, and no doubt he looked forward to a period when, in England at least, king and church would march together to the benefit of all.

There was something in the charter for the rest of Stephen's subjects as well. He would keep the peace, do justice to all and protect all. He would stamp out corruption among his sheriffs and officials. He would observe the good and ancient laws and just customs in relation to murder pleas and other causes and, something that was seen as a really popular move, while holding on to the royal forests established by his grandfather and by William Rufus, he would return 'to the church and to the kingdom' those rather extensive areas that had been added by Henry. This was such a crowd-pleaser that a wild rumour got around that in addition the king had abolished the geld, the land tax that produced much of the royal revenue. No such promise, however, is to be found in the charter.

All these points were faithfully noted down by William of Malmesbury, probably from a copy of the charter held at his abbey since it is known that many copies were made and widely distributed throughout the country. His object seems not to be to praise the king for his noble intentions, however, but to condemn him for his failure to live up to these lofty ideals, for 'he as basely perverted almost everything, as if he had sworn, only that he might manifest himself a violator of his oath to the whole kingdom.'

All that was for the future, however. In the spring of 1136 the crown seemed securely settled on the new head, and the prospects for a successful reign appeared, if anything, rather better than those of either of his immediate predecessors.

4

Distant Thunder

(January – December 1136)

While Stephen's takeover passed off smoothly and peacefully in southern England, it was not without its challenges elsewhere. Indeed, the first year of his reign was punctuated by episodes of extreme violence, but since none of these approached anywhere near his main centre of power in the south-east, they were seen as presenting only minimal threats to his kingship. His handling of these affairs, however, would cast long shadows over later years. The most immediate action took place in southern Normandy, probably before there was even a thought there that Stephen might become king. 'In the first week of December,' says Orderic Vitalis, 'Geoffrey of Anjou, receiving intelligence of King Henry's death, sent forward to Normandy his wife Matilda without loss of time.' Whatever his ultimate intentions this was a shrewd move. Matilda was far more acceptable to the Normans than Geoffrey himself, and the castles she aimed for were part of her long-denied dowry, the very cause of the trouble between Geoffrey and Henry in the king's final year. As anticipated, the border castles of Domfront, Argentan and Exmes were handed over without any fuss, the castellans acknowledging Matilda as their lawful sovereign. Geoffrey himself soon followed, claiming some further castles on the border with Maine, and accompanying William Talvas to the key fortresses of Sées and Alençon. Talvas was the grandson of Hugh of Montgomery, and Sées and Alençon were part of the Montgomery lands in Normandy. They had been seized by Henry in 1112, leaving Talvas only the northern county of Ponthieu, which came to him through his mother. Later, however, Fulk of Anjou had persuaded Henry to return these lands to Talvas, all bar the castles, which were garrisoned by Henry's men. When, in 1135, Talvas had defied the king and been once again stripped of his lands, Geoffrey had supported him. Now William Talvas would prove a useful ally to the Angevin cause. As expected, Sées and Alençon were duly handed over, strengthening the foothold already established on Norman soil.

By this time Stephen's coup in England would probably have been reported far and wide, and it would have been clear to Geoffrey and Matilda that their earlier suspicions had been justified. Normandy and England would not be peacefully handed over to their sworn heir. It was more than likely they would have to fight to hold on to what they had already taken, and certain that they would have to fight to obtain any more of Matilda's promised inheritance. They may have anticipated an immediate attack by Theobald of Blois, but the count, returning south in a sulk, did not immediately take up arms against the Angevins on his brother's behalf. Instead, possibly to give himself some thinking time, he concluded a truce with Geoffrey that was to last from Christmas to Pentecost, a matter of some five months. After this promising start, however, the Angevin campaign ground to a halt and indeed in some respects went into reverse. Matilda established a secure base at Argentan but she was pregnant again and would in due course give birth to her third son, William, in July 1136. Geoffrey, too, had other matters to deal with; the sporadic rebellions that plagued Anjou had broken out again.

The most serious obstacle, though, was the antagonism of the majority of the Normans. Vitalis seems to suggest that initially Matilda and Geoffrey had been if not welcomed, at least tolerated. It was when they attempted to spread out from their bases, in particular when their troops were forced to live off the land they passed through, that trouble erupted. 'His troops, however, spread throughout the neighbouring country, committed many cruelties,

violated the churches and cemeteries ... and caused much injury
and loss to those who had treated them with kindness.' Retaliation
for these 'cruelties' was swift. The Normans, says Vitalis, 'who are
naturally fierce and daring,' made 'furious attacks on the foreign
troops', driving them out and pursuing them to great effect as they
retreated. What he is describing is more or less a rout, with more
than 700 killed. 'The rest ... made an ignominious retreat, and
gaining their own country after being sharply punished at the point
of the sword, had no desire to repeat the experiment.'

Now, if ever, was the time for King Stephen to establish his reign
in Normandy. If he had, there was a good chance he would have
been accepted by the Norman magnates and would have stamped
out the Angevin threat once and for all. But he didn't go, and
though it seemed Matilda's challenge was at least in abeyance, that
was by no means the end of the troubles in the duchy. More than
once Vitalis bewails the fact that Normandy was left with no strong
ruler *in situ* and without such a presence old feuds and grudges
rapidly surfaced to turn one lord against another, to the detriment
of all. Few of those who now fell to fighting were doing so on
behalf of Stephen or Matilda, but with the empress established at
Argentan, the division provided a focus for discontent and a source
of support against older enemies.

As early as December 1135 rebellion had broken out in northern
Normandy where Rabel de Tancarville refused to accept Stephen as
duke ahead of his older brother Theobald. Immediately he fortified
his own castle and seized another, a ducal fortress at Lillebonne.
Then, in February 1136, when Eustace of Pacy died, a more serious
dispute arose over the important lordship of Breteuil in the centre
of the duchy. This had been given to Eustace when he married King
Henry's illegitimate daughter Juliana and was subsequently taken
from him for rebelling against the king. It had since come into the
hands of Robert of Leicester, one of the Beaumont twins, when he
married Amice, daughter of the new lord, Ralph de Gael. Now
William of Pacy, the son of Eustace and grandson of Henry, tried
to reclaim the lordship as his birthright. He was backed in this by
Roger de Tosny, who had had his own castle at Conches taken
from him by Henry when he was suspected of backing William

Talvas and the Angevin cause the previous year. He now attacked and took the ducal castle at Vaudreuil, which action immediately put him and William of Pacy into opposition with Stephen, and into favour with Matilda and Geoffrey.

While these upheavals were being put in motion, Stephen was enjoying his triumphal Easter court and subsequent leisurely progress, first to Oxford, and then on to Salisbury. He did not entirely ignore the situation, but instead of going himself to put down such insurrection, he sent Waleran de Meulan, the other Beaumont twin, who was riding high in the royal favour. As a mark of this favour Waleran had recently been betrothed to Stephen's daughter Matilda. He would have to wait awhile for his wedding, however, as Matilda was around two years of age. Once in Normandy, Waleran lost no time in gathering forces and combating the rebellious magnates. Roger de Tosny held Vaudreuil for a matter of three days before it was retaken for Stephen on 10 May, which happened to be the feast of Pentecost. The following day Roger's own castle at Acquigny was attacked and burnt to the ground, leading him to seek reprisals against Waleran's Norman lands.

At just this time Count Theobald's truce with Geoffrey ran out, and he was rapidly recruited to Stephen's cause by Waleran's twin brother Robert. Despite Theobald's former sulk, he must have already been inclined to accept Stephen's kingship, since he had earlier recommended it to the pope. Now he collected a large force from Blois, and besieged and took the castle at Pont-St-Pierre belonging to Roger de Tosny.

Waleran, too, was actively gathering supporters. Alan of Brittany brought a force of Bretons to the cause, while Richer of L'Aigle, somewhat over-enthusiastic in gathering provisions for his men, incurred the fury of Orderic Vitalis when the lands of the monastery of St Evroult were pillaged. A band of marauders, Vitalis called them, driving off the cattle belonging to monks and others until attacked by the citizens of nearby Ouche, who caught and hanged a number of them. In retaliation Richer burned the settlement of St Evroult to the ground, the monastery itself only being spared when the wind changed.

King Stephen intended to join his lieutenant in Normandy after Pentecost, and indeed a fleet was ready and the king preparing to embark when a rumour reached him that Bishop Roger of Salisbury had died. Along with Stephen's brother Henry, the bishop was one of the foremost supporters of the king's regime at this stage. Stephen was even heard to declare at one point, 'I would give him half of England until the end of time if he asked for it.' Hearing this rumour, the king, in characteristic fashion, instantly cancelled his expedition and hurried back to Salisbury, where he found Roger to be in rude health. However, no more was said about visiting Normandy, and those fighting there on his behalf continued to fight alone.

The campaign was now carried to the Angevins. Richer of L'Aigle attacked both Roger de Tosny and the castle at Gacé, which had been taken by Matilda's supporters, while Waleran's brother-in-law, Gilbert Fitz Gilbert of Clare, pushed even closer to Argentan, attacking Exmes. There, though, he found himself overmatched when William Talvas rushed to defend it. Many men were lost and Gilbert himself only narrowly escaped.

On 21 September Geoffrey of Anjou himself returned to the fray. Marching with a large army he crossed the River Sarthe and pushed rapidly northwards, accompanied by a number of significant supporters. William Talvas was there, along with Duke William of Aquitaine, Count Geoffrey of Vendôme, and the son of Count William of Nevers. It was a short and violent campaign – today we might call it a blitzkrieg – from Argentan in the south to Lisieux in the north, taking six castles in nine days, not all of them by force. Many people joined him, says Vitalis, 'either to support their prince, or from the love of plunder'. Carrouges was taken in three days, and Annebecq was simply handed over by its lord, Robert de Neubourg, who would give solid support to Geoffrey. Not everyone welcomed the Count of Anjou, however. The castle at Montreuil was attacked three times by the Angevins, according to Vitalis, 'but being stoutly resisted by the garrison, they gained nothing but wounds and retired.'

We get the impression of different units of the army, under different commanders, spreading out and targeting castles over a wide swathe of territory in the push northwards. Those that didn't fall easily within an agreed timescale were simply left to be dealt with later. The aim seems to have been to lay claim to all of Western Normandy, including the Cotentin peninsular, which had not yet been visited by Waleran on behalf of Stephen. Lisieux may well have been seen as a base to consolidate, prior to a determined assault on Caen, the city most recently favoured by King Henry.

In fact, it appears that Geoffrey did not get the overwhelming support he was expecting on his journey northwards and by the time he reached Lisieux he seems to have lost confidence in his expedition. This may be, if Vitalis is to be believed, because many of those joining him had turned out to be not magnates or soldiers believing in his cause but an ill-disciplined rabble out for what they could get. 'There were numbers of reckless thieves,' he says, 'for free bands and sturdy plunderers had joined the expedition with no other intention but, like wolves, to devour those who devoured others. Undisciplined vagabonds assembled, like kites, from all quarters ... for no other object than pillage, slaughter and conquest.' This was not the kind of support Geoffrey was looking for, nor was it likely to make the Norman people take to his cause. It was no doubt a failure to control their 'followers' that led Vitalis to note that nearly all the leaders of the expedition 'disgraced themselves'.

Waleran de Meulan, meanwhile, seems to have feared a long-drawn-out siege, and had withdrawn the bulk of the army from Lisieux, leaving the place in the hands of a Breton garrison led by Alan of Brittany. Even before the Angevins arrived, the decision was taken to burn the town, preventing them from getting near the fortress. Geoffrey, no doubt aware that Waleran and his army were lurking nearby, immediately withdrew down the Touques valley. Pitched battles were rare occurrences at this time and clearly he was not prepared to risk everything in a winner-takes-all face-off with Waleran, especially in the absence of King Stephen, who might otherwise have provided a focus for such a contest.

His new target was the castle of Le Sap, which he put under siege. Even here, however, things did not go according to plan. Despite attacking with siege engines and some 3,000 archers,

Geoffrey was unable to overcome the firm defence of Walter de Clare. On 1 October he himself was severely wounded in the foot, and this, with other troubles in the army, brought a swift end to the campaign. Even the arrival of Matilda with several thousand reinforcements on 2 October was not enough to prolong it. The birth of her son barely two months before must have been considerably easier than her previous labour, and that she made the journey at all is evidence of her desire to establish her claims in Normandy. On this occasion, her efforts were in vain.

The Angevins had been in Normandy barely thirteen days, and in that time, in the words of Vitalis, they had secured themselves 'not the dominion but the eternal hatred of the Normans'. With his monastery barely a short day's ride from the events he was describing, he was well placed to receive first-hand accounts of what occurred, but there is something almost gleeful in his account of the retreat of Geoffrey and his army in October 1136. They had, he said, 'Gorged themselves with crude eatables,' and as a result, 'suffered so severely from diarrhoea that, leaving foul tokens of their passage along the roads, numbers of them could scarcely crawl home.' Nor does he show any sympathy for Count Geoffrey. 'The count, who had entered Normandy on a foaming steed with threats in his mouth was now brought home pale and groaning and carried in a litter.' As a final indignity, the ford across one of the rivers was held against them and in seeking an alternative crossing point, the count's chamberlain was killed and his baggage lost, including his 'state dresses and precious vessels'. Altogether it was an ignominious end to Geoffrey's grand design on Normandy.

In the same week, Waleran de Meulan wrapped up most of the other rebels. Roger de Tosny and his mercenaries were defeated with Roger captured and imprisoned and, though Rabel de Tancarville was still defiant, a relative peace was restored to the land under the firm hand of Stephen's lieutenant.

Normandy was not the only place, however, where Stephen's assumption of power was challenged. At around the time of his coronation in December 1135, King David of Scotland was already advancing into northern England with an army. Some have seen this as an opportunistic land grab. Aelred of Rievaulx, one of the northern chroniclers, for instance, declares that the king simply 'gathered an army and harried Northumbria with slaughter and fire.' John of Hexham, another such recorder of the times, takes a more generous view. He first reminds us that David was the uncle of the Empress Matilda, and adds that he was 'not unmindful of the oath which he and the whole realm had sworn to King Henry concerning his successor.' When, therefore, he had stormed and taken the fortresses of Cumbria and Northumbria, 'he received also oaths and hostages from the nobility in pledge that they would keep their faith to his niece.' David, of course, owed everything he had to King Henry, his throne, his wealth, even his wife, and would maybe have felt more obligation than some to honour the dead king's wishes.

Within a few weeks he had covered a wide swathe of territory, taking castles built or sponsored by Henry at Carlisle and Norham, as well as others at Wark, Alwick and Newcastle. This was, in fact, long disputed territory. The area known as Carlisle comprised not just the town itself but all and more of the former county of Cumberland. It had been claimed by both England and Scotland, until King William Rufus decisively annexed it and peopled it with English immigrants. For a while it had been part of the Honour of Lancaster but had been taken from Ranulf Le Meschin by King Henry when Ranulf became Earl of Chester in 1120. Thereafter, Henry had regarded it as an essential part of his border territories with Scotland, part of the same security policy that had led to his illegitimate daughter marrying the neighbouring Scottish lord, Fergus of Galloway.

To the east, Northumbria had been an Anglo-Saxon kingdom and latterly an earldom before the Conquest, though the border with Scotland was frequently rather vague. The earldom had been in abeyance since the last Norman earl, Robert de Mowbray, had led a revolt against William Rufus. However, David's connection with the area came through his wife, Maud, who was the daughter of the last Anglo-Saxon earl, Waltheof. As well as taking over her Honour of Huntingdon, he may well have believed himself entitled to Northumbria, a claim that might have been admitted had the Empress Matilda inherited the throne of England. As it was, his rapid invasion may have been intended to advance both their claims.

This time, however, Stephen was quick to act against the challenge. The chronicler Richard of Hexham, a native of that town, would become prior of the Augustinian abbey there in 1141. He was therefore very close to the action and tells us that David intended to take Durham as well, but 'King Stephen came thither with a great army at the beginning of Lent ... and abode there fifteen days.' The beginning of Lent in 1136 was 5 February, so Stephen had assembled his army and marched north in a matter of weeks, presumably immediately after the funeral of King Henry. There was to be no battle, however.

Possibly David had expected support from the English nobility, many of whom had at that time still finally to declare their acceptance of Stephen. Such support did not materialise and this, together with the size of the opposing army, no doubt persuaded him to negotiate rather than fight. Stephen appeared to be at his charming best. William of Malmesbury declares that King David was 'softened' towards him 'by the natural gentleness of his manners', though he alternatively attributes his easy capitulation to 'the approach of old age'. David was around fifty at the time. Thus, he 'willingly embraced the tranquillity of peace, real or pretended'.

'From David,' says Malmesbury, Stephen 'readily obtained what he wished,' though when we look at the treaty between them it seems to be David who has driven the harder bargain. True, there was no further mention of the rights of the Empress Matilda, but David got away without any offer of homage to the new king because, says Robert of Torigny, 'he was the first of all the laymen who had made oath to the empress.' In fact he almost seems to have been rewarded for the audacity of his invasion. His son Henry, then a youth of some twenty years, took over his father's earldom of Huntingdon and did homage for this, and for Carlisle and Doncaster as well, which seem to have been casually thrown into the bargain. David in response returned Wark, Norham, Alnwick and Newcastle to Stephen. Furthermore, says

Richard of Hexham, 'some say, who testify they were present in this assembly (Stephen) promised him that, if he should wish to give anyone the earldom of Northumbria, he would first cause the claim upon it of Henry, the king of Scotland's son, to be justly adjudged in his court.'

It may well be that Stephen felt it was worth making an effort to secure the support of the Scottish king, but on almost every level it seems that David comes out of this ahead of the game. Not only had he secured Carlisle, but also encouragement amounting to almost half a promise in his designs on Northumbria, albeit through his son rather than in his own person. Stephen, on the other hand, seems to exhibit both the traits assigned to him by Richard of Hexham; first, that in the face of challenges he 'preserved ever a firm courage and a cheerful countenance,' and secondly, that he 'smiled at ... the loss of worldly possessions, however great, as if he did not feel them, or counted them for nothing.' It is quite certain that his uncle, King Henry, who had jealously guarded his borders, would never have allowed such important possessions to slip away so easily.

Peace and tranquillity, 'real or pretended', was established, then, on the Scottish border, and the new Earl of Huntingdon accompanied Stephen when he returned south. Almost at once, however, the first cracks in the new friendly relationship became apparent. Stephen showed great honour to the young man, particularly at his Easter court where he sat him at his right hand at table. This immediately caused an outbreak of anger on the part of the Archbishop of Canterbury and some of the English nobility who felt slighted. The archbishop declared that such a place was rightfully his and promptly withdrew from court, while the nobles, 'enraged at the king, gave vent to their disapproval in the presence of Henry himself.' According to Richard of Hexham, when Henry returned and reported this to his father, King David was 'highly indignant ... and refused to allow him again to visit the king's court, though frequently invited.'

We don't know for sure who the author of the *Gesta Stephani* was, though the name of Robert, Bishop of Bath, has been suggested. Whoever he was, he was no friend to the Welsh. He takes pains to explain exactly where Wales is to be found, and that it is a land well stocked with fish and game and large dairy herds. However, 'the men it rears,' he declares, 'are half savage, swift of foot, accustomed to war, always ready to shift both their habitations and their allegiance.' He seems familiar with the dealings between the Normans and the Welsh, describing how the Marcher lords established by William the Conqueror set about building castles to push their territories into those of the Welsh kingdoms of Morgannwg, Powys, Gwynedd and Deheubarth. 'Reducing the natives to subjection,' he says, 'and settling colonies of their own followers, they introduced laws and courts of justice to promote order,' – a familiar description of a colonial power disregarding any pre-existing system of government.

By the time of the death of King Henry, the border lands were held by Ranulf, Earl of Chester in the north, a pair of sheriffs, Pain fitz John and Miles of Gloucester, between Shropshire and Hereford, and by Robert, Earl of Gloucester in the area of Gloucestershire and Glamorgan. Miles of Gloucester laid claim to lands as far west as Brecon, while the Earl of Gloucester's holdings stretched to the Gower peninsula. In the far west Henry had planted a colony of Flemings in Dyfed, while castles at Pembroke and Carew were held for him by Gerald of Windsor, and Ceredigion came under the lordship of Richard fitz Gilbert of Clare, based in his castle at Cardigan.

To a large extent Henry was lucky in his dealings with Wales. Glamorgan and the far west were, by and large, firmly held. Gruffydd ap Cynan, king of Gwynedd had, after a number of reverses of fortune, settled down to a resigned acceptance of English overlordship, while family feuds in Powys prevented any serious attempt to challenge the Norman influence. Times were changing, however. Gruffydd was growing old, and his sons had their own ambitions. Powys was once more united. Disinherited sons from Morgannwg and Deheubarth were not far away, often in inaccessible uplands, and the Welsh leaders in general had learnt new methods of warfare and the value of castles. Some had even accompanied the English king in his French wars. Henry's fierce reputation had served him well in Wales, but his successor had no such advantage. As the *Gesta* puts it, 'on King Henry's death, when the peace and concord of the kingdom was buried with him, the Welsh, who always sighed for deadly revenge against their masters, threw off the yoke which had been imposed on them.'

It is the *Gesta* that covers the Welsh uprisings most thoroughly, devoting pages to actions and reactions mentioned only in passing elsewhere. According to this source, the first unexpected blow was struck in the Gower. In January 1136 an English force of knights and men-at-arms was attacked and killed by the Welsh of Morgannwg. Such a setback sent shockwaves through the Marcher community but fired the Welsh with dreams of wholesale rebellion. From his home in Cantref Mawr, to the east of Carmarthen, Gruffydd ap Rhys, son of the last king of Deheubarth, set out for Gwynedd to encourage others to join an uprising. At the same time his wife, Gwenllian, led her own force against the English at Kidwelly, seeking a further victory. Sadly, this time the result went against her. Gwenllian was killed – according to Gerald of Wales she had her head cut off – and for a while the flicker of rebellion was stamped out. Barely three months later, however, a greater blow was struck against the hated Norman rulers. On 15 April 1136 Richard fitz Gilbert of Clare, Lord of Ceredigion, was on his way home from Stephen's Easter court. In the pass of Grwyne Fawr to the west of Abergavenny he was ambushed and killed. Whether this was pre-planned or simply a lucky chance, catching an enemy off guard, it served as a trigger for a more general uprising. 'It becoming bruited abroad,' says the *Gesta*, 'that the greatest man in Wales had fallen, the people of several districts, assembling in great numbers, entered his territories.'

Even now a swift response with deadly power might have snuffed out the trouble. Stephen's response, however, was neither swift nor deadly enough. His mind, no doubt, was on other matters; the turbulence in Normandy, perhaps, or maybe the arrival of Robert, Earl of Gloucester, come at last to submit to him. And having finally got the earl to his court, he was not prepared to release him to deal with trouble in Wales, as he might otherwise have done with so prominent a Marcher lord. It could be that he was not certain enough of the loyalty of the border sheriffs, either. Certainly neither Pain fitz John, nor Miles of Gloucester was allowed to leave his court at this time to quell the rebellion. Nor did Stephen go himself with an army, as he had when responding to King David's invasion. Such a move might well have overawed the nascent uprising and brought it to peace in the way that King Henry had done on several occasions. Presumably Stephen felt that Wales was not worth the effort. As the Welsh princes had a history of falling out with each other, maybe he thought the matter would end in similar infighting, without any need for intervention. This time, however, co-operation rather than division was the order of the day. In particular, Gruffydd ap Rhys of Deheubarth and his sons were prepared to join with Owain Gwynedd, son of Gruffydd ap Cynan, to attack the Norman lands of west Wales, while the heirs of the Gwent and Morgannwg dynasty pressed home their advantage in the south-east.

Some response was needed, and it was Baldwin fitz Gilbert, the younger brother of Richard, whom Stephen turned to, to avenge him and take over his lands. 'Entrusting him with a large sum of money,' says the *Gesta*, he 'commanded him to carry relief as soon as possible to his brother's territories, and resolutely strive to crush the enemy.'

The money, of course, came from Henry's well-filled treasury, and the force gathered seems to have been largely made up of mercenaries; both cavalry and archers are specified. No doubt in full confidence Baldwin marched off into Wales and got as far as Brecon unchallenged. 'There he heard that the enemy had advanced to meet him in vast multitudes, and, blocking up the roads by felling trees across them, had summoned their confederates to assemble from all quarters.' Baldwin ventured no farther. According to the *Gesta*, he hoped the Welsh would be 'wearied out' or exhaust the local food supplies if he waited long enough. 'Meanwhile he abandoned himself to gluttony and sloth, until he had prodigally spent all his supplies.' Finally, he withdrew, 'in poverty and disgrace'.

A second expedition, led by Robert fitz Harold, Lord of Ewyas, had a little more success. The *Gesta* describes a great victory over a numerous body of Welsh as he fought his way through to 'a deserted castle', identified as Carmarthen. Here he added 'impregnable fortifications' and a resolute garrison, but no additional resources were forthcoming. Eventually he had to fight his way back to England again, where he found no further support for his cause.

By the autumn of 1136 Owain Gwynedd had already completed one sweep through Ceredigion and returned home with considerable plunder. Now, finding no effective retaliation from England, he returned again with conquest in mind. Burning Aberystwyth, he turned his attention to Cardigan, the last Norman castle, and, incidentally, the refuge of Richard fitz Gilbert's widow, Alice de Gernon, sister of Ranulf of Chester. Robert fitz Martin, Lord of Cemmaes, was the Norman commander at Cardigan. He was convinced he had sufficient forces to defeat this invasion once and for all, and immediately marched out to meet Owain in pitched battle.

Banc-y-Warren, a mound adjacent to the road from Cardigan to Aberystwyth, has been identified as the site of the so-called Battle of Cardigan, which took place in October 1136. The Normans – numbering around 10,000 men, including 1,000 Flemish mercenaries and 2,000 cavalry – took up a position on the slopes, thereby forcing the Welsh to attack uphill, and they expected this advantage to be decisive. It is claimed, however, that this was the first battle where the Welsh employed their soon-to-be-famous weapon, the longbow, and with devastating effect. Infantry were cut down and Norman cavalry stopped by volleys of arrows. The final charge by the Welsh cavalry swept the remaining Normans from the field, in full retreat all the way to Cardigan itself.

The castle there held out but Alice de Gernon was now, according to the *Gesta*, 'strictly enclosed ... short of provisions ... and without hope of relief.' She was, indeed, 'worn out with grief and care'. It was Miles of Gloucester, finally released from service with the king, who undertook to rescue her. The *Gesta* implies it was his own idea, though backed up by royal permission. 'He was,' it says, 'impelled ... as much by compassion and his natural feelings for the distressed lady, as by the king's command, who had written to enforce the enterprise.' The impression is given that without prompting, Stephen might have left the lady to her fate.

The *Gesta* writer is clearly impressed with the commando style of Miles of Gloucester's rescue mission. 'Tracking his way, therefore, through the enemy's posts,' he says, 'among the gloomy recesses of the woods and over the mountain tops, he resolutely approached the besieged castle, and withdrawing the lady and her people in safety, returned triumphantly to his own territories.' Exactly how the lady was 'withdrawn' we are not told.

This, however, was to be the last triumph in Wales for some considerable time. Already the Marcher lords Ranulf of Chester and Robert of Gloucester had given up hope of effective support from Stephen and were making deals with the newly installed Welsh princes on their borders to preserve as much as they could of their Welsh possessions. By the middle of the following year, Gruffydd ap Rhys was firmly established in Dyfed, from which base his sons would progressively regain control over almost all of the former area of Deheubarth. Owain Gwynedd had become the foremost authority in central and north Wales, and the expedition of Pain fitz John to try to relieve the isolated garrison at Carmarthen ended in disaster when Pain himself was killed by a javelin blow to the head.

The policy of King Stephen in relation to these Welsh rebellions is summed up in the *Gesta*. 'The king thought that he was struggling in vain, and throwing away his money in attempting to reduce them, and that the better plan was to suffer for a while their unbridled violence, until ... they should quarrel among themselves, and perish by famine or cut one another's throats.' Quite erroneously the *Gesta* suggests that this, in fact, happened, describing scenes of murder, famine and pestilence until the land was left without men or tillage, and 'scarcely any means of life was left to those who came after.' This misrepresentation perhaps reflects a supreme indifference by the English to what was actually happening in the land beyond their borders. Yet again Stephen had suffered 'the loss of worldly possessions ... as if he did not feel them, or counted them for nothing.' His Marcher lords, however, had suffered considerable loss of life, land and prestige by this royal indifference, and it would no doubt weigh heavily in their minds against the king when it came to choosing sides in future conflicts.

So what was it that was occupying the mind of King Stephen in the summer of 1136, when he should have been either in Normandy or in Wales, securing his dominion over important territories? He chose instead to focus on two very minor rebellions in the south-west of England, both of which, he decided, needed the presence of the king himself.

The first of these was sparked by a property dispute involving an estate at Uffculme in Devon, the Abbey of Glastonbury and one Robert of Bampton. With his zeal for restoring Glastonbury to its former glory, Henry, Bishop of Winchester, laid claim to Uffculme, declaring that it had previously belonged to the abbey and should be returned. Robert responded that it had been given to his father by William the Conqueror, as recorded in Domesday Book, and that he himself had held it at the time of the death of King Henry, such holdings being guaranteed by Stephen's own Oxford Charter. The dispute was heard before the king who, unsurprisingly, found in favour of his brother Henry. Robert refused to surrender the manor, and found himself in rebellion against the king.

With none of this background admitted, the *Gesta* casts Robert as the villain of the piece, a drunkard and glutton who turned, apparently unprovoked, to banditry, and justly had his land taken from him. Having fortified his major stronghold, the castle he had built at Bampton in Devon, he abruptly disappears from the story. The *Gesta* declares he escaped from the king and became a vagabond, who ultimately 'perished miserably in a foreign land'. The castle was briefly besieged by the king, who terrified the garrison into surrender by hanging one of their number who had escaped, and threatening to do the same to the rest unless they immediately submitted. According to the *Gesta*, many of them, being exiled from England, made their way to Scotland, to the service of King David.

The second rebellion was rather more serious and took up a great deal more of the king's time and money. Baldwin de Redvers came from a Norman family with land in the Cotentin peninsular. His father Richard had been an early supporter of Henry in his struggles against his brothers, and had been rewarded with the major Honours of Plympton in Devon, Christchurch in Hampshire and the Isle of Wight. Inheriting in 1107, Baldwin was the wealthiest landowner in the south-west, and in the top dozen in the country. His holdings, among many others, included the borough of Exeter. Why Baldwin rebelled is not entirely clear. With his family loyalty to Henry, he may have thought that if he led others would follow, and flock to support a rebellion against Stephen. The south-west certainly proved later to be solidly behind the empress in her struggle for the throne. Alternatively, it may be that he wanted to emulate Miles of Gloucester, obtaining an hereditary castellanship in Exeter and the role of sheriff of Devon, and was thwarted in this by the king. He may even have been showing support for his brother-in-law Rabel de Tancarville in Normandy.

For whatever reason, he repeatedly refused summons to come to Stephen's court and pay homage for his lands, and the king resolved to make an example of him. The showdown took place at Exeter, and given the wealth of detail supplied by the *Gesta* writer, it is highly likely that he was present himself, or got first-hand accounts from someone who was. Baldwin seized Exeter castle, filling it and the town with armed men and stocking it with provisions commandeered from the surrounding area. The citizens of Exeter, however, did not support his enterprise. Messengers were sent to the king, imploring him to 'come to the help of the citizens in their present distress ... so that, strengthened by his aid, they might oppose Baldwin's power, and maintain their allegiance to the king, their only lord.'

Stephen promptly sent off an advance guard of 200 horsemen to prevent further damage to the town, and followed himself with his own forces, since 'it was as clear as day that the castle of Exeter had always been a royal castle, and that he was justly entitled to its custody.' His welcome, too, would have been gratifying, 'the citizens going out to meet him with offerings and joy' and leading him into the town 'in great triumph'. It would be a while, though, before he triumphed over the castle.

Baldwin had brought his family there, and garrisoned it with 'the flower of the youth of England, who were bound by oaths to resist the king to the last extremity.' In fact the siege lasted three months through the summer of 1136, with both sides pursuing it with great vigour. Stephen had siege engines constructed to hurl stones at the walls, and firebrands over them to set fire to the buildings within. Miners were employed to 'sap the foundations', while lofty wooden towers allowed archers to fire at the defenders on the walls and gatehouse. Judging by the *Gesta* account, the king seems to have taken a strong personal interest, rushing here and there, day and night, to issue orders and even, at one point, apparently mounting the hill and challenging the besieged to come out and fight.

The defenders, meanwhile, lost no opportunity to harass their opponents and smash their war machines. 'Sometimes they made unexpected sallies and fell furiously on the royal army; at others they shot arrows and launched missiles against them from above.' Part way through the siege they were reinforced by a troop of armed supporters, who mingled unnoticed with the king's men before getting a message inside to open the gate and let them in. 'The king,' says the *Gesta*, 'took the affair in good part, saying it would turn out well if it was so ordered by divine Providence.'

Perhaps the surrender and burning of Baldwin's castle at Plympton, and the confiscation of all his property, reconciled Stephen to the delay, but the siege was costing him dear. The *Gesta* estimates some 15,000 marks was spent on the enterprise, and although the outer wall was breached, the garrison simply retired to the inner citadel and continued to hold out. It was lack of water that finally brought matters to a head. The *Gesta* writer attributes it to 'the Almighty Disposer' that, after three months, the springs that fed two wells in the castle dried up. (He completely discounts the idea that it was the hot, dry summer, and possibly the numbers of men and beasts relying on them.) The garrison, he says, was forced to use wine instead, not only for drinking but also for cooking and making bread, and even for putting out fires started by the king's firebrand missiles. When the wine also failed they were forced to negotiate.

At first Stephen refused even to hear their messengers, encouraged to harden his heart by his brother, Bishop Henry. 'For the bishop had remarked their emaciated appearance, their parched and gaping lips,' from which he concluded they would shortly be forced to accept any terms. Even when Baldwin's wife appeared, although the king received her graciously he refused to consider anything but an unconditional surrender.

There were some, however, among those accompanying the king who were related to those besieged, or otherwise favoured a more merciful end to the siege. Persuasively they argued that the king would have triumph enough if he forced a surrender without taking the lives of the rebels, that those in the castle had never actually sworn allegiance to Stephen so should not be treated as traitors and, perhaps especially, that if Stephen ended the siege now, 'he might be at liberty to prosecute other enterprises,' – in Wales, maybe, or even in Normandy. It is tempting to think that the Marcher lords the king had kept with him during this time might have been particularly persuasive on the last point.

Perhaps it was the king's own innate good nature that was decisive, for when he abruptly changed his mind he went rather further than he had been urged. 'He not only allowed the garrison to evacuate the castle without molestation,' says the *Gesta*, 'but permitted them to retain their arms and property, and to take service with any lord they might choose.' This precedent of leniency, according to Henry of Huntingdon, was a big mistake. 'Being ill-advised,' he says, 'he permitted the rebels to go without punishment, whereas if he had inflicted it, so many castles would not have been afterwards held against him.'

Far from Baldwin submitting and attaching himself to the king's interests, as Stephen had no doubt hoped, he immediately took himself off to his Isle of Wight property intending, so the *Gesta* says, 'to weaken the king's resources by collecting a large piratical fleet ... to intercept the merchant ships which plied between England and Normandy and inflict losses on both countries by every effort in his power.' Stephen, though, followed him closely to Southampton, and when Baldwin heard that the king was ordering ships to be made ready, he finally gave in and threw himself upon the king's mercy. Under King Henry, Baldwin would, at the least, have been unlikely to see the outside of a prison cell again. Stephen merely contented himself with confiscating his property and sending him into exile. Crossing the Channel, Baldwin immediately found a welcome at the court of Geoffrey of Anjou. With his encouragement and the support of his own brother on the family lands in the Cotentin peninsular, he began a campaign of banditry, particularly targeting Stephen's followers. 'He mercilessly swept the country of plunder,' says the *Gesta*, 'and became formidable by carrying alarm into every quarter ... continually stimulated to proceed in these outrages by the entreaties and counsels of the countess of Anjou.'

Thus, with what would later be regarded as unfailingly poor judgement, in the first year of his reign Stephen devoted himself to soundly defeating two minnows (letting one escape to trouble him again), while turning a blind eye to the menacing sharks in Scotland, Wales and Normandy that were likely in the long term to prove far more costly. This was the year which most commentators regarded as quiet and successful – but it sowed the seeds for much of the turbulence that would follow.

5

Flickers of Fire

(January 1137 – December 1138)

As he enjoyed the Christmas festivities at his court held at Dunstable in 1136, Stephen may well have felt some satisfaction with his first year as the king of England. Twelve months before, he had barely got the crown on his head. Since then he had ridden out some challenges but now all the major magnates had accepted his rule, he had a treaty with Scotland, Normandy was, if not completely peaceful, at least dormant, and Wales – well, Wales was far enough away not to trouble the king too much. By and large it had been a successful year – and yet even now there were small shifts in the patterns of power that would later bring about significant changes.

On 21 November William Corbeil, Archbishop of Canterbury, had died. He was an old man and his passing was not unexpected. There was at Stephen's court one who confidently expected to step into the vacancy thus created, thereby cementing his position as the most influential person in the kingdom, after the king. Bishop Henry of Winchester had been immensely useful to his brother in the preceding year, and fully anticipated his reward. It is likely many others anticipated it too but, in fact, the post would not be officially filled for some time.

Orderic Vitalis carries a story that Henry was actually chosen as successor, but 'a bishop cannot be preferred from his own see to another without the authority of the Roman pontiff.' He gives this as the reason for Henry's departure from England to Normandy shortly before Christmas 1136, saying that Henry immediately dispatched messengers to Pope Innocent at Pisa, before settling down to await a reply. Wherever Vitalis got this from (and it may even have been a rumour travelling in advance of Henry himself) it is not mentioned in any other report of the time. Henry certainly crossed to Normandy at that time, but the reason usually advanced is that he was on a diplomatic mission, preparing the way for a visit by Stephen in the spring. It might be thought surprising that this should necessitate a journey at the worst time of the year, and just before Christmas at that, but if Henry had any other expectation from his travels, he was to be sorely disappointed. When he arrived in Normandy, according to Vitalis, he was immediately bombarded with demands for justice from those suffering from the lawless state of parts of the duchy. He heard 'doleful complaints of the sad events which filled Normandy with grief' and saw with his own eyes 'houses reduced to ashes, churches unroofed and void, villages in ruins and depopulated'. Whether this was true of the whole duchy, we don't know. Vitalis was living in an area that had fared particularly badly the previous year and no doubt he wrote what he saw. Nevertheless, by the time Stephen finally arrived in the third week of March, his brother had done much to smooth the way for him and make him welcome.

He sailed from Portsmouth to the Cotentin, an area of Normandy that had still not been decisively brought under the control of the king's lieutenant, Waleran de Meulan. No doubt he felt it important the duke should show by his presence that he possessed all the duchy – but he did not stay long. Pausing briefly at Bayeux, his first priority seemed to be to mop up the last of the rebels from the year before. The castles taken by Rabel de Tancarville – at Lillebonne, Mézidon and Villers – fell easily to Stephen and the considerable force that accompanied him, and Rabel himself quickly submitted to the king and was permitted to join the court.

As Robert of Gloucester held the castle at Bayeux, it might have been thought he would have accompanied or even preceded the king to welcome him there. According to William of

Malmesbury, however, he delayed his departure from England and did not join the court before Easter, when it had moved to Evreux. Again, we have to be careful with Malmesbury's account as he always tried to interpret the earl's actions in a way that showed him in the best possible light. He had already excused his submission to Stephen on the basis that he needed to be in England in order to size up the weight of support for the empress, and to encourage others to be true to the oath they had sworn for her. Now he pursues this idea, saying Robert only left for Normandy after he had 'thoroughly sounded and discovered the inclinations of such as he knew to be tenacious of their plighted oath, and arranged what he conceived proper to be done afterwards.' If this is true, Stephen was completely justified in doubting the earl's loyalty. On the other hand, there seemed to be very little organisation or pre-planning in the steps taken later to support the empress in England, so perhaps Malmesbury was simply stating what he hoped his hero had been doing before he left.

The Easter court at Evreux was intended to impress. The area had seen considerable fighting the previous year, and Stephen, with his wife and young son beside him, wanted to show how settled it had since become and how securely it was now under his control. At this time two prominent lords from the region, Rotrou of Perche and his nephew Richer de l'Aigle, came to submit to the king and were rewarded with adjoining castles. Robert de Neubourg also came and was received by the king. The previous year he had handed over his castle at Annebecq to Geoffrey of Anjou, but, having seen Geoffrey's ignominious retreat, he now put himself firmly in Stephen's camp. It was at Evreux, too, that Stephen met his brother Theobald for the first time since his seizure of the crown. Theobald had already written to the pope in support of Stephen's kingship and had fought for him the previous year, but there still seemed to be some lingering resentment. Robert of Torigny says, 'Count Theobald was angry that he, Stephen, being the younger, should obtain possession of the crown, which he said belonged to himself.' As a result, an agreement was made by which Stephen would pay his brother 2,000 marks per year by way of compensation.

Soon after Easter the court moved to the Norman border with France, where a meeting had been arranged between the two kings. They must have made a contrasting pair – Louis in his mid-fifties, obese and ailing; Stephen some dozen years younger and still a prime military figure. One thing they had in common, though, was a solid aversion to Anjou and its rulers, and they soon came to an agreement. In the words of Vitalis, 'being invested by (Louis) in the Duchy of Normandy as a fief of the crown of France (Stephen) made a treaty of alliance with him on the same terms as his predecessor had done.' Apparently these terms included allowing Stephen to avoid paying homage for his duchy; as Henry had done before him, he had his son Eustace perform homage on his behalf.

It was probably on this occasion that Count Theobald was made 'count palatine' by Louis, giving him, within his county of Blois-Champagne, privileges that would otherwise belong to the king. Furthermore, he was appointed guardian to the king's son and heir, Louis the Younger, then seventeen years old, and accompanied the boy on his journey to Aquitaine to escort his promised bride back to France. This bride was the fifteen-year-old Eleanor. Her father, William of Aquitaine, had formerly been an ally of Geoffrey of Anjou, but when he died on 9 April that year on a pilgrimage to Compostela he left all his possessions to the French king, with a strong recommendation that his daughter be married to the king's son. This the king was happy to accept, and the marriage duly took place on 25 July 1137.

The death of William of Aquitaine had robbed Geoffrey of Anjou of a valuable ally, but he may well have been anticipating one even more valuable. 'At this time,' says Orderic Vitalis, 'Robert, Earl of Gloucester, and some others were suspected of favouring the enemy.' According to Vitalis, at some point in May, 'Geoffrey … entered Normandy at the head of 400 men-at-arms, and, taking service on his wife's behalf, carried on an active campaign.' The implication is that he stormed up the duchy expecting the castle at Caen to be handed over to him, 'but the garrison of Caen faithfully preserved their allegiance to the king.' Robert, presumably, was still keeping his options open, not at all ready yet to commit himself to outright rebellion. Some other accounts, however, say that Geoffrey and his army went no further than the border, or perhaps his wife's stronghold at Argentan, and remained there awaiting developments.

It seems clear there was an intention on both sides that there should be a decisive engagement in the summer of 1137. Stephen had mopped up dissent in his duchy and obtained recognition from his overlord. The logical next step was to stamp out the Angevin threat once and for all. Battles were rare at this time; sieges and plundering were the usual activities of enemies. It does seem likely, however, that both Stephen and Geoffrey were contemplating a full-scale battle, with perhaps the death or capture of the chief opponent as a main target. Geoffrey had his army ready, and Stephen had for some time been gathering a mighty force of his own at Lisieux. This, however, was to prove his undoing.

As in the previous year, Stephen put great faith in Flemish mercenary soldiers, and recruited large numbers of them under the leadership of William of Ypres. This William, the illegitimate son of a former Count of Flanders, was the same person who some ten years earlier had tried to claim Flanders for himself. By some accounts he had even been implicated in the murder of Count Charles the Good. After failing in that enterprise, however, he had maintained himself as a sword for hire, at the head of mercenary bands. Stephen had known him for some time and seemingly placed more reliance on him than on his own magnates, which did not go down at all well. 'Stephen,' says Vitalis, 'had great confidence in William of Ypres and the other Flemings and showed them great favour, at which the Norman lords were much incensed, and withdrawing themselves with address from the king's service, took every means of privately annoying the Flemings, of whom they were jealous.'

Stephen's intention had been to march south to attack Argentan or some other fortress held by the Angevins, 'where he should fall in with Geoffrey of Anjou, being very desirous to bring him to a general engagement.' He got no further than Livarot, however, just a few miles down the road, when his army fell apart. 'In this expedition,' says Vitalis, 'there arose a violent quarrel between the Normans and the Flemings who came to blows, and there was a dreadful slaughter on both sides.' Robert of Torigny gives more detail. The quarrel, he says, 'was occasioned by the robbery of a barrel of wine, which a certain Fleming carried off from an esquire of Hugh de Gournay.'

Hugh de Gournay is certainly one of the names mentioned in several chronicles as someone who abruptly left the army at this time, but he was not the only one. Vitalis declares that 'most of the leaders left the camp without taking leave of the king, each body of vassals following its chief.' As if this was not damaging enough to the prestige of a king reported to have 'chafed with fury,' Stephen then put himself in the even more humiliating position of pursuing his deserting lords and trying to placate them. If Vitalis is correct in this, it is hard to overestimate the loss of face this would have involved for the king. One can imagine his grandfather, the Conqueror, pursuing deserters – but not for the purpose of soothing their feelings and persuading them to return. It is a measure of Stephen's overall weakness that even in this he failed. 'Wherefore,' says Vitalis, 'as from certain circumstances he held them in suspicion, he did not venture to recall them to war.' Torigny puts it even more succinctly. The feud, he says, 'compelled the king to return without having accomplished anything.'

It is at this time, too, that William of Malmesbury recites a more sinister incident. He claims there was an attempt on the part of Stephen to ambush and dispose of Robert of Gloucester, 'for the king endeavoured to intercept him by treachery, at the instigation of one William of Ypres.' Robert, however, was warned by an accomplice and 'absented himself from the palace, whither he was repeatedly invited, for several days.' It is not clear whether the earl specifically confronted Stephen about this but Vitalis, who also mentions the incident, seems to hint that the king tried to put the blame entirely on the Fleming. He 'endeavoured by a serene countenance and unrequired confession, to extenuate the enormity of his crime. He swore, in words framed at the earl's pleasure, never again to give countenance to such an outrage.' Furthermore, in order to recover the earl's goodwill, 'he confirmed his oath ... giving his hand to Robert.' He might have given his hand, but Malmesbury clearly believes he did not give his heart with it. 'This he did, it is true,' he says, 'but he never bestowed his unreserved friendship on that man, of whose power he was ever apprehensive.' There was no sharp break between the two men, no violent row and storming out, but if any moment defined the certainty of coming opposition, it was that. It would be a year before Robert formally defied the king, and another beyond that before he actually moved against him, but from that moment onward any chance of a working relationship between the two was gone forever.

With his army in total disarray, Stephen's plans to confront and conquer the Angevin faction were necessarily abandoned. Messengers were exchanged with Count Geoffrey, and a truce arranged that was to run for either two or three years, depending on which account is read. Henry of Huntingdon manages to put a positive spin on this, suggesting it was Geoffrey that needed the truce, 'seeing that at present he could not make head against King Stephen on account of his numerous forces and the abundance of money found in the treasury of the late king, which still remained.' In fact the truce was probably equally welcome on both sides, though the mention of the treasury is timely. Again the price of peace for Stephen was 2,000 silver marks per year, the first instalment being payable immediately.

It is likely that on his progress through Normandy, Stephen paid at least a brief visit to Falaise, where King Henry had kept his Norman treasury. William of Malmesbury estimated that the prudent, careful Henry had left at least £100,000, not counting priceless jewels, gold and plate. This figure may not even include the amount in the Norman treasury, and at the start of his reign Stephen was certainly a very wealthy monarch. To a large extent his early successes were founded upon this wealth. He used it to pay mercenaries and to buy off opponents, but he was not as prudent or as careful as his predecessor. When Henry paid – or more often promised – annuities, it was usually as a temporary measure while he prepared for further action. Stephen seemed to regard the payment as a permanent solution. No doubt the wealth appeared to him almost limitless in those early days, but he would soon find it was not. The Anglo-Saxon Chronicle says the money was 'distributed and scattered foolishly'.

According to several chronicles, the summer of 1137 saw a prolonged heatwave and drought from July to mid-September. In the midst of this Louis VI of France died, a mere six days after the wedding of his son. Thereafter Louis the Younger became Louis VII of France, and Eleanor of Aquitaine became Queen Eleanor. Perhaps to make a point, Stephen is reported as conducting military manoeuvres in the sensitive area of the Norman Vexin, displaying his possession of that region for the benefit of the new king. Vitalis, though, says he was dealing with 'turbulent subjects' and burning castles in a region that was 'a den of thieves'. He made no attempt, however, to move against those rebels in the west of Normandy, Baldwin de Redvers among them, who were causing as much trouble as they could in the Cotentin and Avranches areas.

In November 1137 the king abruptly returned to England, though the reason for this is not entirely clear. There is a consensus of the chroniclers that he had received reports of disturbances in that country, but the account of Vitalis of a conspiracy to massacre all the Normans on a given day and hand over the country to the Scots is scarcely credible. No such conspiracy is mentioned in the English chronicles. There was, though, a truce with David of Scotland, arranged by Archbishop Thurstan, which was due to run out in December, and a Scots army was being gathered. Most of the disturbances, however, seemed to follow the king's return rather than cause it. Another suggestion is that Stephen returned because at least one and possibly two of his young children had recently died. They are named as Matilda, lately betrothed to Waleran de Meulan, and Baldwin. Both would be buried at Holy Trinity Priory, Aldgate.

In another appalling misjudgement of the situation, Stephen took with him to England 'nearly all the great Norman lords', in particular Waleran de Meulan and his brothers Robert of Leicester and Hugh, known as Le Poer, along with their cousin Robert de

Neubourg. In their place he left William de Roumare, half-brother to Earl Ranulf of Chester, and Roger, Viscount of the Cotentin, 'commanding them', in the words of Vitalis, 'to accomplish what he had been unable to effect in person, namely to do justice to the inhabitants, and procure peace for the defenceless people.' Needless to say, they failed in this. The Cotentin in particular rapidly degenerated into violence with constant raiding and plundering, led, on behalf of the empress, by her half-brother Rainauld or Reginald de Dunstanville, another by-blow of King Henry. He was ably supported by Stephen de Mandeville and by Baldwin de Redvers – which must have been uncomfortable for William de Roumare, who was married to Baldwin's sister. William, in fact, is not mentioned in connection with this outbreak of rebellion, but Roger, the viscount, is recorded as resolutely endeavouring to carry out the duty laid upon him by King Stephen, with some success. In January 1138, however, he was lured into an ambush and butchered without mercy, leaving the Cotentin effectively in the hands of the rebels.

One great Norman lord who did not return to England with King Stephen was Robert of Gloucester, who took this opportunity of quietly separating himself from the royal court. Still, though, he made no move to align himself with his sister's cause, and William of Malmesbury is almost certainly overstating the matter when he seems to suggest Robert could have made a decisive move at this time. He declares that Robert 'disguised his feelings, and, allowing the king to depart peaceably to his kingdom, continued in Normandy on his own concerns.'

Stephen, however, was not to be peaceable in England for very long, and his actions at Christmas 1137 give an indication of how power was already shifting from one group to another in that country. The group on the rise was the Beaumont clan, Waleran de Meulan and his brothers. That on the wane was the old clerical administration led by Roger of Salisbury and, more recently, by Bishop Henry of Winchester. Stephen was indebted to the Beaumonts, who had secured Normandy for him the previous year, but his reliance on Waleran in place of the older and wiser Roger of Salisbury, was not likely to be beneficial either to himself or to the country.

Waleran, by all accounts, was a glamorous figure. Some ten years younger than the king, with great wealth derived mainly from his extensive Norman estates, he was connected to most of the major families of the day, including through his mother, Elizabeth of Vermandois, the French royal family. Famed for his literacy and his military prowess, he was not, however, noted for his wisdom or far-sightedness. In his youth he had rebelled, for no apparent reason, against King Henry, and fought and lost a disastrous engagement with the king's men, recklessly charging a well-set line of archers and predictably having his horse shot from under him. Thereafter he had spent some five years as Henry's prisoner. Now, older and possibly wiser, he was typical of magnates of the time in seeking to advance his own family and friends, thereby securing ever greater influence for himself. He and his twin brother, Robert of Leicester, were well supplied with lands in both England and Normandy. Waleran himself had recently been given custody of Evreux when Count Amaury had died, leaving only two young sons to inherit. There was, however, a third Beaumont brother, Hugh, known as Hugh Le Poer, or Hugh the Pauper, who had no lands of his own, and it is likely to be Waleran's influence that led Stephen at Christmas 1137 to decide to advance Hugh to an earldom.

King Henry had had the knack of conferring honour and wealth on his chosen men at no cost to himself, usually by arranging to marry them to wealthy heiresses. This is possibly what Stephen had in mind when he decided that Hugh le Poer should be married to the young daughter of the recently deceased Simon de Beauchamp. The de Beauchamps had long been associated with Bedford. Simon had quickly supported Stephen's rise to the throne and, at the time of his death, he had held Bedford Castle for the king. Stephen's intention was that by his marriage, Hugh would obtain the town and castle of Bedford, with some royal estates in the area, and the title Earl of Bedford. Had this been done by Henry, no doubt all would have gone smoothly, particularly as generous compensation was offered to two of Simon's nephews, Miles and Payn de Beauchamp. For Stephen, however, things were rarely as straightforward. Miles de Beauchamp was then in possession of

Bedford Castle and if the message he received from the king was in similar terms to that recorded in the *Gesta*, it might go some way to explaining his subsequent defiance. He was, in future, says the *Gesta*, to hold the castle from Hugh le Poer instead of from the king, and furthermore, 'if he readily obeyed this command he should have honour and reward; but if he withstood it in any manner, he was to be assured that it would be his ruin.'

Miles replied that he was a loyal servant of the king, but if the king intended to deprive him of 'possessions which belonged to him and his heirs by hereditary right ... he must bear the king's displeasure as best he could.' There is no record that the de Beauchamps did have hereditary rights in the castle, though they might have aspired to this, as did many at the time. Nevertheless, Miles refused to surrender the castle, which reply so infuriated the king that he instantly gathered an army and set out to lay siege to it. Before his arrival, however, Miles had seized all the provisions he could lay hands on from town and countryside alike, 'with whom before he had been on good terms,' and secured a strong garrison inside the place that proved to be impregnable.

Henry of Huntingdon clearly disapproved of the timing of the Siege of Bedford Castle, which began on Christmas Eve 1137 and was continued with vigour throughout the entire Christmas season. This 'was displeasing to God, inasmuch as it made that holy season of little or no account.'

Also disapproving was Bishop Henry, who had tried to persuade his brother to negotiate rather than pursue a siege. Again it is clear that the bishop had lost the influence he had earlier possessed over his brother after assisting him to the throne. Stephen was determined to establish his authority, and continued constructing siege engines and battering the walls through most of January, until called away north by a more serious crisis. Thereafter, according to the *Gesta*, the garrison was starved into submission, while Vitalis declares an honourable surrender was negotiated by Bishop Henry. There is some uncertainty as to whether Hugh le Poer ever did receive his castle and earldom. If he did, he certainly lost them again fairly soon afterwards.

The crisis that drew Stephen away to the north was yet another incursion of the Scots into Northumbria. The original treaty of 1136 had already been broken once when, after Easter 1137, King David had gathered an army and prepared to invade. Peace had been restored by the assembly of a suitably sized opposing army and the negotiations then carried out by Archbishop Thurstan. A truce had been declared, which was to run to the end of the year, but, according to Richard of Hexham, as soon as Stephen returned to England from Normandy, 'the ambassadors of David, king of Scotland, and his son Henry, speedily presented themselves, holding out a withdrawal of the armistice unless he would confer on Henry the earldom of Northumberland, but the king gave no ear to their demand.' Again, Henry of Huntingdon attributes David's invasion to support for the Empress Matilda, but most seem to regard it as nothing more than another attempt by the Scots king to seize the border lands for himself.

In January 1138, while Stephen was assaulting Bedford Castle, King David, with his son Henry and nephew William fitz Duncan, entered Northumbria and attempted to take the castle at Wark, which had fallen to them before. This time, however, it put up a stouter resistance. A three-week siege followed, with the Scots 'applying the whole strength of their resources' but failing to make any headway while losing large numbers of men, either killed or wounded.

At this point David called off the siege and instead, either in a fit of pique or simply to sow terror all around, loosed his forces in a murderous raid across Northumbria. 'And then,' says Richard of Hexham, 'that execrable army, more atrocious than the whole race of pagans ... spread desolation over the whole province, and murdered everywhere persons of both sexes and of every age and rank, overthrew, plundered and burned towns, churches and houses.'

Gruesome details are given of babies being torn from their mothers' wombs, priests butchered on their altars, soldiers drinking the blood of children, in fact all the usual atrocities associated with such raids, 'and by how much more horrible a death they could despatch them, so much more did they rejoice.' The raid had sufficient impact to be awarded its own omen by the *Gesta*, which recorded 'fiery sparks like a furnace, and balls of fire of wonderful brightness streaking across the heavens' – almost certainly a meteor shower – immediately before the awful event.

This was not purely a Scottish army. Richard of Hexham names Germans, Normans and English from Cumbria and Teviotdale, alongside the wild men from Galloway, and others from Lothian. John of Worcester, too, speaks of 'numerous enemies of different races'. The Picts from Galloway were seen as the fiercest, but the whole horde poured down as far as the Tyne, where King David halted at the town of Corbridge. Hexham seems to have been the only place to escape this devastation. An initial raid is reported on a hermit's oratory just across the river from the town, whereupon the two who had killed the hermit and robbed the place became suddenly mad, one smashing his face in on rocks and the other having his legs cut off and drowning in the Tyne. Thereafter David guaranteed the safety of Hexham as long as they kept peace with him, and the town and abbey 'became a secure refuge to numberless poor as well as rich, to whom it offered the necessaries of life and the preservation of their property'.

David's excesses did not last long. By 2 February Stephen had assembled a large army and marched north to confront him. This time there were no meetings and negotiations, but there was no great battle either. As fast as Stephen advanced, the Scots retreated, across the border to the southernmost of David's royal burghs, Roxburgh, where, according to several accounts, they intended to lure the English into a trap. Richard of Hexham describes how Roxburgh was to appear to welcome Stephen, while King David and his soldiers hid in the town, ready to come out at night and surround and capture the king. The plan, if it was a plan, failed because Stephen did not go to Roxburgh. Instead Huntingdon records that he 'carried fire and sword through the southern part of the dominions of King David, who was unable to oppose him.'

This 'tit for tat' was itself of short duration. After a bare two weeks Stephen himself withdrew to the south, leaving David and his army unchallenged. One reason suggested for this is an extended and vulnerable supply line at a time of year when provisions might be in short supply in the local area. Another possible reason is a doubt as to the loyalty of some of the men at present fighting for him. One such was Eustace fitz John, Lord of Alnwick and Malton, and custodian of Bamburgh castle. Like many in the area, Eustace had links with both sides of the border, having witnessed charters of King David as far back as 1124. He was the brother of Payn fitz John, the Marcher lord killed the year before in Wales, and maybe he felt that Stephen had not done enough to support his brother in that turbulent land. Both brothers had risen through service to King Henry, and had been suspected of sympathising with Matilda, though both had quickly submitted to Stephen and been confirmed in their lands. Now, though, Stephen relieved Eustace of custody of Bamburgh and insisted he accompany the court southwards, instead of remaining in Northumbria.

It was the beginning of Lent when Stephen withdrew from Scotland and his Easter court was held at Northampton, a suitably central point for gathering information from all parts of the country. The court was likely to be an uneasy one. Clearly things were moving behind the scenes. William of Malmesbury reports that 'a rumour was pervading England that Robert, Earl of Gloucester, would shortly espouse the cause of his sister,' and Archbishop Thurstan was at court asking for further assistance against the Scots, already massing again along the border. Reports from Normandy would have detailed the continuing troubles there, and the fact that Geoffrey of Anjou was using the time and money gifted to him by Stephen to build up his forces ready for another attempt on Normandy. It seems clear, too, that the Empress Matilda was busy writing letters.

According to the *Gesta*, one such letter was received by David of Scotland, 'complaining that she had been excluded from her father's will, robbed of the crown which had been secured to her and her husband by solemn oaths; that the laws were set aside and justice trodden underfoot; and the sworn fealty of the English barons was broken and disregarded.' It is likely that letters in a similar vein were sent to others, possibly those identified by

Robert of Gloucester as potential supporters, imploring their help for her cause. The *Gesta* implies that David, too, added his voice to hers, and that 'zeal for a just cause ... induced him to foment insurrections in England,' in an attempt to force Stephen from the throne. What is clear is that, at this time, castles were being fortified against the king in a number of areas, most especially in those regions such as the Welsh Marches and the West Country, where Robert of Gloucester had the most influence.

No doubt similar letters, and probably envoys, too, were arriving at Robert's castle at Caen urging him to declare himself, but the earl seems to have been undergoing a crisis of conscience – or possibly, to take a cynical view, weighing where his best advantage lay. He had now sworn oaths to both Stephen and Matilda. Clearly he would get no advancement from the former; with the Beaumonts on the rise, his own star was very much on the wane. On the other hand, if he could obtain a kingdom for his sister ...? Pious and devout, anxious always to do things correctly by the code of his time, surely these practical points must have weighed at least a little in the balance.

We are told only of discussions with clerics and a moral struggle, as the earl 'earnestly revolved how he might escape, before God and man, the imputation of falsifying the oath he had sworn to his sister.' A particular text from the Bible was presented to him. In Chapter 27 of the Book of Numbers, the daughters of Zelophehad came before Moses asking him to rule that they could take possession of their father's inheritance since he had died leaving no son. Moses consulted with the Lord God and was told, 'If a man die and have no son, then ye shall cause his inheritance to pass unto his daughter' (Chapter 27 v. 8) – a most convenient text for Robert of Gloucester to rely on in returning to his first sworn allegiance and abandoning his second. Presumably the clerics did not advise him to read on to where, in Chapter 36, a proviso was added to this, that the daughters must only marry within their own tribe. It was, after all, the marriage of Matilda as much as anything else that had turned the magnates on both sides of the Channel against her.

For just a little while longer Robert would continue his brooding at Caen, and, though Henry of Huntingdon declares, 'After Easter the treason of the English nobles burst forth with great fury,' in fact it was the Scots who moved first. Whether as a result of his niece's letters or otherwise, King David and his son Henry yet again crossed the border and began devastating the coastal areas of Northumbria as far as Durham. Castles at Wark and Norham were besieged in a repeat of earlier invasions, and a separate army under David's nephew, William fitz Duncan, was despatched to Cumbria and the west coast.

With potential troubles on many sides, Stephen clearly decided to split his own forces. The aged Archbishop Thurstan seems to have been told to sort out the north himself 'with the resources available to him there', though Richard of Hexham later speaks of 'the royal warrant with which ... he was provided,' suggesting he might have been given some extra authority to gather and direct men for the defence of the area. Once again Waleran de Meulan and William of Ypres were despatched to Normandy, an additional problem there being the belligerence shown by Roger de Tosny, whom Stephen had rashly released from imprisonment the previous year.

Far more surprisingly, Stephen's queen, Matilda, seems to have been put in charge of the south-east, specifically to neutralise any threat from Robert of Gloucester's castle at Dover through which port an invasion might be expected. She proved herself more than capable of doing this, calling up maritime support from Boulogne to blockade the place while managing her own forces on the landward side.

Stephen himself set off to Gloucester at the southern end of the Welsh Marches, possibly believing that his very presence there might quell any thoughts of rebellion in that quarter. His welcome must have encouraged him. The leading citizens, with his constable Miles of Gloucester, came out to greet him and escort him to the royal palace. There were oaths of loyalty and later in the week, on the feast of the Ascension, the king and his court took a full part in the processions and Masses to celebrate the holy day.

Almost at once, however, trouble broke out at nearby Hereford. Henry of Huntingdon gives a long list of the 'rebels' who at this time held castles against the king. Robert of Gloucester at Bristol was one, although in fact it was his son William who was in residence. Others were William Lovell at Castle Cary, William de Mohun at Dunster, Robert de Nicole at Wareham, Eustace fitz John at Malton, William fitz Alan at Shrewsbury, and Walchelin Maminot at Dover. To these can be added Ralph Paynel at Dudley and Gilbert de Lacy at Weobley. The one who was giving immediate trouble, however, was Gilbert's cousin Geoffrey Talbot, who had recently seized control of Hereford. Gilbert and Geoffrey were as much defying the king over a family land settlement as offering support for Matilda, but Stephen's response was to march an army to Hereford and put it under siege.

For the next month the king sat before Hereford, ignoring the chaos in the north, celebrating the feast of Pentecost with a formal crown-wearing, and gradually weakening the resistance of the garrison until they were prepared to come to terms. The burning of the town by the besieged was a final act of defiance, but when the surrender came there were no savage reprisals. Then, says John of Worcester, who was clearly a fan of the king: 'Since Stephen was, nay is, a loving and peaceable king, he injured no one, but suffered his enemies to depart free.' With so many others poised to challenge him, it was the wrong message for the king to send. 'When the traitors perceived that he was a mild man, and a soft, and a good, and that he did not enforce justice, they did all wonder.' So said the Anglo-Saxon Chronicle, and so it proved. Set free, Geoffrey Talbot immediately joined his cousin at Weobley and after another short siege both fled to Bristol, to the castle that now became the headquarters of a far more serious rebellion. Robert of Gloucester had at last made up his mind.

It was probably at Hereford that Stephen received the messengers from the earl bearing his formal 'defiance'. Robert, says William of Malmesbury, 'renounced his fealty and friendship and disannulled his homage', spelling out his reasons for doing so. Firstly, Stephen had illegally taken the kingdom from Henry's rightful heir. Secondly, he had not kept his faith with Robert and had plotted against him. Thirdly, Robert himself had acted contrary to the law in breaking his oath to Matilda and doing homage to Stephen, and this wrong he now intended to put right, as he had been advised to do by various clerics. He even claimed to have a papal decree ordering him to fulfil the oath he had sworn before his father. Malmesbury promises he will copy this decree into the next volume of his writings but, in fact, never does so, nor has it come to light anywhere else.

No doubt Stephen had been expecting something like this and he had his answers ready. His claim to the kingdom had already been approved by the pope, and he had always treated the earl with all the honour due to him. If he had a complaint, he should come to court and declare it. Robert's messengers were sent on their way and immediately travelled to Bristol with detailed instructions from the earl for putting the castle on a war footing, 'orders full of trouble for the realm of England', says the *Gesta*. The castle was to be provisioned, recruits obtained and 'hostilities should immediately commence with all vigour against the king and his adherents.' Nothing seems to have been said, however, about the arrival of Robert himself and in fact he would be detained for some time in Normandy, assisting Geoffrey of Anjou with yet another invasion. With the earl's castles at Caen and Bayeux surrendered to him, Geoffrey could now count on support across a great swathe of western Normandy. He had some way to go, however, in subduing the whole of the duchy.

In the meantime, Geoffrey Talbot and his cousin seem to have taken the lead in commencing the hostilities required in England. Their first attempt in this area, however, proved singularly inept. The neighbouring city of Bath was the chosen target, but the attack never got started due to a clumsy reconnaissance mission that went badly wrong. In some accounts Geoffrey, Gilbert and a small group of followers were found slowly circling the city. In another, Geoffrey was pretending to help a lost traveller to find his way there. In either case, the newly appointed Bishop of Bath, who seems to have been in charge of defence, realised what was happening and sent out a group of knights. In the scuffle that followed Geoffrey was taken prisoner, while the rest of the party escaped to Bristol.

A rescue mission was sent, summoning the bishop to meet with them 'under a solemn engagement for his safe conduct', so says the *Gesta*. When he appeared, however, they seized and abused him and threatened to hang him unless Geoffrey was immediately released. With his own men having retreated to the city and closed the gates, it is not surprising that the bishop agreed to this. The *Gesta*, however, gives a long explanation as to why he did, declaring that he also gave them a severe lecture on the consequences of breaking their oath. It has been suggested that this bishop, Robert of Lewes, may well have been the author of the *Gesta*. He certainly gives a very detailed description of this incident and its aftermath. For when King Stephen, who had returned from Hereford to London, came storming along with an army, 'though he had enough to do in other parts of the country,' we have, again, a full description of the meeting between king and bishop. Arriving unexpectedly in Bath, says the *Gesta*, 'the king manifested great indignation against the bishop,' and only finally forgave him when Robert convinced him he had been 'well-nigh hanged'.

Stephen's main purpose in the area, however, was to besiege Bristol, whose inhabitants were already putting into practice Earl Robert's commands. 'Wherever they heard that the king or his adherents had estates or property of any description,' declares the *Gesta*, 'they eagerly flocked to them, like hounds snatching rabidly at the carrion thrown into a kennel ... whatever their hearts coveted or they cast their eyes on, was carried off, and sold or consumed.' We are given such a vivid description of Bristol, 'the most opulent city of all these parts', that it is again clear the author knew it well. He describes its position at the confluence of two tidal rivers, and the castle and its defences, and goes into some detail about what he refers to as the 'villainy' practised at this time by its inhabitants. Robbery, extortion and torture are the accusations, and these are backed up by John of Worcester who writes of 'infernal cruelties' and 'bitter torments' devised and implemented by one Philip Gay, variously described as a kinsman of Earl Robert and as tutor to his son.

What they are describing is likely to be the plundering and devastation which, at the time, was seen as a legitimate way of carrying on warfare against an enemy. A lord was supposed to offer protection and prosperity to his people. Devastating his lands not only enriched the raiders and reduced the lord's resources, but also served as a demonstration that he was unable to protect his own, and therefore was not deserving of service. In all this, of course, it was the poorer members of society who suffered most, having their goods taken and crops destroyed, resulting in widespread hunger and hardship. These practices, says John of Worcester, 'which were afterwards introduced far and wide in every part of England, nearly reduced the island to ruin.'

At Bristol, meanwhile, Stephen was finding it almost impossible to put the city under siege. The situation was not helped by the conflicting advice he was receiving. According to the *Gesta*, one group recommended blocking the river access to the sea with huge stones and timber, so the city could no longer receive supplies by that route. This would also lead to the rivers upstream overflowing to drown the place. This, says the *Gesta*, was 'wise and prudent counsel'. Others, though, pointed out the impracticability of the scheme on a wide and deep tidal river, and while they were almost certainly correct, the accusation is made that this group, 'though they were in Stephen's camp, were secretly the earl's adherents.'

In the end Stephen attempted no great engineering works, sitting before the castle for some time before taking himself off to lay waste the earl's lands round about and attack two of Robert's lesser castles at Castle Cary and at Harptree. The first he achieved by a short siege, and the second – held by William fitz John, younger brother of Payn and Eustace – by the rashness of its garrison in marching out to attack a part of the king's forces, leaving the castle itself vulnerable to a sudden assault. Having secured these minor triumphs, Stephen himself was now called away to more urgent matters elsewhere. The *Gesta* likens it to the labour of Hercules in lopping off the heads of the hydra, 'as fast as one of its heads was lopped off more sprung forth, so it was, in a special manner, with the labours of King Stephen,' who was 'constantly in arms, leading his troops from one quarter to another.'

Once again it was the Welsh Marches that were the focus of his attention. Marching northwards from Gloucester in July and bypassing Ludlow, which was still held by the widow of Payn fitz John, he initially attempted to besiege Dudley Castle, perched high on a rock and held for Robert of Gloucester and the empress by Ralph Paynel. Failing to take the castle, he moved on to Shrewsbury. Forewarned of his coming, William fitz Alan and his family had already slipped away, but the man he had left to defend the castle, his uncle Arnulf of Hesdin, proved a tough nut to crack. Using distinctly non-chivalric language, he defied the king for several weeks through August, but this was one siege from which Stephen was determined not to walk away.

John of Worcester details how it was brought to an end. 'A large structure of timber was put together and brought forward; the castle ditch was filled by the king's command; fire was kindled; and the smoke rising in the air smothered all.' The castle gate was then forced and the garrison tried to escape, 'leaping from or creeping out of the castle'. No mercy was shown to them. For once, Stephen was absolutely ruthless. Various accounts describe some ninety-three of the garrison being hanged, among them five of the highest rank, including Arnulf of Hesdin. According to the rules of war at the time he was perfectly entitled to do this. If a garrison refused to come to terms, their lives were forfeit. This sent a very different message, however, from that given at Hereford, and it had immediate results. Bridgnorth surrendered almost immediately. Ralph Paynel at Dudley managed to come to terms, and even far-off Dover capitulated to the Queen. Only Bristol stood out as a major centre of defiance in the south, while in the north the Scots, too, had suffered a severe setback.

Earlier in the year the forces under William fitz Duncan had plundered a wide area of Cumbria and west Yorkshire, down as far as the Ribble Valley. Particular attention had been given to Furness Abbey, founded by King Stephen in 1123, its possessions now 'in a great part destroyed by fire and sword'. On 10 June the crowning triumph of this army was to rout a well-armed and armoured English force at the Battle of Clitheroe.

Meanwhile King David of Scotland was having little success at Wark, but in mid-June the castle at Norham, which belonged to the Bishop of Durham, surrendered in a manner seen by some as shameful, since 'both their wall was very good and their tower very strong, and they had abundance of provisions.' The excellent authorities for these and later activities of the Scots in 1138 are the works of Richard of Hexham, and Ailred of Rievaulx, both of whom were present in the immediate area that year. It is Richard who tells us that David tried to persuade the bishop to convert to the cause of the empress, but was summarily refused. If he failed to obtain one ally, however, David soon received another. Perhaps confirming Stephen's earlier suspicions, Eustace fitz John now firmly allied himself with the Scots, with ambitions not just for Northumbria but for Yorkshire, too. His castle at Alnwick was immediately put at David's disposal, and another at Malton in north Yorkshire was also promised when they should get that far.

Before these troubled times, Eustace had been a justiciar of King Henry, one of the two most powerful men in the north of England. The other was Walter Espec and it is interesting that while Eustace chose one side in the conflict, Walter, who had in fact built the castle at Wark, chose the other. He is named in the list of those leading the defence against the Scots provided by Richard of Hexham. Alongside him we find William of Aumale (also referred to as William Albemarle), Walter of Gaunt, Robert de Brus (ancestor of the Bruce clan) Roger de Mowbray, William de Percy, Richard de Courcy, William Fossard, Robert de Estuteville and Ilbert de Lacy (a member of the northern branch of the Lacy family which was causing so much trouble in the south). Most of these noble men of the north had friendships, and some lands, across the Scots border. They were not a coherent group, however. Hexham declares that they hesitated in moving against the Scots, not only because they had no natural leader, the king being engaged in the south, but also because they did not entirely trust each other. There were rumours of treasons. Eustace had joined the enemy. Would anyone else?

It was Archbishop Thurstan, 'a man of great steadfastness and courage,' says Hexham, who 'roused them by his speech and counsel.' 'Burdened with years, weak in body', as he is described, he had ample evidence of earlier atrocities to turn the matter into a religious campaign, and he urged all who could, to hurry to arms. They should be 'preceded by the priests with cross and banners and relics of saints, to defend the church of Christ against the barbarians.' He would have gone to war himself, Hexham declares, carried in a litter, only they compelled him to stay behind and pray for them instead.

King David crossed the Tees at the end of July and paused for the part of his army led by William fitz Duncan to join him. When they did so, his force was estimated at 26,000 strong. They were full of confidence and, says Hexham: 'Not Yorkshire alone did they purpose and threaten to depopulate, but also the greater part of England.' They were, however, the same mixture as before, some Normanised Scots and Anglo-Normans, well trained, armed and armoured, and a large collection of other wilder Scots from Galloway and beyond, with little training and no armour – Thurstan's 'barbarians'. It was these latter that Walter Espec was referring to in his rousing pre-battle speech, as 'worthless Scots with half-bare buttocks' who 'oppose their naked hides to our lances, our swords and our arrows, using a calf-skin for a shield.'

The armies came together near Northallerton on 22 August, a foggy morning by all accounts. There was a suggestion that the Scots intended to take the English by surprise, but instead found they were ready and waiting, blocking the road to the south. Nor did the battle commence immediately. Negotiations were attempted by the elderly Robert de Brus, a man 'of great resources, grave in manner, scant of speech'. He had been a friend of David and had done homage to him for lands in Annandale and, like Robert of Gloucester, wanted to do all things correctly. According to Ailred he got permission to go and speak with the Scottish king, 'either to dissuade him from war, or lawfully to renounce allegiance to him after ancestral custom'. He came straight to the point. Why, he asked David, are you making war on the Normans and English when it was they who put you on your Scottish throne and supported you against other Scots? How, indeed, do you intent to support yourself without our help, 'as if the Scots would suffice alone for thee, even against the Scots? New to thee is this confidence in Galwegians.' The only reason the Scots hated the

English, he added, was because of their support for David and his family, and David himself would be blamed for the atrocities they had committed, even though he claimed they were done against his commands. Ailred suggests David was swayed by this speech, that the two erstwhile friends were in tears together, and all might have ended well but for the intervention of William fitz Duncan, 'a man of high spirit and the chief provoker of war'. Thereupon Robert formally renounced his fealty to David and returned to his own side.

As both armies now put themselves into battle order, there was a fierce argument on the Scottish side as to who should be in the front rank. The knights wanted that role 'so that armed men should attack armed men, and knights engage with knights, and arrows resist arrows.' On the other hand, the Galwegians demanded that they should go first, so their courage could inspire the rest. After all, they pointed out, they had defeated armoured knights at Clitheroe. They almost came to blows about it but in the end the Galwegians got their way. David's son Prince Henry, who seems by all accounts to have been a paragon of every virtue, arranged the second rank consisting of himself, knights, archers and the men of Cumbria. A third rank was made up of men from Lothian and Lorn and the isles, while King David was in a fourth rank, with a picked bodyguard of Scots, English and French knights.

By this time the archbishop's force had received some small assistance from Stephen in the form of a number of Midland knights, Robert de Ferrers (who was in his late sixties) from Derbyshire, and William Peverel and Geoffrey Heslin from Nottinghamshire. Nevertheless, the English were still far fewer in number, and they fought in a single block with the most vigorous knights in front, mingled with lancers and archers, all dismounted, with their horses far to the rear. Shield to shield, the knights protected the archers, while behind, older men clustered about the 'Standard' that they had devised, both as a rallying point and to give them protection. Richard of Hexham describes how this was made. 'Some of them soon erected a mast of a ship in the middle of a frame which they had brought, and they called it "The Standard" ... and upon the summit of this tree they hung a silver pyx with the body of Christ, and the banners of St Peter the apostle, and of Saints John of Beverley and Wilfrid of Ripon.' Thus, the Lord Jesus Christ, in the form of a consecrated host, was to be their leader, while the local saints and the patron of York Minster were to protect them in the battle. Hexham also claims that, when King David and his men drew near and saw this standard and its banners, 'immediately the hearts of the king himself and his followers stood still with fear and dread.' It was too late to stop now. The Galwegians were already making a charge.

Ailred describes their war cry as 'a yell of horrible sound', while Henry of Huntingdon, who was not there, claims they cried, 'Albany, Albany', an old name for Scotland. As they crashed into the English front line, says Ailred, some of the lancers fell back but the strength of the knights held, and in their midst the archers soon got to work. He describes with some delight the effect of their arrows. 'But the southern flies swarmed forth from the caves of their quivers, and flew like closest rain; and irksomely attacking their opponents' breasts, faces and eyes, very greatly impeded their attack. Like a hedgehog with its quills, so would you see a Galwegian, bristling all around with arrows, and nonetheless brandishing his sword and in blind madness rushing forward, now to smite a foe, now to lash the air with useless strokes.'

Nonetheless the battle lasted several hours. At one point Prince Henry rallied the Scottish knights in a cavalry charge around the English left wing, attacking those left with the horses and the rearguard. A brisk manoeuvre by the third English line, however, left him surrounded. His charge was not followed up and by the time he had extricated himself, King David and his men, 'overwhelmed and distressed,' were fleeing the battlefield.

John of Worcester declares the king 'escaped with some difficulty through the woods and thickets to Roxburgh,' while three days later his son made his way to Carlisle. Ailred claims the latter had escaped by telling his men to throw away their banners and badges and mingle with those who were pursuing the Scots until they could outstrip them and get away. Others say he arrived on foot at Carlisle with only one companion. The numbers of the dead are variously given as 10,000, 11,000 and 12,000, the vast majority of them Scots, and despite the claim of Richard of Hexham that they were left unburied to be eaten by wild animals, they were, in fact, interred together in an area known as Scotpit Lane.

'The king of England received the news of this event with extreme joy,' says Hexham, as well he might. His immediate response was to reward two of the major figures. William of Aumale became Earl of Yorkshire, and Robert de Ferrers, Earl of Derbyshire, though he was to die the following year. The fires of rebellion had been stamped out – or at least damped down – in the south. Archbishop Thurstan had won his battle in the north. But if Stephen thought for a moment that his war was over, he was a long way from the truth. To quote Winston Churchill, it was only the end of the beginning.

6

Shifting Sands

(January – September 1139)

Stephen's 'firefighting' campaign in 1138 has been described as a military achievement of the first rank. Certainly in terms of dividing his forces, with an effective commander in each area, it showed a good grasp of strategy, while his own rapid deployment of men in operations up and down the country probably justifies his reputation as a military commander. His tendency to abandon a siege when it became wearisome, however, would prove costly in the long run. True, he saw to the end the sieges of Hereford and Shrewsbury, using the second to reverse the mistakes of the first. Dudley and Bristol, however, were left unconquered, and while the first was induced eventually to surrender, Bristol, apparently commanded by the twenty-one-year-old son of Robert of Gloucester, survived to form a focus for further rebellion.

Stephen's task would have been immeasurably more difficult had there been an invasion from the Continent on behalf of the Empress Matilda. He had set his queen to guard Dover, but there were many other places along the coast where such an invasion could have been attempted. That none came is probably due to the efforts of his commanders in Normandy, Waleran de Meulan and William of Ypres, and also to the ambitions of Geoffrey of Anjou. It seems fairly clear that, whatever dreams the empress may have had of gaining a kingdom, Geoffrey's thoughts, initially at least, went no further than the Duchy of Normandy. When in May 1138 Robert of Gloucester finally declared for Matilda, there were no great preparations to send a force with him to England on her behalf. Instead, Geoffrey, now in his mid-twenties, seems to have persuaded him to join first in the conquest of the duchy.

There was already plenty of trouble in Normandy. The Cotentin, which had never been securely Stephen's, was a hotbed of violence and banditry, where, under the leadership of Reginald de Dunstanville, Baldwin de Redvers, among others, was taking a prolonged revenge on the king for his losses in England. At the other end of the duchy Roger de Tosny had renewed his attacks on Breteuil and its surrounds, continuing in the third generation his family's claim to lands, now held by Robert, Earl of Leicester, which they felt should have been theirs as far back as 1103. No wonder, then, that Vitalis says Waleran and William of Ypres were dispatched to Normandy 'to relieve that afflicted country'. They found Roger de Tosny more than ready to stand up to them and when, in June, Geoffrey of Anjou invaded for the fourth time, in all probability they were overmatched.

By July Vitalis declares that the enemy were prevailing 'through intestine treason', with Robert of Gloucester's castles at Caen and Bayeux now held for the Angevins, and a great sweep of lands in the north-west of the duchy open to them.

Now Waleran used his connections to the French court to call in reinforcements from that country, along with other auxiliary troops all 'determined to march against the Angevins'. Geoffrey, however, had no intention of taking the risk involved in engaging such forces and, warned in advance, rapidly retreated to Anjou leaving Waleran's forces, according to Vitalis, 'extremely disappointed'. Thwarted in his aim of a decisive battle, Waleran turned his attention instead to Robert of Gloucester in his castle at Caen. It is Vitalis again who tells us that this was 'in order that a thousand soldiers might not appear to have been embodied to no purpose and return home without any feat of arms.' By wasting the country all about, no doubt the intention was to draw the earl out to fight. Robert, though, was not going to play, and 'wisely shut himself up in the castle with a hundred men-at-arms.' The only engagement was a short but fierce skirmish involving some forty horsemen.

Throughout the summer, as a sort of peace was restored in England, violence continued in Normandy. 'The Normans,' says Vitalis, 'were spending their fury in the bosom of their mother country, and crimes of all sorts were perpetrated in every quarter.' The crowning outrage came on 7 September when Roger de Tosny made a surprise attack on Breteuil. The inhabitants had been threshing corn in the streets and the piles of straw and chaff were ready fuel for firebrands thrown by the raiders. The town was burnt to ashes, including the church of Saint-Sulpice where some had fled and where many possessions had been stored for safety. Strangely enough, immediately after this, Vitalis records that Roger made peace with Waleran and his brother, the lord of Breteuil, without a word as to how this transformation was brought about. The three of them then returned to England, where Roger was also reconciled to Stephen.

On 1 October Geoffrey of Anjou came again to Normandy. Falaise was the main target this time, but the great castle on its rocky crag was securely held for King Stephen by Roger de Lucy. Vitalis gives a detailed account of his defiance, claiming that every day the castle gates were thrown open, and Geoffrey, by now accompanied by Robert of Gloucester, was challenged to try to storm them. For eighteen days the castle was besieged, while Geoffrey 'toiled before it in vain.' Then, on 19 October, the Angevins changed tactics and withdrew to waste the country all about; churches were robbed and everything possible was plundered, until, as Vitalis again records, the army suddenly fled away by night, 'in sudden panic inspired by God.' Whatever the cause of this abrupt retreat – possibly to regroup or resupply – it was by no means the end of the campaign. Ten days later Geoffrey was back, this time skirting Falaise and pushing his raids and plundering further up country towards the Channel coast. 'For three weeks,' says Vitalis, 'Normandy was unceasingly subjected to slaughter and ravage by the count's fierce inroads, and great losses were sustained.'

This was the same policy pursued by King David in the north of England, and in neither case did it endear the native population to the cause of the empress. If anything it hardened resistance against her. Those who had lost family or goods to these marauders, or suffered hunger through the winter as a result of their plundering, would be unlikely to give them their support, whatever their original inclinations in the dispute between the royal cousins.

Early in November Geoffrey and his army came to the town of Touques at the mouth of the river of the same name. Nearby was the fortress of Bonneville, held by William Troussebot, which they intended to attack the following day. The town, however, seemed to be entirely deserted, no doubt due to a warning of their approach. Whether this had become a regular occurrence, or if on this occasion they were unusually lax, we don't know, but Vitalis tells us that finding all the houses empty, and 'quartering themselves in them without any precautions, they sat down to carouse in a splendid manner.' William Troussebot, however, was well aware of their presence and was not going to wait to be attacked.

At some point he sent out to Touques 'some wretched boys and common women', presumably those least likely to arouse suspicions. Their aim was to set fire to the town and, Vitalis suggests, some forty-five fires were kindled. The Angevins 'were awoke to the crackling of flames,' and fled the town. Troussebot and his garrison were waiting outside in full armour ready to ambush them, but apparently the smoke from the fires was so thick that the raiders were able to scatter and escape. At dawn, says Vitalis, Geoffrey of Anjou managed to assemble his forces in a nearby cemetery but rather than returning to the attack, he 'fled with the utmost speed and ... never held bridle till he arrived, not without disgrace, at Argentan.'

That was the end of campaigning in Normandy for the year. Apart from the fact that the weather was bad and that the holy seasons of Advent and Christmas were upon them, Geoffrey and Matilda would at this time have been engaged in preparing the brief for Bishop Ulger of Angers to present to the pope the following year. Despite the fact that Stephen had already had a letter of support from Pope Innocent, they still hoped that the presentation of their side of the case might persuade him to change his mind. In such a matter, especially one involving the violation of sworn oaths, the backing of a pope could well be crucial and the papal circumstances had themselves been altered by the death of the rival Pope Anacletus in January 1138, allowing Innocent, at last, to take possession of St Peter's Basilica in Rome.

In fact at the end of 1138, a papal legate, Alberic, Bishop of Ostia, had been in England for some months. His mission was essentially one of unity within the church and acceptance of the authority of Pope Innocent everywhere; but as the pope's representative, he also carried great weight as a diplomat and peacemaker. By late September he had travelled via Hexham as far as Carlisle, where he met King David of Scotland still licking his wounds after the Battle of the Standard. David had initially supported Anacletus, but now accepted the legitimacy of Innocent and also permitted the Bishop of Carlisle, who had been ousted by the year's disturbances, to return to his see. Then, Richard of Hexham tells us, over three days Alberic negotiated with David, not without some difficulty, 'for the re-establishment of peace between him and the king of England'. A truce was put together whereby David agreed to 'bring no army and no evil upon the land of the king of England' (except around Wark Castle, which was still besieged) before 11 November 1139. Terms were also made with the Picts of Galloway and the other wild Scots, who promised to return all the captive girls and women they had carried off during the recent campaigns, and 'would thenceforth slay no one at all unless he opposed them.' By and large, these terms were obeyed. The siege at Wark castle continued until the garrison was starved into submission immediately before 11 November 1139. They were given 24 hours to leave, with their arms, and the town and castle were then burned to the ground.

Returning to the south, Alberic seems to have continued with his mix of church business and diplomacy. A church council was summoned to meet at London on 6 December, and a great host of clerics attended from around the country. Much of the business concerned canon law, repeating matters laid down in previous councils such as the prohibition of laymen investing bishops. It was a sign of the times that nuns were threatened with excommunication if they were found wearing sable or ermine, gold rings or braided or made-up hair. More seriously, anyone who killed or imprisoned a person who was in any form of holy orders could also be excommunicated, while the clergy themselves were forbidden to bear arms or engage in warfare.

An important item on the agenda was the appointment of a new Archbishop of Canterbury to replace William Corbeil, who had died more than two years previously. It was no secret that Henry of Blois wanted the job, he had even been dropping hints to the pope, while several other senior clerics were conveniently in the area. That Henry was not going to get it was probably no secret by the time the election took place on 24 December. He was not present on that day, apparently engaged in an ordination ceremony at St Paul's Cathedral. Some have suggested he was deliberately got out of the way, and stormed off in a fury when he heard what had happened. It seems unlikely, however, that an election under the supervision of a papal legate would be that concerned about the anger of a mere bishop, and a counter-suggestion is that he was tactfully offered a way to avoid an awkward situation before his colleagues.

The man chosen for the post, and subsequently consecrated by the legate, was Theobald, the abbot of Bec, a candidate with impeccable credentials, several of whose predecessors at Bec had earlier proved to be notable archbishops. Had Stephen backed his own brother for the post, there would likely have been accusations of royal interference in church matters – though this did not prevent the king's illegitimate son Gervase from being appointed abbot of Westminster about this time. More than likely Stephen left the matter entirely to the church authorities, subject to giving final approval to the candidate chosen. The matter is often cited, however, as evidence of a cooling between the brothers and a slackening of the bishop's earlier influence over the king, particularly as there is a suggestion that Theobald of Bec was proposed by Waleran de Meulan.

In the event, Henry's lobbying of the pope was not entirely wasted. Less than two months after the new archbishop's consecration, Henry was given a very substantial consolation prize, being appointed as standing papal legate to England. Thus, although inferior to Theobald as a bishop, he now, when occasion demanded, wholly outranked him as the pope's representative. Whether Alberic had anything to do with the appointment we don't know, but possibly Pope Innocent felt that in this way honour was satisfied all round.

Throughout the period of the church council, and at the royal Christmas court immediately afterwards, Alberic was also pursuing his role as diplomat and peacemaker between England and Scotland. In this, as Richard of Hexham is careful to point out, he was ably assisted by Queen Matilda, who was 'warmly attached to her uncle David of Scotland and his son Henry, her cousin, and on that account took great pains to reconcile them to her husband.' With the queen as mediator, and 'backed by her feminine shrewdness and address,' the need for a settlement could be frequently raised with the king, though at first he was solidly against their proposals. The magnates, especially those with lands or interests in the north, wanted revenge against the Scots rather than peace, and Stephen was inclined to give them their way. It is possibly this feeling that Henry of Huntingdon reflects when he writes that, after Christmas, the king 'went into Scotland, and by fire and sword compelled the king of the Scots to come to terms.' At this time, however, Huntingdon was on his way to Rome, accompanying Alberic, Theobald and a number of English bishops to the Lateran Council called by the pope, and his account is entirely wrong. In fact Queen Matilda refused to take 'no' for an answer, and 'the zeal of a woman's heart, ignoring defeat, persisted night and day ... till it succeeded in bending the king's mind to its purpose.'

One factor in her favour was the increasing likelihood of an invasion into southern England on behalf of the Empress Matilda. Stephen may well have counted himself lucky that no such invasion had come the previous summer, and he may have decided it was better to seek peace in the north in order to avoid the prospect of fighting on two fronts simultaneously. Since David at least claimed to be fighting on behalf of the empress, detaching him from her supporters could also be seen as something of a coup. On his side, too, David may have been disappointed that his efforts in the north had not been backed more strongly in the south, and in particular by some move on the part of the Angevins themselves, and he may have been more ready to come to terms because of this failure of support.

When the two sides came to agreement, the treaty gave the Scots king virtually all he had asked for. Prince Henry was to become Earl of Northumbria, with the exception of the strongholds at Newcastle and Bamburgh, which Stephen kept in his own hands. The Northumbrian barons were given the option of swearing fealty to the new earl, saving the fealty they owed to the king, and most of them did so. It was, however, stipulated that Northumbria was not to become part of Scotland, and that Prince Henry was obliged to keep all the 'laws, customs and statutes' of Northumbria that had existed in King Henry's time. In return for this, King David, Prince Henry and all their dependants bound themselves to remain at peace with, and loyal to, King Stephen for the rest of their lives. To ensure this, the sons of five earls of Scotland were given as hostages. The treaty was signed at Durham on 9 April 1139 by Prince Henry and Queen Matilda, with a number of barons from both sides. The queen and prince then travelled south to Nottingham where Stephen confirmed the agreement, and Prince Henry remained for some time with the English court, marrying Ada, the daughter of William of Warenne, whom, according to Richard of Hexham, he dearly loved.

By the end of 1138 at the latest, Stephen seems to have accepted that he would need to fight to hold onto his kingdom. This would appear to be the reason behind the unusual number of new earls he created around this time. Henry had created only two in his entire reign, one being his chief counsellor and the other his illegitimate son. In the space of a few years in the late 1130s, however, Stephen created half a dozen or more. There has been a great deal of argument as to whether or not these were simply 'sweeteners', handed out to keep men loyal to a weak king. William of Malmesbury, for instance, refers to greedy magnates 'who did not hesitate to ask the king for estates or castles, or in fact anything that had once taken their fancy,' and he criticises the king for giving away, in some cases at least, not only the title, but the whole of the royal revenue he would otherwise have drawn from the county concerned. Waleran de Meulan, for example, refers to revenues 'that were once the king's and are now mine'.

A further criticism is that almost all the new men were connected in some way to the Beaumont family. Thus, Waleran himself became Earl of Worcester, his brother Hugh was, in title at least, Earl of Bedford, his brother-in-law Gilbert fitz Gilbert of Clare became Earl of Pembroke, while Gilbert's nephew, also called Gilbert, became Earl of Hertford. Added to this, the new husband of his half-sister Ada of Warenne was now Earl of Northumbria as well as Earl of Huntingdon, his brother Robert was already Earl of Leicester and would soon become Earl of Hereford, and his cousin Roger was Earl of Warwick. It is easy to see why some felt the Beaumonts were exerting a stranglehold on the country, quite apart from their influence on the king himself.

When we look at the other earls created around this time, however, a different pattern emerges. Simon de Senlis, for example, probably became Earl of Northampton as compensation for losing Huntingdon, his claim to that county having been recently passed over in favour of Prince Henry of Scotland. In any case, he was and continued to be a close and loyal supporter of King Stephen. William d'Aubigny became Earl of Lincoln around the time he married Queen Adeliza, the widow of King Henry. Within a short time, however, he gave up that title to become Earl of Sussex, in which county lay Arundel Castle, their principal seat. If these might be seen as appointments required by circumstances, the remaining two are clearly rewards for military service. Thus, as already noted, William of Aumale became Earl of York while Robert de Ferrers became Earl of Nottingham and Derby as a reward for their prowess at the Battle of the Standard.

These last two seem to be the key to Stephen's thinking. Disregarding family connections, if we see where he has placed his new earls it becomes apparent that they are strategically positioned to hold down areas of the country for the king, where he feared he was most likely to face a challenge in the times ahead – the far north, the Midlands and especially the Welsh March, and far west Wales where a new boundary was set with the native Welsh. The men appointed were military men, not administrators, and clearly their role was to be military, a return to the policy of William the Conqueror immediately after 1066. This might also explain the generosity of the revenue grants that accompanied the appointments. If these men were to fight for the king they needed the resources to do so. True, they mostly had extensive estates of their own but giving them access to royal revenues might be seen as tying them that bit closer to the royal cause. While this may have had benefits in the short term, however, in the longer term it impoverished the king, and as William of Newburgh comments, 'having exhausted the treasures of his uncle, he became himself less powerful and efficient.'

On 4 April 1139 the Lateran Council summoned by Innocent II opened in Rome. Its most important business was the re-assertion of the position of the papacy as, in his words, 'head of the world', but it was here too that Matilda's case would be heard for the first time and ruled upon. Her representative, Bishop Ulger, was a learned and holy man, but apparently quite unused to the sharp cut and thrust of international affairs at a papal court. He has been described as 'a lily among thorns'. He set out his case clearly and succinctly, basing it on two major propositions. Firstly, that the crown should have gone to Matilda by clear hereditary right, and secondly, that it had been promised to her by oaths sworn by all concerned, including Stephen and the archbishop who crowned him. These arguments must have seemed to him unanswerable, but he was completely unprepared for the counter-attack presented on behalf of Stephen by Arnulf, Archdeacon of Sées.

Matilda, he claimed, had no hereditary right to the English crown because her parents had not been legitimately married. Without expressly calling her a bastard, he brought out the story that Henry's wife Edith had been a professed nun and that, therefore, her marriage could not be recognised by the church. Completely nonplussed, Bishop Ulger had no answer to this, though if he had been aware of the writings of Eadmer he could easily have refuted the claim, as several did, explicitly, in later years, when it was far too late to do much good for the empress.

Matilda's mother had indeed been brought up in a convent, where her aunt Christina was abbess. She had on occasion worn a veil, though she claimed this was at her aunt's insistence, to protect her from 'the lust of the Normans', and when that lady was out of sight she tore it off and stamped it underfoot. All this had been fully examined in 1100 at the time when her marriage to Henry was first proposed. A council of enquiry had questioned her, as had the saintly Anselm, Archbishop of Canterbury, and each had concluded that she had never become a nun and was free to marry. Even at the very church door Anselm had demanded of the onlookers if anyone could establish that she was unfit to marry he should speak up, but no one did.

If Ulger had had these facts to hand the outcome might have been different. Instead, apparently unaware of this backstory, he could only bluster and offer insults to Arnulf, and the session broke up without a resolution. The odds seem to have been stacked against him from the start, however. Pope Innocent had already recognised Stephen once, and the king had cunningly sent the same men again to represent him. The pope may also have been weighing up the likely outcomes of any decision he made.

If he found for Stephen, it was possible there might be a civil war in England whereas, if he found for Matilda, that possibility would become a certainty. He had, too, a glowing report from Alberic as to the present situation in England, the respect for the church and the probable reconciliation of Stephen with Matilda's most active supporter, David of Scotland. The pope's inclination was to let well alone, and in the event he accepted graciously the gifts King Stephen had sent him and confirmed him on the throne of England.

It is tempting to think he might not have been so happy with Stephen as a friend of the church had his decision been postponed a few months to the summer of that year. An event occurred then, which Robert of Torigny describes as 'a transaction of unprecedented infamy', which marked the final severance of Stephen's ties to the regime he had inherited. Bishop Roger of Salisbury and his family were about to undergo a mighty fall from power.

In June 1139 the court assembled at Oxford. There, according to William of Newburgh, the king 'became so depraved by evil counsel that, through his greediness for money, he laid his impious hands on ecclesiastics, and, paying no deference to holy orders, sullied his royal character with an indelible stain.' The ecclesiastics were 'the most noble and powerful bishops in England,' and 'as though they had been the vilest characters, guilty of the most heinous crimes, he seized them and shut them up, and confined them with chains, as well as despoiled them of their property and castles.'

These castles were, in fact, the crux of the matter. Roger of Salisbury and his nephews, bishops Alexander of Lincoln and Nigel of Ely, had each in recent years been enthusiastic builders and improvers of castles in their dioceses. Roger himself had built a mighty edifice at Devizes, 'than which,' says Robert Torigny, 'there was not a more magnificent fortress within the whole of Europe.' Another at Sherborne was only a little less grand, and he had begun another at Malmesbury, disapproved of by William of Malmesbury as being 'even in the churchyard, and scarcely a stone's throw from the principal church'. He had even taken over the royal castle at Salisbury (present-day Old Sarum) and surrounded it with a wall. Bishop Alexander, too, had built himself a splendid castle at Newark, which he claimed was for the defence and dignity of the church. Another on flat fenland at Sleaford, however, was probably more of a residence for the bishop, with a tithe barn for the collection of the crops due to the diocese. Bishop Nigel also had a well-fortified castle near his cathedral at Ely, and another a few miles away at Aldreth.

It is unsurprising that these edifices, and the magnificence of the bishops' entourages, became a source of jealousy. The *Gesta* rather sniffily records that Roger and his nephews, 'neglecting the duties befitting the purity and simplicity of their Christian profession, surrounded themselves with secular pomp,' while Malmesbury declares that 'some powerful laymen, hurt at the probability of being surpassed by the clergy in extent of riches and magnitude of their towns ... fostered the latent wound of envy in their bosoms,' and 'poured forth their imagined grievances to the king.' The laymen are specifically named by Vitalis as Waleran de Meulan and his brother Robert, and Alan of Brittany, holder of the Honour of Richmond in Yorkshire.

In the heightened tensions of the summer of 1139, with the arrival of Matilda and her champion Robert of Gloucester expected at any time, it is hard to separate allegation from fact. Vitalis tells us that, at this time, Roger of Salisbury had 'obtained a bad reputation above all the great men of the realm for being disloyal to his king and lord, Stephen, and favouring the party of Anjou.' This may, however, be simply the story reported in Normandy, where the Beaumonts had extensive lands and the Angevins were hated. The *Gesta*, which generally seems to favour Stephen, suggests this claim is more a plot on behalf of the magnates to cut their rivals down to size, saying that 'setting no bounds to their jealousy and hatred, they instilled in the king's mind many weighty charges against them.' Malmesbury, too, talks of 'frequent insinuation of the nobility', telling the king that 'the bishops ... were mad for erecting castles, that none could doubt but that they were designed for the overthrow of the king, for as soon as the empress should arrive, they would ... immediately greet their sovereign with the surrender of their fortresses.'

The *Gesta* account is particularly ambivalent, since earlier it seemed to add weight to these very claims. Bishop Roger, it stated, 'was more attached to the children of the late King Henry, and disposed to serve them faithfully.' Not only had he built the castles, but he had made sure they were 'profusely stored with arms and provisions, watching the opportunity ... of rendering (the Angevins) prompt and vigorous aid on their landing in England'. It also suggested there were regular communications between the bishop and the party of the empress in Normandy, and that knowing of their imminent arrival, 'he strengthened himself by enlisting large bodies of troops to be turned over to their service.'

We will probably never know the truth. Roger of Salisbury had certainly been strongly against Matilda's marriage and the Angevin connection, and had virtually handed the country to Stephen when he arrived. It is possible he had changed his mind in the meantime and regretted going back on his sworn oath. He may even have been one of those whom Robert of Gloucester came to England to persuade of their errors, as Malmesbury describes, and who had then returned to the party of the empress.

For some time, according to Malmesbury, King Stephen pretended not to listen to the tale of his magnates, though they 'gratified his ear so much'. The suggestion is that this was partly out of respect for the bishops, 'or, as I rather think, from apprehension of the odium he might incur by seizing their castles.' This is spelt out by the *Gesta*: 'For if it is wrong and forbidden to injure any man ... much more is it disgraceful and unallowable to exhibit violence of any sort against the highest minister of the holy altars.' When Stephen did eventually act, the *Gesta* declares, 'He was led to this by foolish, not to say mad counsels.'

The opportunity arose as people were still assembling at Oxford on 24 June. It seems an uncanny degree of foresight when William of Malmesbury reports Bishop Roger as reluctant to travel to the court. 'I heard him speaking to the following purport,' he says, '"I know not why, but my heart revolts at this journey."' It was the bishop's followers, however, who became involved in a quarrel over quarters with the followers of Alan of Brittany, 'as though fortune would seem subservient to the king's wishes,' says the *Gesta*, though Vitalis is fairly clear the quarrel was a put-up job. What began with words, ended with swords. Supporters of the bishop left a meal unfinished as they rushed to join the fray. Blood was shed. Malmesbury's version says that Alan's servants were defeated and his nephew almost killed, while the *Gesta* declares that partisans of Waleran de Meulan joined the fight and put the bishop's men to flight, 'slaying some, taking others prisoner.' And all this happened within the compass of the king's court and under his peace.

Bishops Roger and Alexander had already arrived in Oxford, but hearing of this clash they were preparing to fly when the king's officers burst into their lodging and arrested them. 'All present were in amazement at the violence,' says the *Gesta*, and possibly more amazed still when Stephen demanded they hand over the keys of their castles, 'as pledges of their fidelity'. When they hesitated to do this they were ordered to be held in close confinement.

The one family member outside this net was Nigel, Bishop of Ely. Hearing of the fate that had befallen his relations, he now fled away, not to his own possessions at Ely, but to Bishop Roger's sturdy castle at Devizes, 'where,' says the *Gesta*, 'he prepared to offer a stout resistance to the king.' Stephen, stirred to action at this defiance, immediately followed him there, 'bringing with him the two bishops strictly guarded, and commanding them to be separately confined in two foul places, and to be subjected to severe fastings.' William of Malmesbury in fact declares it was Bishop Roger that went on hunger strike to persuade his nephew to hand over the castle, but Torigny seems fairly sure it was the king who 'pinched him with hunger'.

Either way it failed to have the desired effect, so Stephen's next move was to have Bishop Roger's son, Roger le Poer, who at the time was his own chancellor, arrested, 'thrown into chains' and brought along. Possibly he was aware that Bishop Roger's mistress (or maybe wife), Maud of Ramsey, the man's mother, was within the castle. According to Vitalis, who gives a lively account of the whole proceeding, Bishop Roger tried to persuade Nigel to surrender, but the 'arrogant nephew' persisted in his defiance. Whereupon Stephen had a gallows built before the castle gate and threatened to hang young Roger le Poer. At this, says Vitalis, his mother, who had possession of the main part of the fortress, 'leapt up and said, "It was I that bore him, and I ought not to lend a helping hand to his destruction. Yea, rather I ought to lay down my own life to save him."' She then began to bargain with Stephen – her fortress in exchange for her son's life – which so humbled Bishop Nigel that he 'sorrowfully' consented to hand over the castle. 'This castle, therefore,' says the *Gesta*, 'and the others they possessed, being surrendered to the king's hands, the bishops, humbled and mortified, and stripped of all pomp and vain glory, were reduced to a simply ecclesiastical life, and to the possessions belonging to them as churchmen.'

For it was not simply the castles that Stephen took over, but also the arms and treasure that he found therein, a move that is clearly approved by the *Gesta*. 'We cannot but admire the king's unexpected turn of fortune,' it says, 'for when he had nearly exhausted his treasury in the defence of his crown … what report said was stored in the castles for his injury and detriment, fell into his hands to his honour and profit, without any care of his own.' These treasures, says Torigny, in fact enabled the king to arrange for the marriage of his son Eustace to the sister of the new French king.

Many of the chronicles have a strangely inconsistent approach to this incident. On the one hand they condemn the use of violence against the churchmen and accuse Stephen of greed and of listening to depraved counsels. On the other, there seems to be a strong suggestion that the over-mighty bishops got what they deserved. William of Newburgh goes so far as to say that Stephen was 'appointed God's avenger' against Roger of Salisbury. One who had no such divided attitude, however, was the king's own brother, Bishop Henry of Winchester.

For a number of reasons Bishop Henry must have felt a chill at the arrest of these three powerful men. He too had been building castles and fortified palaces in recent years, more than all the other bishops put together. There was Merden Castle near Winchester, Bishops Waltham Palace on the way to Portsmouth, Downton Castle near Salisbury and Farnham Castle in Surrey. In Taunton he had a three-storied stone keep with massively thick walls, while possibly his favourite was Wolvesey Castle near Winchester Cathedral, begun by a predecessor but continually added to by Bishop Henry. If keeping castles was to be seen as an offence against the king, he was certainly in line to be the next to fall. Not the least of his worries about the arrests must have been the fact that he had not seen them coming, and clearly was not consulted in the matter. If he had had any doubts before about his waning influence on the king, these must all have been swept away by this one incautious action on Stephen's part. Had Bishop Henry been asked, no doubt he could have devised other ways to deal with the situation without leaving the king open to censure – but he was not asked, and was the first to lead the condemnation that followed.

He summoned a church council to meet at Winchester on 29 August. Almost all the bishops came, with a few exceptions such as Archbishop Thurstan of York, who was excused from making the journey due to his age and infirmity. A number of other clerics, abbots and archdeacons would also have attended, one of whom was William of Malmesbury, thus well-placed to give a detailed account of proceedings.

Bishop Henry began by revealing his appointment as papal legate, something he had apparently not done before, and this was 'received with much good will'. Having established his superior authority, he then launched a severe attack on the king, although shifting some of the blame onto his advisors. 'It was a dreadful crime,' he said, 'that the king should be so led astray by sinister persons as to have ordered violent hands to be laid on his subjects, more especially bishops, in the security of his court.' This was a double charge, firstly that the arrest had been made at court, where all should be under the protection of the king and free from such actions, and secondly that those arrested had been bishops. To this was added the further offence of 'despoiling the churches of their possessions under the pretext of the criminality of the prelates'.

The king, he said, had been repeatedly asked to 'amend his fault', to put right what he had so obviously done wrong, but he had refused to do so. Therefore, he should be summoned by the council to answer for this, and the bishop felt this outrage so strongly 'that he would rather himself suffer grievous injury, both in person and property, than have the episcopal dignity so basely humiliated.' Nor need they fear that he would fail to execute whatever the council decided was proper to be done, 'through regard to the friendship of the king, who was his brother, or loss of property or even danger of life.'

At this point the king, who was clearly nearby, sent envoys to demand to know why he should be summoned to answer to this council. He received the sharp reply that 'it was the act of heathen nations to imprison bishops and divest them of their possessions.' He should now either account for his actions or submit to the judgement of the council. Furthermore, he was reminded that it was not by force but by the 'fostering care' of the church that he had achieved his crown in the first place, and it was therefore incumbent on him to repay this debt by favouring the church and its ministers. It may have been this last barb that stung the king into sending a detailed response to the accusations. This was presented by Aubrey de Vere, a chamberlain and justiciar of the king, who was, needless to say, related by marriage to the Beaumont/de Clare group, so prominent in the king's favour.

Malmesbury, writing much later, gives a precise summary of the king's arguments. Firstly, that although Bishop Roger was seldom at court, his people were troublemakers, the incident at Oxford being only the latest example of this. Secondly, that Bishop Alexander, whose men were also involved, was carrying on a feud with Alan of Brittany and encouraged his followers in the violence. Thirdly, that the king had discovered beyond doubt that Bishop Roger was secretly favouring the king's enemies, and that 'it was in every person's mouth that, as soon as the empress should arrive, he would join her party.' It was for these reasons that Roger of Salisbury had been arrested, 'not as a bishop but as the king's servant who had administered his affairs and received his wages.' It was furthermore claimed that the bishops had surrendered their castles 'voluntarily' in order to escape the punishment due for their crimes, and that the 'trifling sums of money' found in the castles must lawfully belong to the king, 'as bishop Roger had collected it from the revenues of the exchequer in the times of his uncle ... Henry I.'

Of course, Bishop Roger denied the allegations made against him, while the papal legate, 'mildly as usual', declared that such allegations should be properly tried in an ecclesiastical court according to law before guilt should be assumed and sentence carried out. Since this had not been done, he said, the bishops should get their property back in the meantime. Malmesbury says that many arguments of this kind were used on both sides, but in the event the council was adjourned to await the arrival of a more senior cleric, the Archbishop of Rouen, who was expected to deliver some profound theological thoughts on the matter.

'When he came,' says Malmesbury, 'all were anxious to hear what he had to allege,' but his reasoning would have been deeply disappointing to Bishop Henry. Yes, he said, the bishops could keep their castles – if they could show where, in the canons of the church, it said that bishops could rightly possess castles. Since they could not do that, 'it was the height of impudence to contend against the canons.' Further, even if it had been right for them to have castles, in these troubled times they ought to hand over the keys to the king, whose job it was to defend national security. 'Thus,' says Malmesbury, 'the whole plea of the bishops was shaken.'

At this point Aubrey de Vere spoke up again on behalf of the king. There had been mutterings, he said, among the bishops, that they intended to take their case to Rome, to the pope himself. The king advised against this move, 'for if any person shall go from England to any place, in opposition to him and to the dignity of his kingdom, perhaps his return may not be so easy.' In any case, being aggrieved, the king himself might take his case to Rome.

It is interesting to see two ancient weapons being used on behalf of King Stephen in this council. First the claim that Roger of Salisbury was arrested not as a bishop but as a servant of the crown. Just such an argument was used by William the Conqueror against his half-brother Bishop Odo of Bayeux when he was arrested and imprisoned in 1082. Further, the threat that if you go you may not return, was used frequently by both William Rufus and Henry in their dispute with Archbishop Anselm about lay investitures. In Anselm's case he was quite happy to go, and to settle abroad until the political climate had changed. The bishops in 1139 were not as keen to do so.

When the king's message was received, says Malmesbury, 'partly advising and partly threatening', the council broke up. Stephen would clearly not submit to their judgement, and they held back from excommunicating him without the specific authority of the pope. Besides, he adds, 'they understood, or some of them even saw, that swords were unsheathed around them. The contention was no longer of mere words, but nearly for life and for blood.'

There is a sharp divergence here between different accounts of the aftermath of this council. Both Malmesbury and Henry of Huntingdon describe Bishop Henry and Archbishop Theobald as prostrating themselves before the king in his chamber, and begging him to reconsider his actions and avoid any division between king and church at that time. Huntingdon declares the king was unmoved and refused to grant their request, while Malmesbury says he went a little way towards conciliation 'by condescendingly rising to them, yet, prevented by ill advice, he carried none of his fair promises into effect.' Completely at variance with this is the account in the *Gesta*, which says the king was 'justly declared and clearly adjudged by the whole clergy' to be guilty of unlawfully laying hands on the Lord's ministers. He then submitted himself to them, 'and, laying aside his royal robes, with a sorrowful mind and contrite spirit, he humbly acknowledged the guilt of his offence.'

It has to be said that the weight of available evidence lies with the account given by Malmesbury. The castles were not returned to their previous owners, being instead garrisoned with the king's men. The bishops themselves were released, but Roger of Salisbury, 'worn down by grief and driven to madness', according to William of Newburgh, died a few months later on 11 December 1139.

This action of the king and his refusal to admit his fault, says Henry of Huntingdon, 'prepared the way for the eventual ruin of the house of Stephen,' but if the king justified his actions on the basis of a looming national emergency, he was soon to be vindicated. The council at Winchester broke up on 1 September and before the month had ended, the Empress Matilda and her faithful brother, Robert of Gloucester, had finally landed in England.

7

Triumph and Disaster

(September 1139 – February 1141)

There is very little agreement as to when the civil war between Stephen and Matilda actually began. Some date it from the time of the formal defiance of Robert of Gloucester, others from the arrest of the bishops, while the Anglo-Saxon Chronicle declares that the entire reign was discord and evildoing. It is clear, however, that the arrival of Matilda in person – and perhaps more especially Robert of Gloucester – marked a distinct change of gear. Henry I had used an elaborate network of spies, keeping him informed of threats to his peace on both sides of the Channel. It is unlikely Stephen maintained this practice, but it was certainly no secret in the autumn of 1139 that some sort of invasion was imminent. A watch was posted along the south coast in places where a landing might be attempted, and the king was clearly on tenterhooks as he waited to see where the blow would fall.

Different writers give details of a number of actions at that time, which might be seen as diversionary tactics. The *Gesta*, for example, with its special emphasis on West Country affairs, describes the 'formidable insurrection' that William de Mohun launched from his castle at Dunster on the north Somerset coast. This took the usual form of plundering and burning all the area around, whereby 'he reduced to subjection by violence not only his neighbours but the inhabitants of remote districts.' This was the kind of distraction the king could do without and, when forced to take notice, he wasted very little time on it. Arriving with a strong force outside the castle, he could see at once that it was impregnable, 'inaccessible on one side where it was washed by the sea, and fortified on the other by towers and walls with a ditch and outworks.' Instead of attempting the impossible, he delegated the task to Henry de Tracy, 'a good knight of much experience in war', who by a series of resolute attacks, 'so reduced and humbled William' that he gave up his raiding, 'and left the country in tranquillity.' We are not told what happened to William de Mohun at the time, but there seems to have been some kind of showdown where Henry de Tracy took 104 knights in a single encounter, thus putting an end to the disturbances.

Henry de Tracy seems to have been given a licence to subdue the whole area, for we next find him taking action against William fitz Odo, an apparently exemplary landowner in times of peace, 'taking not even a twig from his neighbours', but who, when trouble broke out, also took arms against the king. This William, too, was defeated by the indefatigable Henry de Tracey. William's castle was burnt, says the *Gesta*, and 'all his possessions, with immense hoards of money, with the king's permission, fell to the lot of Henry.' Payment for a job well done, no doubt.

A far more serious challenge to Stephen was made at Wareham. This may have been simply another diversion, or perhaps a real attempt to seize a Channel port for the empress. Around the beginning of September, Baldwin de Redvers landed there, 'with a bold and spirited band of soldiers'. They marched straight to Corfe Castle, commanding a gap in the Purbeck hills where, according to the *Gesta*, they were admitted at once. As this was the time of the legate's church council, it is likely that Stephen was hovering somewhere in the Romsey area, close enough to Winchester, while keeping an eye on the important landing places around Southampton and Portsmouth. As soon as he heard of Baldwin's arrival, however, 'he put himself without a moment's delay at the head of such of his people as could be soonest mustered, and appeared suddenly before the castle for the purpose of besieging Baldwin.' He was apparently there for several weeks, attacking the castle perched high on its crag with his siege engines and attempting to starve the inmates into submission.

The *Gesta* claims the king was still before Corfe Castle when he heard of the landing of Matilda and Robert of Gloucester at the end of September, but John of Worcester declares he was at that time besieging Marlborough Castle, which until very recently had been held for him by John the Marshal. This John, more properly John fitz Gilbert, the son of King Henry's Marshal of the Horses, inherited his father's post when he died in 1129. Initially he accepted Stephen as king, and was granted custody of two castles, Marlborough and Ludgershall in Wiltshire. With further land at Hamstead outside Newbury, this made him virtually master of the Vale of Pewsey, between Devizes and Reading. What made him change sides, we don't know. Possibly he was another man sounded out by Robert of Gloucester during his time in England, and he may have been receiving regular communications from the Angevins across the Channel. If John of Worcester is right, his sudden declaration for Matilda in the autumn of 1139 could have been part of a co-ordinated plan to divide the royal forces and draw royal attention away from the real landing place of the empress, at Arundel in Sussex.

This was, perhaps, the least likely place for an invasion along the whole south coast, and may therefore have been watched less closely than other areas. A few miles inland, up the broad Arun River, Arundel Castle was already an impressive fortification, though considerably smaller than the mighty edifice of today. More importantly, it was the residence of King Henry's widowed queen, Adeliza of Louvain, who was Matilda's step-mother, even though she was probably a year or so younger. Adeliza had made no fuss when Stephen became king and there is no evidence she had previously favoured Matilda's claim to the throne. William of Malmesbury, though, insists that Adeliza was in regular communication with the Angevin court and had invited the empress to come to England, later breaking faith with her.

More improbably, Robert of Torigny claims it was the widowed queen's new husband, William d'Aubigny, who invited Matilda. William was and always would be a staunch supporter of Stephen, and it is most likely that Robert's sources simply said an invitation had been issued from Arundel, and he had concluded it must have come from the male partner holding the castle.

If Arundel was an unlikely place for an invasion, it is only fair to say it would be stretching things to describe the party that landed there on 30 September 1139 in quite that way. Malmesbury, getting the story straight from the top, says that no more than 140 horsemen accompanied the empress and her brother – an escort rather than an army – and violent invasion may have been the last thing on the mind of at least one of those involved.

One of the accepted functions of a medieval queen was to act in the role of peacemaker, and if Adeliza did invite Matilda to Arundel, that may well have been the part she envisaged for herself. She may even have had the backing of her husband for such a project. Whether Matilda or Robert of Gloucester shared this aim or had more aggressive intentions, we cannot be sure, but if Baldwin de Redvers and John the Marshal were part of a co-ordinated plan, it could well be the latter.

The actions of Robert of Gloucester, once his sister was safely installed in the castle, could be compatible with either option. If there were to be peace talks, it might be better that he was absent, especially as his lands, castles and adherents in the west would be a valuable lever and bargaining chip. If it was to be war, the sooner he rallied support for the empress the better. Either way, he was not going to let himself be imprisoned in a siege situation, or taken as a hostage should the castle be surrendered. In fact, knowing or guessing that Stephen was already marching an army towards Arundel, Robert left almost as soon as he arrived and, in the words of Robert of Torigny, 'boldly marched through the middle of the king's land, accompanied only by ten knights and ten mounted archers.'

There are a number of different versions of what happened next. According to the *Gesta*, Stephen left part of his force at Arundel to blockade the castle, and immediately set out in pursuit of Robert. He failed to catch him, however, as 'the earl had not gone by the high road, but had betaken himself to byways,' and the king quickly returned to Arundel. It would have been clear to him that

Robert would head towards his main base at Bristol, but if Torigny is correct that he went via Wallingford to consult with Brian fitz Count, that could be another reason why Stephen missed him. Malmesbury, too, describes a meeting with Brian, though he does not say where this took place. The two had been close friends since childhood, and though Brian had done nothing so far to support the empress, it was always likely that he would join any serious uprising on her behalf. The arrival of Matilda and Robert was simply a trigger for his declaration of fidelity to her, and he would prove a most faithful follower.

It is the *Gesta* that carries a story not found elsewhere about an encounter on the road between Robert and Bishop Henry of Winchester. Clearly from the account given, it was the bishop who initiated this, posting men at all the crossroads until the earl appeared. Then, says the *Gesta*, 'encountering the earl, (he) entered into amicable relations with him and allowed him to proceed without opposition.' Wherever this story came from, the *Gesta* writer finds it preposterous. 'It is utterly incredible,' he says 'that the king's brother should receive with a friendly embrace the invader of his brother's kingdom.' If it was just a rumour that reached his ears, however, it is a plausible one on several levels.

The least likely is that Bishop Henry was aggrieved at his brother's actions in relation to his fellow bishops and the failure of his legatine council to make him reverse, or at least repent, what he had done. Some of the advice later given by the bishop might lend substance to this suspicion, but the *Gesta* is probably right to discount Henry as a traitor to his brother's cause. It must be remembered, however, that the bishop had another hat to wear in all these times of trouble. As papal legate, the pope's representative in England, it would have been his duty to act as peacemaker between the rivals, and he may have sought a meeting with Robert in order to do just that, or at least to urge restraint on the Angevin faction.

Whether or not such a meeting took place, Bishop Henry soon joined his brother at Arundel, 'as if he had not fallen in with the earl,' and proceeded to offer advice to Stephen concerning the dilemma that now faced him. Stephen was, in fact, in an awkward situation. He had rushed back to Arundel and taken steps to put the castle under siege, but Matilda was there under the protection of the erstwhile queen, and making war on women – at least high-born women – was not in the rule book. He could eventually starve them out without resorting to bombarding the castle, but he was in enough trouble already with the church over the arrest of the bishops, without giving them further grounds to condemn him. Nor could he claim that Matilda had committed any act of war against him, which might have justified imprisoning her or forcing her submission. Indeed, Adeliza, whom John of Worcester describes as being awed by the king, 'swore solemnly that no enemy of his had come to England on her invitation,' – a rather ambiguous statement – and that she was simply showing hospitality to a person who had formerly been attached to her.

Bishop Henry's advice was that Stephen should allow Matilda to join her brother, advice that Henry of Huntingdon describes as 'perfidious counsel'. The reason for this advice, however, as stated in the *Gesta*, was that 'while the king sat down to blockade the Countess of Anjou in one corner of the kingdom, her brother would speedily raise an insurrection and disturb the country in another quarter,' while if they were together, he 'might combine all his own troops in an immediate and sharp attack of their position,' which argument makes a good deal of sense. It is likely that both Robert of Gloucester and King Stephen seriously overestimated the level of support Matilda's presence would raise in the country, and quite possibly both were expecting a mighty confrontation in the near future.

The final decision was that Matilda would receive a safe conduct to her brother in Bristol, escorted for part of the way by Bishop Henry and Waleran de Meulan and then from Calne onwards by the bishop and Robert himself. Such a safe conduct was, says William of Malmesbury, 'a favour never denied to the most inveterate enemy by honourable soldiers', though Orderic Vitalis takes a far different view. 'It may be remarked,' he says, 'that this permission given by the king was a sign of great simplicity or carelessness.' Then, working himself up into a real rant, he continues, 'it was in his power at this time to have easily stifled a flame which threatened great mischief.' Stephen should have 'driven away the wolf from the entrance to the fold ... nipped the growth of malignancy in the bud', and been like his uncle in crushing the efforts of those who threatened the country, 'by smiting them with the sword of justice'. Whether he was really advocating driving Matilda away or smiting her with a sword is not entirely clear, but in the event Stephen did neither. While winning for himself praise for his chivalrous treatment of a woman, and a cousin at that, it is highly possible that in later years he regretted his decision. Others certainly did. Even John of Worcester is driven to remark: 'He is the king of peace, and would that he were also the king of vigour and justice.'

Arriving in Bristol, Matilda met the other significant defector to her cause, Miles of Gloucester, who now declared he held Gloucester Castle on her behalf. Within a few days she had travelled on with him to take up her residence there. Some have queried why she did not remain at Bristol, which is generally seen as the headquarters of her cause, the place from which, as John of Worcester puts it, all calamities flowed. Bristol, though, belonged to Earl Robert, while Gloucester was a royal castle. In years past it had been part of an annual royal tour, and a place where, at Christmastime, the king would hold court with a formal crown-wearing. If other royal castles were closed to her, she was at least able to claim Gloucester for herself.

The idea that if she were present in England the country would rise up to support her was quickly shown to be untrue. In Robert of Gloucester, Brian fitz Count and Miles of Gloucester she had three strong and able leaders, good military commanders and truly loyal servants, but no great magnates rushed to join them. She was four years late in coming, and most had already adapted to, and profited by, the new regime. There would be lesser lords who would defy the king on her behalf, particularly in the Welsh Marches and the West Country, and others who would take advantage of the troubled times to get benefits for themselves – the Welsh kings might be numbered among these – but nothing like the overwhelming numbers needed to topple an established and consecrated king such as Stephen. When the *Gesta* declares that 'all their adherents who had hitherto paid a faithless and hollow submission to the king ... with one mind ... rose against him in all quarters with great vehemence,' it seems well wide of the mark. Nevertheless, although the empress could not conquer the king, neither could the king dispose of the empress. One advantage she held was that, by and large, those who had declared for her formed a compact territory in the western part of England. She had, of course, the tacit support of King David in the north as well but after the stinging defeat at the Battle of the Standard, not much could be expected from that quarter at this time.

The most easterly of her adherents was Brian fitz Count at Wallingford. Situated between Oxford and Reading, both held for the king, he appeared by far the most vulnerable to attack, and it was at Wallingford, therefore, that Stephen made the first attempt to carry what was clearly now a civil war, to his opponents. Wallingford, though, was a tough nut to crack.

Strategically sited at a crossing point on the Thames, it had been an Anglo-Saxon stronghold and base for the warrior 'housecarls' before the Conquest. Immediately afterwards a Norman castle was begun and it had been strengthened and added to ever since. Brian fitz Count had had plenty of time to provision and garrison it with a strong force, and it soon became clear to Stephen that any siege was likely to be a long one, and even then might fail to achieve its object. He stuck it out for a few weeks and then, wearying of the effort, established and garrisoned two counter-castles to continue the struggle and marched away.

While this was happening, the supporters of Matilda in other areas were not idle. Miles of Gloucester, accompanied by Geoffrey Talbot, had already laid siege to Hereford, and his son-in-law Humphrey de Bohun claimed Trowbridge Castle for the empress. Robert fitz Hubert, a Flemish mercenary captain, had also seized Malmesbury, though it is not at all clear on whose behalf. He is said to have been a relative of William of Ypres, and at this time may or may not have been in the pay of Robert of Gloucester.

Trowbridge was Stephen's new target, but on the way he surprised the garrison at Miles of Gloucester's castle at South Cerney, while a combination of siege and negotiation resulted in Malmesbury being handed over by Robert fitz Hubert. The

Gesta says Robert was taken prisoner but, if so, he must have been very soon released for he quickly found his way to Robert of Gloucester at Bristol.

After these easy victories Stephen would find Trowbridge a far more difficult task. Like Wallingford it had been well prepared for a siege, and Humphrey de Bohun was ready to put up a stubborn resistance. Nevertheless, the king set about constructing his siege engines and bombarding the castle, though, according to the *Gesta*, 'the besieged were neither injured by his machines, nor at all daunted by his blockade.' While he was thus engaged, however, Miles of Gloucester, 'a man of a most active mind, and always ready for bold deeds', took a picked body of soldiers to Wallingford where, arriving by night, they fell on those the king had left there 'with so much impetuosity that they were forced to yield.' Some were killed, some wounded and some taken prisoner, before Miles withdrew just as rapidly to his own area, 'with the glory of a brilliant victory'.

This lightning raid must have come as a great shock to Stephen when news of it was brought to him. If he'd thought this war would be a matter of picking off the castles of his opponents one by one, he was rapidly disillusioned. There at Trowbridge, he himself might become the target of just such a raid. The *Gesta* records that it was the barons who accompanied him, however, who, weary of the long sieges, became 'united in apprehension' that Robert of Gloucester would fall on them with all his force. They advised the king to withdraw and after strengthening the garrison at nearby Devizes he took that advice, returning to London 'to rally his strength, and then advance where fortune summoned him to some safer enterprise.' Cautious rather than cowardly, it is likely the king now appreciated he was in for a prolonged struggle, and setting himself up as a target was the last thing he should be doing in these opening weeks.

The first serious blow of the war was landed by Robert of Gloucester, deliberately striking at his nemesis Waleran de Meulan, recently made Earl of Worcester. A detailed eyewitness description of the attack on that city has been left to us in the *Chronicle* of John of Worcester, and it is clear from that account that the attack was not unexpected. He describes the citizens in the days beforehand carrying their goods into the cathedral and other churches, in the hope of saving them from the burning and pillaging to come. 'Oh, wretched sight!' he exclaims, 'behold the house of God ... where the sacrifice of praise should have been offered ... seems now but a warehouse for furniture.' Soon the townspeople themselves were taking shelter in the churches, where only the sacred area behind the roodscreen seems to have been kept free of them. 'Within is heard the chant of the clergy, without the wailing of children; and the notes of the choir are mingled with the sobs of infants at the breast, and the cries of sorrowing mothers. Oh, misery of miseries to behold!' Needless to say, the clergy themselves stripped from the churches and hid away all plate and images and anything that might be deemed of value.

The blow fell on Tuesday 7 November at daybreak, as the monks were chanting the service of Lauds. A great army had marched up from the south, which John calls the centre of mischief. 'The city of Gloucester had risen in arms, and ... marched to attack, pillage and burn the city of Worcester.' The response of the monks was to don their finest vestments and to carry the relics of their beloved St Oswald through the streets 'in supplicant procession', which noble action seems to have had little effect on the course of events.

The first attack was made on the south side of the city, near the castle held for King Stephen by William de Beauchamp, hereditary sheriff of Worcester. That attack, though, was beaten off. 'Our people made a brave and obstinate resistance,' says John. The attackers soon discovered, however, that the north side had no such protection, and there, he says, 'the entire host rushed tumultuously in, mad with fury.' It soon became apparent that plunder and destruction were the aims, rather than conquest.

Houses were set alight in many parts of the city, and a considerable number burnt down, though he says most of it survived unburnt. Goods and animals were seized in large numbers and people made captive for ransom, 'whether they have the means or have them not.' Then, having done their worst, the attackers drew off 'never to return on such a foul enterprise'. All this, he says, took place on the first day of winter, 'which will, doubtless, be very severe to the wretched sufferers.'

Around a week later, on 13 November, Waleran de Meulan came to visit. According to John, he 'mourned over the city, and felt that the evil was done to himself,' which, of course, was exactly what was intended. Even more so, however, it had been done to the citizens of Worcester, and there is no record of him offering any practical help. Instead he went off to sack Sudeley Castle, held for Robert of Gloucester by John fitz Harold, 'returning evil for evil' on the supporters of the empress. This John fitz Harold and his brother Robert were grandsons of Ralph of Mantes, who in turn was a nephew of Edward the Confessor, and generally regarded as the first 'Frenchman' to be given lands in England. More pertinently, Robert had been the leader of that expedition against the Welsh in 1136 that had been left stranded in Carmarthen by lack of support from Stephen. Like many of the Marcher lords, they had more reason than most to turn against the king when given an alternative cause to support, and this attack by Waleran would have done nothing to change their minds.

The king also came to view the damage at Worcester, bringing with him, according to John of Worcester, a large army. He stayed only long enough to appoint William de Beauchamp a royal constable before marching on towards Hereford. Miles of Gloucester had already taken the city and was besieging the garrison in the castle, but if it was Stephen's intention to launch an attack on him, he quickly changed his mind. Stopping at Leominster, some 12 miles away, he found the town extremely reluctant to swear allegiance to him, and instead of pushing on 'retired with disgrace', as Malmesbury puts it, first to Worcester and then back to the security of Oxford.

The Christmas court that year was held at Salisbury, for the very good reason that Stephen wanted to get his hands on the wealth left behind by Roger of Salisbury. The bishop had died of a 'quartan fever', probably influenza or a form of malaria, early in December, and the chroniclers seem to have had mixed feelings about his passing. While most draw biblical lessons about the folly of laying up treasures on earth, William of

Malmesbury at least shows some sympathy. 'There were very few who pitied him,' he writes, 'so much envy and hatred had his excessive power drawn on him, and undeservedly too, from some of those very persons whom he had advanced to honour.'

The bishop seems to have spent his last days trying to reimburse places he had wrongfully deprived, but the *Gesta* describes 'immense sums of money and a vast quantity of plate, both of gold and silver', left in the church at Salisbury. All of this was taken over by King Stephen on the basis, as he had earlier claimed, that it had been obtained from the exchequer and therefore rightfully belonged to him. The *Gesta* declares that the canons at Salisbury thoroughly approved of this and had even offered it to the king, though the truth is that they probably had little choice. Very generously Stephen confirmed the return of assets that the bishop had already promised, and even gave the canons a little towards their building works. A very different version of this transaction appears in John of Worcester's account. Here the canons 'presented' the king with £2,000 and were given in return an exemption from taxes. Furthermore, he promised he would refund this sum 'when peace was restored' – probably the first specific admission that the country was now at war.

Immediately after Christmas King Stephen had new challenges to face, the first of these in the hitherto quiet area of East Anglia. Bishop Nigel of Ely had already proved himself the most volatile of the family of Roger of Salisbury, and the death of his uncle and its aftermath hit him hard. He felt, says John of Worcester, that he had 'lost, as it were, his right hand'. His reaction was to fortify his castle at Ely on land below his cathedral, and also another castle a little distance away at Aldreth, guarding the way through the fens. The *Gesta* sees this as a vindication of the earlier claim that the bishop had 'long plotted against the king'. He acted, it says, 'both that he might ... have satisfaction for the injuries his uncle had suffered at the king's hands ... and also aid the children of King Henry in recovering the crown.' Henry of Huntingdon, however, who was closer to the situation, only says that King Stephen hated Bishop Nigel because of his loathing for Roger of Salisbury, and that 'his anger extended to all his kindred.' He makes no mention of any links to the empress and indeed, there was no support for Nigel from that quarter in his defiance of the king.

Ely at that time was truly an island, rising above its surrounding marshes and fens. When Stephen arrived with his army in January 1140, therefore, it took some ingenuity to actually get at the bishop. The king quickly took the castle at Aldreth and then was advised to construct a bridge of boats across the part of the fen where the water current was slackest. With these tied together and bundles of 'wattled rods' laid across, the army got over the worst of the water, and was then guided through the 'slimy marshes' to the island itself. It is the *Gesta* that gives us these graphic details, and which also states that the advice was given by 'a clever monk of Ely', who was rewarded by being made the abbot of Ramsey, a famous monastery nearby. This promotion was clearly disapproved of, for it adds, 'and we know that afterwards he was subjected to much trouble and affliction, the Almighty justly punishing secret offences, on account of his unlawful intrusion into the church.'

Isolated as he was, Bishop Nigel had little chance of achieving anything meaningful by his defiance. Indeed, as soon as the king gained a foothold on the island he escaped, though with some difficulty, and made his way 'in poverty and distress' to Gloucester. Stephen, meanwhile, took possession of Ely, along with 'great booty and large sums of money' that were found there – another boost for the royal coffers at a time when it was much needed.

A more serious insurrection occurred about this time on the other side of the country. In Cornwall William fitz Richard, Lord of Cardinham, who had previously held the area for Stephen, abruptly declared for Matilda. He married his daughter Mabel to the empress's half-brother, Reginald de Dunstanville, delivering with her, so the *Gesta* says, the whole county of Cornwall. This was clearly a nominal delivery since Reginald is then described as 'compelling the inhabitants to submit to him by force of arms', though 'with more courage than prudence'. In fact, despite initial successes and the garrisoning of castles with his own men, Reginald seems to have so upset the population, including the clergy whose churches were robbed, that when Stephen arrived in the area accompanied by Alan of Brittany, they were not lacking local support.

William of Malmesbury claims that Reginald was created Earl of Cornwall by his half-brother, Robert of Gloucester. It would be unlike Malmesbury to slip up on facts so close to home, but such a creation – of one earl by another – would have been unprecedented. Reginald was confirmed in that office by Matilda the following year, however, and it may be that he has simply backdated the deed to the intention. On firmer ground we have a further demonstration of Stephen's policy of creating earls as military governors to hold down or, in this case, to recover areas on his behalf. Alan of Brittany, already Earl of Richmond, now became Earl of Cornwall as well, a title to which he claimed some right as it had previously been held by his uncle Brian of Brittany.

A short but vigorous campaign by king and earl quickly succeeded in recovering most of the land taken by Reginald, leaving that 'proto-earl' with only the one castle he resided in, which may possibly have been Launceston. This, the *Gesta* declares, showed the wrath of God for Reginald's failure to prevent the plundering of churches. Furthermore, it declares that 'the wife of his bosom was driven to madness and became subject to demoniacal influence' for the same reason. That he was not entirely beaten is indicated, however, by Stephen leaving an active body of soldiers with the new Earl Alan, and instructions to continue activities against Reginald until he was driven out of the county.

It is clear Stephen didn't want to remain too long in Cornwall. Though he had strong adherents in the south-west – Henry de Tracy in Barnstaple, for instance – he was still a long way from his main power base, and concerted action on the part of Robert of Gloucester and his supporters could well have cut him off from London and the south-east. Indeed, the *Gesta* suggests that just such an idea occurred to Robert and that he assembled troops ready for a decisive showdown with the king, only to think better of it when Stephen called up 'all the barons of Devonshire to his aid'. Yet again the war was to be carried on, not by battle, but by siege and chevauchée.

In just such a violent progress the king passed through the West Country, taking easy castles and plundering the land, while at the same time Miles of Gloucester was doing the same to the royal possessions in the Severn valley, though not for a moment taking his eye off the main prize at Hereford. For a while it seemed Stephen might be intending to raise the siege in that beleaguered city, but once again he stopped short. Instead Robert of Leicester, the younger Beaumont twin, was granted 'the city and castle and whole county of Hereford', in essence a second earldom, albeit over an area at present in the hands of the enemy. Whether or not the intention was that Robert and his brother, the recently created Earl of Worcester, should combine forces and wrest the whole region away from the empress, in practice very little was done. Waleran, no doubt still smarting from the sack of Worcester the previous year, did indeed lay waste a large part of the Vale of Gloucester, including Robert of Gloucester's town of Tewkesbury, but soon after this the Siege of Hereford was brought to a successful conclusion by Miles of Gloucester and Geoffrey Talbot.

This was achieved, to the 'insufferable horror' of the *Gesta* writer, by a two-pronged artillery assault, one part, commanded by Geoffrey Talbot, being based in the cathedral itself. 'The citizens ran about wailing when they saw the churchyard dug up to make a rampart for the fortified post, and the mouldering or newly interred corpses of their parents and relations rudely thrown up from their graves.' The tower, too, was utilised as 'a station for engines of war, from which missiles were hurled to crush the king's troops.' Unable to withstand this double assault, the castle was finally surrendered, adding one more stronghold to the firm base of the empress in the Welsh Marches.

In mid-March 1140 the tensions within the royal camp were once more exposed at a council in London where, among other business, the replacement of the Bishop of Salisbury was proposed. Henry of Winchester put forward the name of Henry Sully, son of his eldest, overlooked brother, William of Sully, and therefore nephew of both himself and the king. This nomination was countered by Waleran de Meulan, who instead proposed his own cousin, Philip de Harcourt, who, since the expulsion of Roger le Poer the previous year, had held the post of Lord Chancellor. To the fury of Bishop Henry, Stephen approved Waleran's candidate, prompting the bishop to pull rank as papal legate and veto the appointment. Not only was the kingdom divided against itself, with desolation the likely consequence – as quoted from St Luke by William of Newburgh – but even those on the same side were frequently at loggerheads. In such a climate it is hardly surprising that others attempted to take advantage of the lack of firm government to benefit themselves.

One such, Robert fitz Hubert, had already had his fingers burnt once but that did not deter him from trying again. In late March 1140 he and a band of followers managed to get possession of Devizes Castle from the king's garrison. This they did, according to the *Gesta*, by scaling the walls at night using ladders 'strongly and cleverly formed of thongs', which could be thrown over the battlements without disturbing the guards. Under the impression he had taken the castle for the empress, Robert of Gloucester is said to have sent his son with reinforcements, only to have them repulsed. The castle was not to be given up to any other party. Fitz Hubert had taken it for himself and, according to William of Malmesbury, intended to carve out for himself a lordship stretching from Winchester to London. He met his match, however, in the person of John fitz Gilbert the Marshal.

The various accounts disagree both as to whose side John was on, and how fitz Hubert came to fall into his hands. Malmesbury and the *Gesta* say he was for the empress, John of Worcester for the king. The important point is that John held the royal castle of Marlborough, and it was the castle that fitz Hubert wanted. The *Gesta* claims he offered a peaceful alliance, while Worcester talks of threats, but either way John could see which way the land lay. Declaring, 'I would rather make another man my prisoner than be taken myself,' he invited fitz Hubert into the castle, promptly seized him and 'threw him into the dungeon to die of hunger and suffering'.

In fact he was not there long. He was handed over to Robert of Gloucester – Worcester says for money, while the *Gesta* says because John was a faithful adherent of Gloucester's – and taken to Devizes where he was hanged in front of his own men. This was simply 'a just and divine retribution' for his cruelties, declares the *Gesta*. The other sources, however, say his hanging was threatened in order to make his followers hand over the castle, and carried out when they refused, fitz Hubert having previously made them swear never to give up the castle even if he was hanged. What might appear as their high-minded faithfulness is rather undermined, though, when soon afterwards the king offered a very large sum of money in exchange for the castle, which offer was immediately accepted. The agent of this transaction, Hervey Brito, or Hervey of Brittany, was rewarded by marriage to an illegitimate daughter of the king, being granted the wealthy Honour of Eye, and becoming earl of Wiltshire.

Robert fitz Hubert was not the only one to chance his arm at this time. In East Anglia, Hugh Bigod is reported to have seized the castle at Bungay, though this may well have been a strike at the Beaumonts rather than at the king, since the land in question was part of an estate belonging to Robert of Leicester. It may also have been intended to draw the king's attention to the fact that Hugh, who had helped put him on the throne in 1135, had since received no advancement from Stephen, while honours aplenty had been showered on the Beaumonts. When, after Whitsun, the king took back the castle, there seems to have been little violence involved. Within a short time the two were fully reconciled, and although the records are not entirely clear, it is possible that later that year Hugh was created Earl of Norfolk, at the same time as another major East Anglian landowner, Geoffrey de Mandeville, was made Earl of Essex.

According to William of Malmesbury, 'The whole of this year was embittered by the horrors of war,' and yet it was in the summer of 1140 that the first attempt was made to negotiate a peace between the rival factions. One reason for this may have been that both sides were running short of resources to carry on the conflict. There was a general lack of provisions – hardly surprising when so much had been plundered and destroyed – and Malmesbury reports a scarcity of money and widespread counterfeiting.

Matilda's faction was perennially short of money, but he even accuses the king of reducing the weight of the silver penny as he had run out of money in trying to keep so many soldiers in the field. Henry of Huntingdon, too, gives a depressing account of the state of affairs. 'Where the king spent Christmas and Easter it matters not,' he says, 'for now all that made the court splendid ... had disappeared. The treasury, left well filled, was now empty.'

It was against this background that, around midsummer, a peace conference was held at Bath. Again, it is Malmesbury who gives us the details. The meeting was mediated by Bishop Henry of Winchester, and, depending on how cynical a view is taken, he was either attempting to regain some power over the king, or, acting as papal legate, simply carrying out his proper role as peacemaker. The king was represented by Queen Matilda, by Archbishop Theobald of Canterbury and by Bishop Henry himself, while on the side of the empress only Robert of Gloucester is specifically named, along with 'others of her friends'. If this was to be a general clearing of the ground to produce concrete proposals for a lasting solution, it was not a resounding success.

'They wasted words and time to no purpose,' Malmesbury says, 'and departed without being able to conclude a peace.' Nevertheless, it seems some progress might have been made. He reports that the empress was inclined towards letting the church settle the matter, though the king, listening to the warmongers among his advisors, vetoed this. This little detail suggests that the issue had moved on from simply replacing Stephen with Matilda. That had already been turned down by the pope as recently as the previous year. More likely the matter under discussion was what should happen at the end of Stephen's reign. Both parties had sons, and it seems that the question now to be decided was solely concerned with the succession.

Clearly, enough had been said for the papal legate, 'who knew that it was the especial duty of his office to restore peace,' to undertake a diplomatic journey among other interested parties. At the end of September, therefore, he crossed the Channel and had 'a long and anxious discussion' with both the King of France and Count Theobald.

Once again this suggests it was the succession that was at issue. Stephen's son Eustace had recently become betrothed to Constance, the sister of the French king. This had been negotiated by Queen

Matilda and, according to most accounts, facilitated by paying a large sum of money to King Louis, money drawn from the treasure left behind by Roger of Salisbury. Clearly, though, this marriage was in the expectation that Eustace would become King of England and any suggestion that he would not would necessarily involve the brother of the bride, as, indeed, would arrangements for the future of the Duchy of Normandy. We don't know what outcome there was from Bishop Henry's discussions. If William of Malmesbury ever knew what proposals were brought back by the bishop at the end of November, he does not disclose them. He does say that Empress Matilda and Robert of Gloucester immediately agreed to them, while King Stephen hesitated a long time before finally refusing to do so, which suggests there must have been at least enough in them to have tempted him.

By that time, however, events had already moved on. John of Worcester reports a violent skirmish near Bath between Robert of Gloucester and some of the king's men, which may have rapidly followed upon the breakup of the conference. It was in this action that the adventurer Geoffrey Talbot received a fatal wound. Later, an attack on Nottingham by Robert, which resulted in the burning of the city, would have done nothing to soften Stephen's heart towards his cousin's cause. Then, at the very end of the year, the king's attention was turned to Lincoln, the mightiest city of the East of England, with its castle and cathedral sitting high above the surrounding countryside. Ranulf, Earl of Chester, and his half-brother William of Roumare had somehow entered the castle and were now apparently holding it against the king, who had garrisoned it with his own men the previous year. How and why they did so depends on which of a number of different accounts is accepted as true.

John of Hexham alone declares that Ranulf wished to attack Prince Henry of Scotland on his way north from the king's court, and when, by the intervention of the queen, he was frustrated from doing so, 'this hostility was transferred to plots against the king's safety.' Quite what this has to do with Lincoln is hard to see, though the link is possibly to do with lands Ranulf felt he should have inherited. Through his father he believed he had a claim to Carlisle and Cumberland, which had now been given to Prince Henry. Through his mother he believed he had a claim to at least part of the castle at Lincoln, and it is this that also links him to his half-brother William of Roumare.

The mother of them both was Lucy of Bolingbroke, the much-married heiress who carried her rich inheritance of lands in Lincolnshire and Carlisle to each of her husbands in turn. William of Roumare was the son of her second marriage, and Ranulf of Chester the son of the third (after which she paid 500 marks to Henry for the right not to be married again). On her death in 1138 her property was split between the two of them, but there was also the matter of Lincoln Castle. Most unusually, at Lincoln there were two separate mounds and two separate keeps, one clearly a royal castle, but the other, known as Lucy's Tower, part of the estate of Lucy of Bolingbroke. It is highly possible that, in garrisoning the castle after the disgrace of Bishop Alexander, the rights of Lucy's sons had been overlooked and that it was Lucy's Tower that had now been seized.

William of Newburgh says the castle was entered 'by a stratagem', but it is Orderic Vitalis, the farthest from the scene, who gives us full details, which may or may not be accurate. Ranulf and William, he says, cautiously chose a time 'when the garrison of the tower were dispersed abroad and engaged in sports'. They sent their wives in first, as if on a social visit, 'under pretence of their taking some amusement'. Then, when the ladies were engaged in talking and joking with the wife of the knight in charge of the tower, Ranulf arrived, 'without his armour or even his mantle, apparently to fetch back his wife'. He had with him only three companions, and no one suspected anything until they were inside, whereupon they seized upon available weapons, ejected the guard, and let in William of Roumare with a body of men who proceeded to take over the castle, and, he claims, the whole city.

It makes a good story and may possibly be true, but it does not seem to be the cause of the trouble that followed. Malmesbury, introducing his explanation of 'the mazy labyrinth of events' in 1141, begins by stating: 'King Stephen peaceably departed the county of Lincoln before Christmas, and had augmented the honours of the Earl of Chester and his brother.' Far from ejecting them from the castle, it seemed he had been confirming them in their possession, and it has been plausibly argued that this was the occasion when he bestowed the position of constable of the castle on Ranulf, and created William of Roumare Earl of Lincoln. Within a matter of weeks he had abruptly changed his mind, so much so that in the middle of the Christmas festivities the king stormed back up to Lincoln and put the castle under siege.

None of the chroniclers seem to have a plausible explanation for this. Several declare that it was the citizens of Lincoln who called him back, with the *Gesta* claiming they were being oppressed by the earls. William of Malmesbury simply says they wanted to curry favour with the king by pointing out that the brothers were peacefully residing in the castle and 'might very easily be surprised'. He adds that Stephen's response was 'unjustifiable' as he had 'left them before the festival without any suspicion of enmity'.

It has been suggested that during the Christmas feast Stephen may have realised he had given away more than he intended in his settlement with the brothers at Lincoln. Evidence exists of grants of estates and privileges across the midland shires to Ranulf of Chester, including the town of Derby and a castle that may have been Belvoir Castle on the Lincolnshire border. This may well have gone down badly with other magnates with interests in the area, particularly Robert of Leicester, especially when it was realised Ranulf now held interests across a swathe of land from Cheshire in the west, through the north midlands, and into Lincolnshire in the east. Should he decide to change his allegiance, Stephen might find his southern powerbase completely cut off from the north, where King David of Scotland must still be reckoned a potential threat.

Whatever the reason, the king arrived outside the walls of Lincoln, achieving the surprise that had been predicted. Both Ranulf and William of Roumare, along with their families, were residing in the castle, but Ranulf somehow managed to get away before the circle of the besiegers was completely closed. Although it is later suggested that Stephen had relatively scanty forces with him, it was clearly enough for Ranulf to realise he would need more than his own resources in order to lift the siege. He needed a powerful backer and he knew just where to find one.

Some years previously he had married Mabel, daughter of Robert of Gloucester, and it was to his father-in-law that he now appealed, 'although,' says William of Malmesbury, 'he had long since offended him on many accounts.' The main bone of contention between them was that Ranulf had thus far tried to remain neutral in the struggle between Stephen and Matilda. He had 'appeared staunch to neither party.' Now, however, he was prepared to declare himself. In return for aid from Robert, he promised 'eternal fidelity to the empress,' and the earl took him at his word.

It was not only Robert of Gloucester who turned out, but all the leading figures in Matilda's campaign. Miles of Gloucester was there, and Brian fitz Count, along with those referred to as 'the disinherited', and all the Welsh they could muster, led by the princes Cadwaladr (the brother of Owain Gwynedd), Madog ap Maredudd of Powys, and Morgan ap Owain of Glamorgan. Needless to say, it took a little while to assemble this force, and it was not until the beginning of February that they approached Lincoln. John of Hexham suggests the king was aware of their approach, since he declares the magnates with him urged him to 'levy an army' as they had not brought large enough forces with them to fight a battle. Vitalis, though, says Stephen could not be persuaded it would come to that. He was wrong.

We know the date for it was a major Christian feast day; 2 February was Candlemas Day, or the Feast of the Purification of Our Lady, and though several accounts claim it was the very day Robert of Gloucester and his men arrived, after crossing an almost impassable marsh, it is more likely they actually reached Lincoln the day before. We know, too, what Stephen was doing early that morning, for the *Gesta* and Robert of Torigny together give us full details, complete with an omen. He was hearing Mass in the cathedral, a service led by the newly humbled Bishop Alexander. Stephen, says Torigny, 'was offering to God the usual waxen taper', but it broke as he placed it in the bishop's hand. (The *Gesta* says it was extinguished.) 'The king took this as a sign that his own power was broken'. Furthermore, a pyx holding the consecrated host above the altar suddenly fell as its chain broke, and 'this also was an omen of the king's downfall.' On a more positive note, the *Gesta* declares that the candle was stuck together again and relit, a sign that his losses would only be temporary.

The king was then informed that his enemies were close at hand, and if he did not retreat at once there must be a battle. He was, indeed, urged to retreat, to put off the battle, to raise a larger army, and not to fight on a holy day. Stephen brushed off this advice, and you have to wonder if he had in mind his father's ignominious retreat from battle all those years before in the Holy Land. On 2 February 1141 King Stephen refused to retreat. Instead he would fight the Battle of Lincoln.

We have a very good idea of who fought on each side in this battle, and how they were drawn up in battle array, as Henry of Huntingdon gives us pages of speeches allegedly delivered before the fighting. Thus he has Robert of Gloucester tell his forces, 'There is no possibility of retreat over the marshes ... Here, therefore, you must either conquer or die,' before going on to shower insults on the leaders of the opposing army. While these speeches must be seen as largely fictitious, it is likely the actual insults would have had some basis in reality, at least as seen at the time. Their opponents, and the insults linked to them, included Alan of Brittany – 'polluted with every sort of wickedness'; Waleran de Meulan – 'crafty, perfidious ... the last in fight, the first in flight'; Hugh Bigod – doubly perjured in claiming Henry changed the succession; William Earl of York – so wicked his wife left him; William of Warenne – the 'flagrant adulterer' who took her away; Simon of Senlis – 'who never acts but talks, who never gives but promises'; and William of Ypres – words failed in describing the 'crooked paths of his treasons'.

For the other side, Huntingdon declares that the address on behalf of the king was given by Baldwin fitz Gilbert, as Stephen's voice was not clear enough to be heard. In this only Robert of Gloucester and Ranulf of Chester come in for specific insults, the former having 'the mouth of a lion and the heart of a hare', while the latter was 'a man of reckless audacity ... with designs beyond his powers'. The Welsh were described as 'ill-armed and recklessly rash; and ... unskilled and unpractised in the art of war.'

Both sides, of course, claimed to have right on their side. Even before the royalist speeches were concluded, says Huntingdon, the enemy was advancing upon them, 'the blast of their trumpets and the trampling of the horses making the ground quake'. We don't know the exact site of the battle but it is likely to have been on the flat land below the western gate of the castle, an area broad enough to hold the three divisions of Robert's army, and the more unusual formation adopted by the king, of two lines of cavalry in front and the mass of infantry clustered around the dismounted king in the rear. Robert of Torigny comments that 'the cavalry, however, appeared to be exceedingly scanty when drawn out in battle array.'

Robert of Gloucester had placed the 'disinherited' in the centre, among them, presumably, Baldwin de Redvers, though he is not named. On one flank were Ranulf of Chester and the Welsh, and on the other Robert himself. It was the disinherited who led the charge, falling on the king's cavalry and disconcerting them, according to Malmesbury, because they didn't fight like gentlemen. They 'did not attack from a distance with lances, but at close quarters with swords', a practice that made it far more likely that someone would get hurt. However they fought, it was effective, the royal cavalry being 'routed in the twinkling of an eye', says Huntingdon, with the earls that led them fleeing the field. A counter-attack by the mercenaries, led by William of Ypres and William of York, was effective for a time against the Welsh, until they too were routed by Ranulf of Chester. At this point William of Ypres, as a seasoned commander, decided that the royal position was hopeless and 'deferred his aid for better times', abandoning the battle and taking the remnant of his men with him.

That left Stephen and his infantry alone on the battlefield facing the whole of Robert's army, which now closed in around them, cutting off any hope of retreat even if they had not all been on foot. The fight was not ended, however. Huntingdon describes Robert's mounted forces repeatedly attacking 'as if they were assaulting a castle', trampling and slaying and taking prisoners, while in the centre Stephen himself made his assailants recoil 'from the unmatched force of his terrible arm'.

The chronicles are united in admiration for his courage. 'King Stephen,' says Robert of Torigny, 'kept his ground like a lion, standing single-handed in the field ... grinding his teeth and foaming at the mouth like a wild boar.' Had there been a hundred such, he declares, they would have carried the day, and even then 'it was no easy matter to take him prisoner.' Ranulf of Chester tried and failed, and, says Vitalis, 'as long as three of his soldiers stood by him he never ceased dealing heavy blows,' first with his sword, and when that shattered, with 'a Norwegian battleaxe with which some youth had supplied him.'

According to Malmesbury, the end came when the king was struck on the head by a blow from a stone, 'but who was the author of this deed is uncertain.' For Huntingdon the end was when the last of his weapons was shattered, whereupon 'William de Cahagnes, a brave soldier, rushed on him, and seizing him by his helmet, shouted, "Here, here, I have taken the king."' So he had, but according to John of Hexham that was not the end of the matter. The king refused to surrender to a mere knight, and it was only when, at his own suggestion, Robert of Gloucester was called over, that Stephen formally surrendered himself into the hands of the earl.

8

Disaster and Triumph

(February – December 1141)

The chroniclers are unanimous that the outcome of the battle and the capture of the king were God's judgement on Stephen for his wrongdoing. The *Gesta*, in fact, declares that when a crowd had gathered round the king and he was being disarmed, 'he frequently exclaimed in humiliation and grief that this shameful disaster had befallen him as a punishment for his sins,' though he goes on to point out that those who had broken their fealty and rebelled against him were no less guilty.

Robert of Gloucester took charge of the king and, says Malmesbury, 'the person whom he had just before fiercely attacked … he now calmly protected.' He would not allow anyone to injure him, 'not suffering him to be molested even with a reproach', though the violence of the day had not yet abated. Finding that Stephen's supporters had now either fled or been taken prisoner, the attackers, or at least some of them, took out their aggression on the citizens of Lincoln, many of whom were slaughtered and the town sacked. This, says Malmesbury, with little sign of clerical forgiveness, showed the 'just indignation of the victors', since these citizens 'had been the origin and fomenters of this calamity'.

By 9 February the captive king had been taken to Gloucester for a meeting with his cousin Matilda, the one defeated but still an anointed king, the other not yet a queen. Even Malmesbury is not able to tell us what passed at this meeting, but the upshot was that Stephen was to be held prisoner in Bristol Castle, the strongest of Matilda's fortresses and the farthest from Stephen's power base in the south-east. Initially, at least, he was held as a royal captive, with 'every mark of honour', in the same way that before him Robert Curthose, the brother of King Henry, had been held for nearly thirty years. Curthose, though, had never been a crowned king, seemed resigned to his imprisonment and had no party in the country prepared to fight for his release. Stephen would prove a very different proposition.

Delighted though she must have been at this abrupt and possibly unexpected change of fortune, Matilda would have known she had a long way still to go before she could become Queen of England. There were no immediate precedents for deposing an anointed king, and no great rush of magnates to submit and acclaim her. Taking Stephen's seizure of power for a model, it seemed clear she would have to win over the church, the administration and probably the citizens of London before she could settle a crown upon her own head.

The first point of contact with the defeated regime was Henry, Bishop of Winchester. As papal legate and brother of the king, he could have a double influence on those whose backing Matilda needed, and if the chroniclers are correct he had kept at least a channel of communication open with the Angevin camp through the previous year. Messengers were sent to the bishop and a meeting arranged at Wherwell, near Winchester, on Sunday 2 March, the third Sunday of Lent. It was a dark and rainy day, according to Malmesbury, and a certain amount of dark negotiating must have gone on as each side sought to get what it needed, while being more than a little wary of the other. In his role as papal legate, of course Bishop Henry could claim he was acting in the interests of the church and of peace for the country, which would cover any changing of sides with an air of respectability. He certainly seemed to achieve a good bargain. In the end, Matilda 'swore and pledged her faith' to give the bishop exactly what he had sought and failed to achieve under Stephen. 'All matters of importance in England,' and in particular the giving of the higher church offices, 'should await his decision, if he, with the holy church, would receive her as sovereign and observe perpetual fidelity to her.' In return Bishop

Henry swore to keep faith with Matilda as 'Lady of England' as long as she held to this promise. There has been much discussion about that title. 'Lady of England' certainly falls short of 'Queen of England', though it could well have been accepted as an important step on the way, and a pledge that Henry would use all his powers, as he had for Stephen, to obtain the throne itself for Matilda. It is noticeable that the promises on both sides were conditional.

The *Gesta*, as partial to Stephen as Malmesbury is to Matilda, takes pains to explain Bishop Henry's behaviour at this time. His problem was that, while 'it was a serious affair, and indecent in the eyes of the world ... to desert (his brother) suddenly in his adversity,' yet 'there was the greatest difficulty in supporting the king's cause,' since his castles were not provisioned or garrisoned properly for a fight. His agreement with Matilda was, therefore, on the same footing as Robert of Gloucester's submission to Stephen in 1136 – a way to watch and wait for a change of circumstances, when 'he might promptly and freely stand up for his brother.'

The immediate consequence of the pact with Matilda was that she and her supporters moved on to Winchester, where they took up residence in the royal castle on the hill overlooking the town. She was also put in possession of the royal treasury ('small in amount' says the *Gesta*) and regalia, a sign that the administration of royal finances was now in her hands. Then the bishop had her 'proclaimed sovereign lady and queen in the market place before the people,' before leading her in a splendid procession to the cathedral. In this procession she was accompanied not only by the Bishop of Winchester, but also by Bishop Bernard of St David's, who had been her mother's chancellor, the bishops of Lincoln, Ely, Bath, Hereford and Chichester, and many abbots. 'Thereupon', says John of Worcester, 'the famous city of Winchester was delivered over to her: she received the royal crown of England, and the legate himself cursed those who cursed her, blessed those who blessed her, excommunicating her adversaries and absolving those who submitted to her.'

It might be thought, therefore, that Matilda had clearly achieved the support of the church, but there was one notable absentee from all this. Theobald, Archbishop of Canterbury, did not appear on the scene until a few days after this great occasion, and he went not to Winchester but to Wilton. He was summoned by the legate, according to Malmesbury, or came to pay his respects, according to John of Worcester. Either way, he was not yet prepared to submit to Matilda. He claimed, says Malmesbury, it would be 'beneath his reputation and character to change sides till he had consulted the king.' Therefore, being given permission to do so, he led a delegation to visit the royal prisoner at Bristol. There Stephen seemed resigned to the realities of his situation and quickly gave permission for them to break their fealty to him. 'Graciously obtaining leave to submit to the exigency of the times,' the archbishop finally agreed to back the position taken by the legate, and to submit to Matilda.

By this time Easter was upon them. While many departed to their own homes, Matilda herself spent the feast at Oxford, where the castle formerly favoured by Stephen had been handed over to her by the castellan, Robert d'Oilly. Though many of the lesser barons had now come forward, either voluntarily or otherwise, to submit to the empress, a number of the bigger fish were still at large, and it was probably with an eye to winning them over, as well as justifying his own actions, that Bishop Henry summoned a full church council to meet at Winchester on the Sunday after Easter.

The purpose of this, as declared by the bishop himself, was 'to deliberate on the peace of the country which was exposed to imminent danger', and we have an excellent eyewitness to the proceedings. 'As I was present,' writes William of Malmesbury, 'I will not deny posterity the truth of every circumstance, for I perfectly remember it.' He can tell us nothing, though, of what was said on the first day, for Bishop Henry took away each group in turn – first the bishops, then abbots, then archdeacons – 'and discoursed with them in secret of his design'. The second day, however, saw the bishop at his most persuasive, addressing the whole assembly with a great speech.

Having first recited his authority from the pope to call such a meeting, he then launched into the story to be presented to the world to explain, first the acceptance of Stephen, and now his deposition in favour of Matilda. He recalled the peace England had

enjoyed under King Henry, and the oaths sworn to accept Matilda
as sovereign in order to prolong that peace. Matilda, however,
had delayed too long in Normandy, said the bishop, and, falling
back on the tale of riots and confusion that the *Gesta* would claim
followed the king's death, he smoothed over his own role in the
succession, declaring 'we provided for the peace of the country,
and my brother was allowed to reign.' However, he went on, there
was no peace, nor any justice 'against the daring'. Bishops were
held captive, abbeys were sold, churches were robbed – perhaps a
reference to Stephen's seizure of the treasure of Roger of Salisbury
from his cathedral. He had tried to remonstrate with his brother,
he declared, reminding them of the council held the year before
to protest against the arrest of the bishops. 'I gained by it nothing
but odium,' he said. Then, distancing himself still further from the
reign he had helped to establish, he added, 'I ought to love my
mortal brother, but ... I should still more regard the cause of my
immortal Father.' Stephen had failed the church, and in return 'God
has exercised his judgement' by allowing him to be defeated and
imprisoned. The kingdom, he said, must not be allowed to decay
for lack of a sovereign – and here he reminded them of what he
had said privately to them before, which may, perhaps have been
a different message to the different groups. It was, he claimed,
the clergy who should elect and crown a sovereign, and now he
recommended that they should duly elect Matilda and offer her
their full support and fidelity.

If he was expecting roars of approval for this oration he did
not get them. Malmesbury reports drily that those who approved
'becomingly applauded', while those who did not remained silent.
Their silence, though, was not contradiction, and that was good
enough for Bishop Henry. He had, he told them, sent to London
for a delegation of citizens to come and hear their reasoning, and
explained he had done this as the importance of the city made them
'almost nobles', and therefore entitled to a voice at this time.

In fact for some time past London had been attempting to
copy the major wool towns of the Continent, which had set up
'communes' or corporate bodies, to a large extent running their
own affairs. Stephen, who in his previous existence as Count of

Boulogne was used to such ideas, had probably encouraged this, particularly as the Londoners had been the first to acclaim him king. Certainly the importance of London was growing, as that of Winchester was declining. Malmesbury, on the other hand, seems to disapprove of such new-fangled ideas. When the delegation of Londoners arrived the next day, he says they had been sent 'by the fraternity, as they call it, of London'. Nor were they prepared to fall in with the wishes of Bishop Henry. He had possibly thought a group of citizens would be easily cowed by the eloquence of a papal legate, but this delegation had ideas of its own. Far from simply accepting Matilda as sovereign, they asked for the release of the king. Nor did the bishop's repetition of his speech from the day before have any great effect, even when he pointed out that Stephen's policies had drained them of money due to the bad advice of people who had deserted him at Lincoln.

At this point, says Malmesbury, proceedings were interrupted by a clerk, 'whose name, if I rightly remember, was Christian.' He came bearing a letter from Stephen's queen, Matilda, and boldly presented this to the bishop in front of the whole assembly. Having glanced at the contents, Bishop Henry refused to read it, but the clerk, determined to carry out his mission, 'with notable confidence, read the letter in their hearing'. In it the queen entreated the clergy, and especially Bishop Henry, 'the brother of her lord,' to release King Stephen from the prison where he was held in chains, and to restore to him the kingdom.

The boldness of this was likely to have caused a considerable stir, as, no doubt, the queen intended, but there was no likelihood of the bishop agreeing to her demand. On the other hand, it may have encouraged the Londoners to stand firm against his persuasion. They decided that they would return to London and report what the church council had agreed, 'and give it their support as far as they were able'. If the queen had not achieved her objective, neither, it seemed, had Bishop Henry, and it would take several more months of negotiations before the empress could approach the city of London with any prospect of a coronation in the abbey at Westminster.

In the meantime events were not standing still. Geoffrey of Anjou may have had different objectives from his wife, but nevertheless his activities in Normandy were of the greatest value to her, not least in detaching important magnates from Stephen's cause. Similarly, her success in England was for him a golden opportunity, and he lost no time in seizing it. As soon as he heard of the triumph at Lincoln, Vitalis tells us, he sent messengers to the lords in Normandy who had previously supported Stephen, telling them to surrender their castles to him and to maintain the peace. He may have been a little premature in assuming Matilda would be Queen of England, but it was certainly apparent that Stephen was in no position to resist Geoffrey's claim to Normandy.

By and large the lords agreed. For some it was the old problem of lands on both sides of the Channel and deciding where their primary interests lay. Others had their own quarrel with Stephen and were not sorry to change their allegiance. Among the latter was Rotrou of Perche, who is named by Vitalis as the first to offer his submission to the Count of Anjou.

Around the middle of Lent, a council of the principal lords of Normandy once again tried to interest Count Theobald of Blois in becoming king of England. 'However,' says Vitalis, 'like a religious and prudent man, he declined to burden himself with the weight of such vast cares.' Theobald then offered his own backing to Geoffrey, on condition that the count gave up to him the city of Tours, and obtained the release of Stephen and his return to the lands he had held in the time of King Henry.

As it was now clear they could find no lord to lead them against Geoffrey, from this time onwards the more significant defections from Stephen began. The most important of these involved the Beaumont twins and Bishop John of Lisieux. It was Robert, Earl of Leicester, with significant lands in England and Normandy, who entered into a truce with Geoffrey on behalf of himself and his brother, at least until Waleran should return from England and speak for himself. Robert soon returned to England, where he would later prove to be a nominal but inactive supporter of King Stephen. Waleran, on the other hand, fought on for Stephen in the

Worcester area until later in the year, when he finally submitted to Matilda, crossed to Normandy, and threw his weight behind Geoffrey's campaigns in that land. Thus Stephen lost the foremost of the magnates who had supported him throughout his reign.

Similarly, Bishop John of Lisieux, long the right-hand man of King Henry in Normandy, found himself before Easter 1141 surrounded by garrisons that had peacefully surrendered to the Angevin cause, and gave in to the inevitable. The bishop himself did not long survive this submission, but the surrender of Lisieux was a major gain for Geoffrey. Soon after this Falaise, Verneuil and Nonancourt also fell into his hands, giving him the most substantial hold yet on central Normandy. All the land on the left bank of the Seine now acknowledged him, with the exception of Rouen itself, and any English lord with lands around the area could have had no doubt where the power in the duchy now lay.

Sadly, this is the last that Vitalis contributes to our knowledge of his times. 'And now, he says, 'worn out by age and infirmities, I have a strong wish to bring this book to a close.' He was sixty-six years old, and viewed the current events in England and Normandy with pessimism, citing the imprisonment of Stephen and the submission and death of John of Lisieux as examples of 'great men of this world crushed by severe disasters.' He thanked his God that he had instead been called to serve Him in poverty, and closes by asking forgiveness for his sins, and the blessing of eternal salvation for himself, his friends and benefactors. We don't know exactly when he died, but it is certain that our understanding of his times and his contemporaries would be immeasurably the poorer without the detailed and vivid word pictures that flowed from his pen.

In England, meanwhile, the Empress Matilda – Lady of England – was steadily gaining ground. According to the *Gesta*, the greatest part of the kingdom gradually submitted to her, though the writer calls them 'a servile and despicable crew' for doing so while their king yet lived. Not all came voluntarily. Alan, Earl of Richmond, was captured by Ranulf of Chester and chained in a 'foul dungeon' until he agreed to do homage to Matilda, giving up his recently acquired county of Cornwall to Reginald de Dunstanville, and his castles to the service of the empress. Hervey Brito was besieged in Devizes Castle by a 'rude multitude of country people', until he agreed to hand it to the empress, whereupon he left the country and never returned. Hugh, Earl of Bedford, on the other hand, seems to have simply handed Bedford back to Miles de Beauchamp and gone off to live up to his nickname, 'The Pauper'.

Through all of this, as the empress made a slow progress towards London, Robert of Gloucester was 'assiduously employed in promoting her dignity by every becoming method.' By turns persuading, promising, threatening, he was 'already restoring justice, and the law of the land, and tranquillity' through all the regions which had submitted to her. Bishop Henry, too, was showing 'laudable fidelity', but Malmesbury admits it was 'a work of much difficulty to soothe the minds of the Londoners'. Possibly this was due to the fact that the remaining supporters of the king, notably his queen, Matilda, and the formidable William of Ypres, were close by in Kent. Indeed, at this time Henry of Huntingdon records that all England now acknowledged the empress as sovereign, 'except the men of Kent, who with the Queen and William of Ypres, made all the resistance in their power.'

At the beginning of May the empress was at Reading, praying at her father's tomb and gathering around her a suitable court. She was already acting as a sovereign, issuing charters, granting and confirming lands and privileges in the name of Matilda, Lady of England. There is no clear evidence she ever referred to herself as Queen of England. That title could only be claimed after a suitable coronation at Westminster, and even to get there she had to go roundabout as the royal castle at Windsor was still held against her. By the end of May, King David of Scotland decided that the new regime was sufficiently established for him to join her. He would have been a major figure at her court when she met further delegations of Londoners at St Albans, to negotiate her entry into their city. That step was finally taken just before midsummer. John of Worcester records that the empress came 'with a great attendance of bishops and nobles, and being received at Westminster with a magnificent procession, took up her abode there for some days.'

At last the throne of England was within touching distance – and then it all began to go wrong. One after another the chroniclers lay the blame for this solely on the shoulders of Matilda herself. She was 'elated with insufferable pride', says Henry of Huntingdon, 'so that she alienated from her the hearts of most men.' 'She assumed a majestic haughtiness of demeanour,' says John of Hexham, 'and so she provoked the nobles by arrogant denunciations.' The *Gesta* says she conducted her affairs 'imperiously and rashly', receiving people 'with coldness and at times with manifest displeasure'. It offers proof of her 'superciliousness and arrogance' that, when the highest in the land, King David, Bishop Henry, or even her brother Robert of Gloucester came to kneel before her with requests, she did not ask them to rise and listen to them but 'dismissed them, slighted, with some haughty reply'. Nor would she listen to advice, 'but ordered all affairs at her own will and mere motion'. Even the ever-loyal William of Malmesbury is driven to comment, 'if his party had trusted to Robert's moderation and wisdom, it would not afterwards have experienced so melancholy a reverse.'

How far this is true we have no way of knowing. The refrain seems constant, though the repeated phrases are similar enough to suggest a form of Chinese whispers. It also sits uneasily with the reports of Matilda's demeanour when acting as Empress of the Romans. Possibly in the time between, 'Matilda the Good' had become embittered enough to become 'Matilda the Haughty'. It could also be an example of the misogyny of the times; men were not used to taking orders from women. Time after time Matilda is accused of not showing 'the gentleness of her sex', while still possessing a 'womanish vanity'. Very likely the problem was that the men wanted to be wooed, persuaded and cajoled, while Matilda expected to command. It is interesting that the *Gesta*, without a shred of irony, praises Stephen's queen for her 'clear understanding' and 'masculine firmness'.

Initially the empress's actions seem reasonable enough. The man she confirmed as Bishop of London, Robert de Sigillo, was an acceptable candidate, and securing the support of Geoffrey de Mandeville, custodian of the Tower of London, was an eminently sensible move. It is not at all surprising that he should have been willing to transfer his allegiance, though he would have alienated the Londoners by doing so. Nor is it surprising, given the shrewdness of the man, that he should have driven a hard bargain.

Geoffrey was the son of William de Mandeville. He, too, had been custodian of the Tower, but had lost his post and his lands as a punishment for letting Ranulf Flambard, a most important prisoner of King Henry's, escape from his custody. Geoffrey had spent his life in the service of Henry, and latterly King Stephen, gradually recovering what his father had lost, and he had no intention of letting it slip away now through being on the wrong side. On the other hand, the Tower of London was an important bargaining chip. From Stephen, Geoffrey had obtained the earldom of Essex. Now Matilda trumped that by confirming the earldom and adding hereditary posts of sheriff of Essex, Hertfordshire, Middlesex and London, along with some valuable lands.

At this time, too, Matilda rewarded some of her faithful followers. Baldwin de Redvers becomes Earl of Devon, and William de Mohun, Earl of Dorset. It is in handling the still-touchy Londoners, however, and the issue of what to do about Stephen and his family, that the empress appears to lose her balance and descend into vindictiveness. The Londoners, says the *Gesta*, 'fancied that they had now arrived at happy days when peace and tranquillity would prevail.' They would soon be informed that peace would come at a price. William of Malmesbury offers no account of what passed in London, possibly because he was not there, or possibly because he wanted to gloss over the actions and their consequences. We therefore have no counterbalance to the story in the *Gesta* that Matilda summoned the wealthiest of the Londoners to her and demanded from them, 'in an imperious tone, an immense sum of money'.

Needless to say, they pleaded poverty: their resources were diminished in these troubled times, they had been supporting the poor, and they had 'subsidised the king to their last farthing' – which last was unlikely to please the empress. They asked for moderation in her demands, and a delay in imposing a 'new and vexatious tax' until disturbances had ceased and they could build up their wealth again. Then they should be 'better able to supply her wants'. On hearing this, says the *Gesta*, Matilda 'broke out into insufferable rage'. The Londoners had frequently paid large sums to Stephen. They had 'opened their purse-strings wide to strengthen him and weaken her'. They had, therefore, no reasonable excuse for asking now to be let off any part of the sum demanded. The Londoners, we are told, then 'departed to their homes, sorrowful and unsatisfied'.

Interestingly, John of Worcester has a different version of this confrontation. Instead of Matilda demanding money, he has the citizens making a petition of their own. They 'prayed her that they might be permitted to live under the laws of King Edward, which were excellent, instead of under those of her father, King Henry, which were grievous.' Leaving aside the fact that this seems no way to get on the right side of King Henry's daughter, it is not at all clear why they should hark back to laws that had ceased to exist before any of them were born. It is possible that the supposed laws might refer to restricting the right of the sovereign to claim arbitrary taxes, but in any case, the result of the petition was that the empress refused to listen to them, again sending them away with a grievance.

It was at this time, too, that Queen Matilda renewed her efforts to get her husband released. John of Worcester provides details. Envoys were sent on behalf of the queen and 'the highest nobles of England', offering castles, money and hostages 'if the king were set free and his liberty, though not his kingdom, was restored to him.' They would persuade him to abdicate, to become a pilgrim or even a monk. Here again the empress refused to listen to them – and one can hardly blame her. Liberating an anointed king would scarcely make for peace in the kingdom, whatever was promised on his behalf. The *Gesta* claims she answered them 'with words of cruel and shameful abuse', whereupon Queen Matilda resolved to try force where honeyed words had failed. With the help of William of Ypres, she gathered a great army and marched on London, laying waste the lands around it until the Londoners decided they had been too hasty in abandoning Stephen and re-opened communications with his queen.

In the Christian calendar, 24 June is a feast day commemorating the birth of John the Baptist. According to the *Gesta*, the Empress Matilda had just sat down to dinner on that day when the city bells began to ring. This was not a celebration, however, but a signal for war and 'the whole city flew to arms.' Warned that she was about to be attacked, the empress 'fled shamefully with her retinue' says John of Worcester, 'leaving all her own and their apparel behind', not to mention the food on the table. The *Gesta* tells us that even galloping at full speed they had barely cleared the town 'when a countless mob of townsfolk burst into the quarters they had quitted, and pillaged everything which their unpremeditated departure had left in them.'

William of Malmesbury has a slightly different version, declaring that the party 'gradually retired from the city, without tumult and in a certain military order,' but even he has to admit that the Londoners plundered everything 'which they had left in their haste.' Whichever way one looks at it, Matilda had been chased out of London by an angry mob. Not all was lost, of course, but the crown had certainly retreated from her grasp, and the humiliation would have offered encouragement to those who had not yet submitted to her, and maybe brought a shadow of doubt to those who had.

She still held the king prisoner, secure in Bristol Castle, and Henry of Huntingdon suggests that it was in revenge for her treatment by the queen and the Londoners that 'with a woman's bitterness', she now caused him 'to be bound with fetters'. On the other hand, he may have been chained for some time before this, as John of Worcester reports the queen, in her pleas for her husband, describing him as being 'captive in close custody and fetters'. William of Malmesbury claims he was chained because he had 'either eluded or bribed his keepers, (and) had been found more than once beyond the appointed limits, more especially in the night-time.' It seems Stephen had not given any undertaking that he would not try to escape and, after recovering from the despair of Lincoln had shown some enterprise in attempting to do so.

According to the *Gesta*, the disorder of Matilda's retreat from London is evidenced by the way so many of the party, 'forgetting their mistress and thinking only of their own escape ... took the first turnings of the road which presented opportunities for effecting it, and made for their own estates.' Bishop Henry is specifically named as doing this, and he certainly ended up in Winchester, while the empress, Robert of Gloucester, 'and a few other barons whose course best lay in that direction' made their way with all speed to Oxford.

It was probably just before the retreat from London that cracks had appeared in the relationship between the bishop and the empress. He may well have expressed some sympathy with Queen Matilda's plea for Stephen and had, on his own account, asked that Stephen's counties of Boulogne and Mortain should be given to his eldest son, Eustace, at least while his father was a prisoner. 'Offended at the repulse' when the empress abruptly refused his request, this was not, however, her only crime in the eyes of the bishop. Some weeks earlier, Geoffrey, Bishop of Durham, had died, and with unseemly haste and against the wishes of the local clergy King David of Scotland had inserted his own chancellor, William Cumin, as bishop-elect, on his way south to the court of the empress. John of Hexham, in fact, claims the king had forbidden the burial of Geoffrey until Cumin had been 'admitted within the fortress of Durham', and this gives a clue as to the sensitive nature of the appointment. From the time of William the Conqueror, the bishops of Durham had been 'Prince-bishops', with wide civil powers equivalent to an earl's. They were expected to act as a buffer between England and Scotland, initially over the whole area of the diocese, which covered the old Anglo-Saxon earldom of Northumbria, and later over the smaller area south of the rivers Tyne and Derwent. King David had achieved mastery over the northern part of the diocese through his son's appointment as Earl of Northumbria. If his own chancellor was to be appointed Bishop of Durham, he would effectively have moved his area of control even farther south.

It may be that Matilda was not aware of the political implications of this when she agreed to her uncle's suggestion that Cumin should be confirmed in the post, but Bishop Henry most certainly was. Yet again his protests were waved aside, and the Durham chronicler suggests that the empress was on the point of conferring on Cumin the temporalities of his see, when matters were interrupted by the arrival of the London mob. This is plausible, as a major feast day would be an appropriate time for such an investiture, and, if true, lends some support to the *Gesta's* claim that Bishop Henry was 'privy to and at the bottom of this conspiracy' which brought the mob there at that time – if he could not prevent the appointment in one way, he would do so in another.

Safely in Winchester, well separated from the empress and her court at Oxford, Bishop Henry now began to slide away from his newly expressed fidelity to Matilda. This division, laments William of Malmesbury, 'may be justly considered as the melancholy cause of every subsequent evil in England.' Stephen's queen was working 'manfully and resolutely' – compliments when applied to her by the *Gesta*, but not when applied to the empress – to persuade all those who still favoured the king to join her in achieving his deliverance from prison. 'Still more earnestly she supplicated the Bishop of Winchester ... that ... he should unite his endeavours with hers for the king's release,' and her entreaties bore fruit. After a secret meeting with the queen at Guildford, the bishop began to spread complaints about the empress. According to William of Malmesbury, he claimed that 'she observed nothing which she had sworn to him' and that 'she knew not how to use her prosperity with moderation.' At the same time, he lifted the sentences of excommunication he had earlier imposed on the followers of the king.

The Lady of the English, meanwhile, was regrouping at Oxford, gathering again those who were still loyal to her, and even receiving a few new recruits. One such was William de Beauchamp, sheriff of Worcester. He had always resented being forced to submit to Waleran de Meulan when the latter was made Earl of Worcester, and with Waleran at that time in possession of the city and doing what damage he could to the neighbourhood in the name of King Stephen, William travelled south to see what he could achieve by submitting to the empress. He was immediately received as her liege man, and confirmed in what he regarded as his hereditary position in Worcester. This was, of course, conditional on him being able to recover the city, but Waleran's position as earl was not recognised, and even if he submitted, the empress promised this would not affect William's position without his consent. In fact Waleran did submit a few weeks later, but his main interests were in Normandy, and he soon left the country to offer his services to Geoffrey of Anjou in his continuing conquest of the duchy.

For around a month the Empress Matilda remained at Oxford, and during this time further honours were handed out, some as rewards for service, some better seen as bribes or inducements to remain loyal to her cause. Among the former, Miles of Gloucester achieved his ambition of becoming Earl of Hereford. Among the latter, Geoffrey de Mandeville received a new and enhanced charter, extending and giving more detail to the honours already awarded to him in the earlier grant made in London. This charter was to be backed by guarantees from Geoffrey of Anjou and their son, the young Henry, and even by the King of France 'if I am able to arrange this.' A similar doubt attaches to many of the gifts made at this time.

For example, Aubrey de Vere was to be given Colchester Castle 'when I obtain it,' a rather distant prospect as it was at the heart of Queen Matilda's Honour of Boulogne. De Vere was, however, at the request of his brother-in-law Geoffrey de Mandeville, given a choice of earldoms, opting in the end to become Earl of Oxford. This Aubrey was the son of the man who had represented King Stephen when he was summoned to answer before Bishop Henry's church council the year before. According to some accounts, that Aubrey had submitted to the empress and been killed by the London mob in May 1141. Despite the honours received, neither Geoffrey nor Aubrey de Vere would remain long in the service of the empress.

By this time it seems clear that there were suspicions as to the loyalty of Bishop Henry. At some point, William of Malmesbury tells us, Robert of Gloucester rode over to Winchester with a small body of retainers, presumably to find out at first-hand how the land lay. If he was attempting to keep the bishop on side he did not succeed as, 'failing in his endeavours', he soon returned to Oxford. It was shortly after this that the empress took more decisive action, no doubt on her brother's advice.

What Robert may have seen at Winchester was work going on to strengthen and provision Bishop Henry's residence, Wolvesey Castle, just to the east of the cathedral. As a result, says the *Gesta*, the empress, 'shrewdly suspecting the bishop's secret intentions, hastened to Winchester with a body of disciplined troops, to endeavour to forestall his movements.' Malmesbury says as soon as she was settled in the royal castle on the hill above the town, she sent for Bishop Henry, who made vague excuses and promised to come later, before fleeing the town. The *Gesta*, however, declares that 'as she was entering one gate of the town with a numerous retinue ... the bishop, mounting a swift horse, escaped at another gate, and made all haste to secure himself in one of his own castles.' Both now called for all the support they could get, and the town of Winchester between the two castles became a battleground, with the forces of the empress attacking Wolvesey Castle and the bishop's men defending it.

Initially, it seems, the advantage was with the empress. Despite Malmesbury's claim that few attended her, the *Gesta* gives a decent list of earls and others who were present with her army. David of Scotland heads the list, along with Robert of Gloucester; Miles, Earl of Hereford; Baldwin de Redvers, Earl of Devon; Reginald de Dunstanville, Earl of Cornwall; William de Mohun, Earl of Somerset and/or Dorset; Roger, Earl of Warwick, and a group of barons 'nowise inferior to the earls in faithfulness and merit, in courage and gallantry', including John Marshal, William fitz Alan, Robert d'Oily and Brian fitz Count. It will be noticed, of course, that only one of these earls was a defector from the king's side, and many of the others were the usual suspects from the west of England, newly elevated to the rank of earl. Ranulf of Chester is also listed, but Malmesbury declares that he 'came late and to no purpose'. Useful though he had been, his conversion to the empress seems not to have been entirely trusted, or indeed trustworthy. Of his partner at Lincoln, William of Roumare, there is no sign on either side.

Against this onslaught Bishop Henry, unsurprisingly, 'summoned to his relief the queen, and William of Ypres, and almost all the barons of England'. So says Henry of Huntingdon, although few are actually named. The long-standing solid supporters, William of Warenne, Earl of Surrey and Simon of Senlis, Earl of Northampton were there along with William d'Aubigny, Earl of Arundel, but a considerable proportion of this army seems to have been made up of professional soldiers. William of Ypres, of course, had his mercenaries, and the *Gesta* claims Bishop Henry had also 'taken into his pay, at great expense, a number of stipendiary soldiers.' The same source declares that London had provided 1,000 men 'well-armed with helmets and breastplates', who, judging by their equipment, must have been an established militia. They certainly set about their task with a high degree of professionalism, although Malmesbury snipes that many of those present were only there because they 'preferred military enterprise to peace', and that 'many of them were ashamed at having deserted the king in battle … and thought to wipe off the ignominy of having fled.'

It took some time for all these forces to assemble and meanwhile the original siege of Wolvesey Castle was continued with full force. 'There were daily engagements,' says Henry of Huntingdon, 'not, indeed, regular battles, but desultory skirmishes,' and 'every man's gallantry was seen by all and he gained renown according to his deserts.' He makes it sound more like a joust, particularly when he adds: 'This interval was therefore universally pleasing, as exhibiting the splendour of their illustrious achievements.' Things were about to get more serious, however, for, as the *Gesta* reports, 'while the (empress's) party pressed the siege of the castle by every invention of skill and art, the garrison from within shot lighted brands, with which they reduced to ashes the greatest part of the city.' Possibly they were attempting to drive their besiegers further away, or possibly preventing the townspeople giving them assistance, for several writers claim the town sided with the empress rather than the bishop.

The result was widespread devastation including the loss of at least one abbey, that of the nuns of St Mary's, close to Wolvesey Castle. Malmesbury claims another abbey was also destroyed but as this was outside the city walls, it may have been a separate incident. There a large cross coated with gold, silver and precious gems – donated by King Cnut, no less – was seen to sweat as if weeping, before the fire reached it and toppled it from its place. Malmesbury also declares that afterwards Bishop Henry stripped the ornamentation from the cross and used it to pay his mercenary soldiers. John of Worcester backs up this story, but claims the bishop kept this booty for himself.

It was the arrival of the Londoners that tipped the balance away from the empress. Now suddenly, says the *Gesta*, 'the forces engaged in the siege of the bishop's castle were themselves besieged by the royal army, which closely hemmed them in from without.' The siege was 'of extraordinary character ... unheard of in our day. All England was there in arms.' With the numbers now available, the royal party were able to keep a close watch on all the roads around the city. Plentifully supplied from the east, they could lift the siege on Wolvesey Castle, and close off almost completely the supply line of the empress from the west. Andover was taken and burnt by William of Ypres to prevent the town being used to protect a possible route for provisions, and seven weeks after beginning the siege on the bishop's castle, the situation of the empress and her many followers within the walls of Winchester was becoming desperate. In fact there were fewer followers than there had been. Geoffrey de Mandeville and Gilbert of Clare had already slipped away to join the queen's army, and the late-arriving Ranulf of Chester would probably have done the same if he hadn't been suspected of treachery and his approaches rebuffed.

By the middle of September it was clear that something must be done quickly or all would be lost. The *Gesta* describes a decision taken to send out 300 troops under John Marshal to establish a post at Wherwell. It implies that this was to prevent the royal army from completing its stranglehold on the town, but his raid has also been suggested as a diversion, to distract the attention of the royalists while the empress effected an escape from the city. Whatever the intention, the raid went badly wrong. Again, it was William of Ypres who, attacking with great numbers, forced the raiders to retreat into the church of Wherwell Abbey, no doubt displacing the nuns who would have gathered for safety in that strongest part of their compound. The church was set on fire, and the *Gesta* gives a graphic description of the 'horrid and lamentable spectacle', where 'in one quarter there was butchery, in another the prisoners were dragged along bound with thongs.' Then the flames burst through the roof, and almost all those within were forced out – all but John Marshal, who, by at least one account, was left for dead inside. This same account declares that the roof was at least partly of lead, and when this melted in the heat, it dripped onto the unfortunate John, who, in consequence, lost the sight of one eye.

Perhaps suspecting that this was a diversion, William of Ypres and his men were already returning towards Winchester when, on the morning of 14 September, the gates were abruptly thrown open and the empress and her entourage made a break for freedom. John of Worcester claims that it was in fact Bishop Henry who opened the gates and let them out. Perhaps he was suffering a crisis of conscience over the many different things he had sworn over the past months, or possibly pursuing a rather more noble policy of refusing to make war on women.

They marched out in a body, according to the *Gesta*, the whole army in close order. The empress was towards the front, closely escorted by Brian fitz Count with Reginald de Dunstanville and their men, while, expecting the strongest attack from the rear, Robert of Gloucester commanded a rearguard. John of Worcester gives this as 200 horsemen, while Malmesbury specifies that these were 'a chosen few, who had spirit enough not to be alarmed at a multitude.'

Making their way towards a crossing of the River Test at Stockbridge, they had not gone far before the royal army were in pursuit, whereupon a speedy but orderly retreat turned into something quite different. 'The king's troops,' says the *Gesta*, 'poured in upon them from all sides in countless numbers with so much impetuosity that they were routed and dispersed.' Matilda was got away over the river, flying over Danebury Hill in the direction of Ludgershall, while Robert of Gloucester's determined rearguard stand at the crossing allowed many others to escape, among them King David of Scotland and Miles of Gloucester.

Four Kings: This fanciful medieval representation of the four Norman kings shows, from left, William the Conqueror, William Rufus, Henry I and Stephen.

Eye Castle remains, Suffolk. The Honour of Eye was Stephen's first landholding in England, with Eye Castle as its 'caput' or administrative centre. It had formerly been a royal castle.

Barfleur, Normandy. William Adelin, only legitimate son and heir of Henry I, drowned when *The White Ship*, which was to carry him to England, sank after striking a rock off this dangerous coast.

Reading Abbey was founded by Henry I. Between that king's death in December 1135 and his burial here in January 1136, Stephen had seized the throne of England.

Domfront Castle, Normandy. A favourite castle of Henry I, Domfront was one of the first to be handed over to his daughter Matilda.

Exeter Castle. Baldwin de Redvers seized this castle in 1136 and held out for three months against King Stephen, until starved into submission.

Medieval Walls of Bath. Bath was one of the first targets of the supporters of Robert of Gloucester when he formally defied Stephen in 1138. A botched raid led to the kidnap of the Bishop of Bath.

River Avon below Bristol. During the Siege of Bristol in 1138, it was suggested the river below the town should be dammed to flood the place, however, this impracticable scheme was never attempted.

Dudley Castle. High above the town of Dudley, this castle was briefly besieged by Stephen in 1138. It surrendered after the fall of Shrewsbury.

Shrewsbury Castle. Here Stephen carried through his siege to the end, and when the castle was finally stormed and taken, ninety-three of the garrison, including those of highest rank, were hanged from the castle walls as a lesson to others.

Henry I's castle at Caen. This was inherited by his son, Robert of Gloucester, who eventually sided with Matilda and Geoffrey of Anjou against King Stephen.

Falaise Castle. Falaise was one of the strongholds of Henry I. Handed to Stephen in 1136, it was finally secured for the Angevin faction in 1141.

Great West Door, Lincoln Cathedral. This lower west end of Lincoln Cathedral dates from the time of Bishop Alexander. Much of the rest of that early building was destroyed in an earthquake in 1185.

Newark Castle. Built by Bishop Alexander of Lincoln, this was one of the sumptuous castles that led to the downfall of the bishops. It was confiscated by King Stephen in 1139.

Ely Castle and Cathedral. In the foreground is the site of Ely Castle, built by Bishop Nigel of Ely. There he briefly defied the king before fleeing to Bristol.

Malmesbury. The Old Bell Hotel beside the abbey is believed to stand on the site of Malmesbury Castle, built by Bishop Roger of Salisbury. Held for King Stephen, it was the subject of a number of sieges before being handed over to Henry Plantagenet in 1153.

Dunster Castle. Raiding from here in 1139, William de Mohun may have been attempting to draw Stephen away from the south coast, where Matilda was imminently expected to land. At that time, the sea filled all the flat land before the castle.

Arundel Castle. Much larger today than in 1139, it nevertheless provided a secure landing place for the Empress Matilda and Robert of Gloucester.

Site of Wallingford Castle. The original castle was established on this mound immediately after the Norman Conquest.

Wallingford Castle. By the time of King Stephen, Wallingford had been expanded to fill all the space between the original castle and the remains in the far distance. Extremely well-fortified and garrisoned by Brian fitz Count, it withstood all attempts to take it by siege.

Salisbury, 'Old Sarum'. This hilltop site was once occupied by, in the foreground, the cathedral of Roger of Salisbury, and, in the background, Salisbury Castle.

Approach to Ely. At the time of Bishop Nigel's revolt, all the land in the foreground would have been water or marsh. A monk called Daniel guided King Stephen safely through it to Ely.

Bungay Castle. Seized by Hugh Bigod, Bungay became his power base. He was later created Earl of Norfolk.

Lincoln Castle. This original castle mound at Lincoln was the site of the royal castle.

Lucy's Tower, Lincoln Castle. This second castle mound at Lincoln, beside the royal castle, is attributed to Lucy of Bolingbroke and was inherited by her sons, William of Roumare and Ranulf of Chester.

West Gate, Lincoln Castle. It was from this gate that King Stephen and his forces advanced to fight the Battle of Lincoln in February 1141.

Site of Bristol Castle. Bristol was the major stronghold of Robert of Gloucester. It was here that King Stephen was held prisoner for most of 1141.

Winchester Cathedral. Here the Empress Matilda was proclaimed 'Lady of the English' by Bishop Henry of Winchester in 1141. It was seen as a step towards becoming Queen of England.

Wolvesey Castle. This was the palace and stronghold of Bishop Henry of Winchester. It was besieged by Matilda and her supporters in 1141.

Rochester Castle. Rochester was held for King Stephen by William of Ypres. It was here that Robert of Gloucester was kept a prisoner while negotiations proceeded between the Empress Matilda and Stephen's queen, also named Matilda, for an exchange of captives.

St George's Tower, Oxford Castle. It is claimed the Empress Matilda escaped by letting herself down from this tower when she was besieged in the castle in 1142.

Gatehouse of Ramsey Abbey. This abbey was seized and used as a power base by Geoffrey de Mandeville during his revolt of 1143–44.

Pevensey Castle. Held by Gilbert, Earl of Pembroke, until 1147, Pevensey was subsequently taken from him after a siege and given to King Stephen's son, Eustace.

Robert himself, though, was eventually overwhelmed and taken prisoner by the mercenary Flemings under the command of William of Warenne. It is to be hoped that Malmesbury's declaration that 'he thought it disgraceful and beneath his dignity to fly,' is simply an example of the writer's hero-worship. It would be a shame if such a valuable commander was stupid enough to allow himself to be taken for such a spurious reason.

Ludgershall was by no means a safe haven for the empress, and she probably stayed only long enough to obtain a fresh horse. So great was the haste of the party that she then rode from there to Devizes astride – 'male fashion' says John of Worcester – drawing a rare compliment from the writer of the *Gesta*. 'Always superior to womanly weakness,' he says, 'and with a heart of iron in times of adversity, she made her escape before them all to Devizes, attended only by Brian and a small retinue.' This headlong race of some 20 miles, however, would have been a severe test of endurance, and when even Devizes was deemed too vulnerable, Matilda could ride no further. Then, says John of Worcester, 'She was placed, already nearly half-dead, upon a hearse, and being bound with cords like a corpse, and borne upon horses, was carried ignominiously enough to the city of Gloucester.' Presumably he is describing her carriage in a litter, but his choice of words does seem to be overdoing suggestions of doom.

Behind her, at the scene of the rout, all was confusion, and from the vivid details given in the *Gesta* it seems highly likely that the writer was actually there. He describes the countryside as strewn with valuables left behind by the scattered followers of the empress, and being thoroughly looted by the victors, even as they pursued and captured the fugitives. Valuable horses that had lost their riders galloped about. Shields, mail, weapons and armour lay about, while 'rich robes, precious vessels and valuable ornaments, lying in heaps, were everywhere ready to the hand of the first comer.' Among those casting off all distinguishing marks of rank were some of the greatest magnates, and even the Archbishop of Canterbury and other bishops had their possessions looted, 'their horses and clothes carried off, or barbarously torn from them.'

One of those successfully escaping was John Marshal, who made his way, wounded but free, back to his castle at Ludgershall. Another, William Cumin, managed by various means to get himself to Durham at the end of September. There he found David of Scotland, who had arrived only the day before after being captured, bribing his captor to let him go, and then being smuggled away by one of his godsons, who was actually one of the queen's men. This, as several accounts comment, was the third time the king had successfully escaped from England in the last half dozen years. Miles of Gloucester, too, had an adventurous journey to Gloucester, where, according to the well-informed John of Worcester, he arrived 'weary, alone and half-naked', though no doubt hugely relieved to find the empress safe. Less happy was his son-in-law, Humphrey de Bohun, the earlier hero of Trowbridge, who now found himself a prisoner of William of Ypres.

By far the most important prisoner, however, was Robert of Gloucester. He was taken first to Queen Matilda, though we have no details of that meeting, and thereafter committed to the custody of William of Ypres in the great keep at Rochester Castle. This was a fairly liberal captivity, if Malmesbury is to be believed. He declares the earl went freely to the cathedral below the castle, and could talk with anyone he pleased. He claims he even managed to purchase some valuable horses during the time he was held there.

Nevertheless, says Malmesbury, 'during the whole of his captivity ... he was enticed by numberless and magnificent promises to revolt from his sister,' but stood firm for her cause. Nor would he agree to any scheme to set him free unless this was also agreed by the empress.

Negotiations went on for weeks between the two parties, with messengers and 'confidential friends' passing between the empress and Queen Matilda. Some accounts suggest a peace treaty might have been accomplished to put an end to all the violence. John of Worcester, for example, suggests a rather unlikely idea that the king should be returned to the throne, with Robert of Gloucester 'being invested with the dominion of the whole of England under him' – a sort of universal justiciar – 'whereby both could work together to restore the peace that they themselves had so disturbed.' This, like all other proposals, came to nothing. There was, says the *Gesta*, 'no possibility of a mutual concurrence between the parties on terms of peace and amity, each betraying much arrogance in negotiating the treaty.'

Malmesbury also refers to this idea, and to the earl's response that he was not his own master to decide such things, being bound to his sister. 'Irritated and incensed at this,' says Malmesbury, 'they began to menace,' threatening to send him to Boulogne as a captive for life. He had expected nothing else, was the earl's reply, though he pointed out that, in that eventuality, the king would surely be sent to Ireland for similar imprisonment.

In the end they settled for a straightforward prisoner swap, 'an exchange of the king for the earl, the one for the other; the affairs of the civil war returning to their former state.' So says the *Gesta*, adding that 'this was cheerfully ratified on both sides.' This transaction was carried out with all the finesse of a Cold War spy swap at Checkpoint Charlie. Such was the suspicion of all parties that serious hostages were needed to guarantee that the deal would go through.

Malmesbury gives copious details a few pages further on in his book, saying that he did not put them in the right place when writing of the year 1141, because 'I did not know them then,' adding, 'I have always dreaded to transmit anything to posterity ... the truth of which I could not perfectly vouch for.'

The hostages, he says, were to be the queen and her son (presumably Eustace), while Bishop Henry and the Archbishop of Canterbury also bound themselves that if, when the king was released first, he did not liberate the earl, they themselves would 'deliver themselves up into Robert's power, to be conducted wherever he pleased'. For additional security, in case Stephen felt he could well do without his brother and the archbishop, the earl obtained letters from them addressed to the pope, requesting that, in that eventuality, the pope himself might obtain the liberty of all of them.

On 1 November Queen Matilda and her son travelled to Bristol where the king was released, leaving them in his place. Stephen then hurried to Winchester where Earl Robert had been brought from Rochester, arriving there on 4 November. Malmesbury records a 'friendly interview' between the two, when each tried, without success, to persuade the other to his own point of view. 'Thus failing of peace,' he says, 'they severally departed.' Robert was released in turn, and departed for Bristol leaving his own son William as surety for the queen's return. When he arrived there the queen and her son were duly set free. They then completed the deal by returning to Winchester, and finally the earl's son was himself liberated.

Thus, by the end of the year the situation was exactly as it had been at the beginning, and all the suffering, triumph and tragedy of the intervening months might never have happened. The *Gesta* calls this, 'a cruel and unwise conclusion, pregnant with evil for every part of the land.'

9

An Endless Winter

(1142 – 1147)

It seems generally accepted by all the writers that both Stephen and Earl Robert had behaved with dignity and honour throughout their captivities. Even their opponents might grudgingly admit that their personal reputations had been enhanced, though their military powers had, no doubt, been diminished. The one person whose reputation had been severely damaged by all the changes of an eventful year was Bishop Henry of Winchester, and we find him at the end of the year earnestly striving to rescue what he could from the wreckage. He was, says Malmesbury, 'a prelate of unbounded spirit, who was never inclined to leave incomplete what he had once purposed,' and it was quite beyond him to move forward without making some attempt to justify his actions. As a result, a legatine church council was called by him and held at Westminster on 7 December 1141. Reporting on this, Malmesbury points out that he cannot be as detailed as he was about the last council in April, as this time he was not actually present. However, he still offers a full account of proceedings.

The bishop opened by reading a letter he had received from the pope at some point in the year, which 'gently rebuked' him for not working to obtain his brother's freedom, and told him he must make every effort, 'whether ecclesiastical or secular', to obtain that end. Stephen himself was also present at the council, and he too seems to be rebuking his brother when he complained that 'his own subjects had both made captive, and very nearly killed him by the injuries they had inflicted on him,' injuries, presumably, resulting from the chains that had held him during the latter part of his imprisonment. After this, says Malmesbury, Bishop Henry, 'by great powers of eloquence, endeavoured to extenuate the odium of his own conduct.'

In a masterly speech he claimed he had been forced to accept the empress because with all the king's earls dispersed, she had surrounded Winchester and, by implication, threatened him. Thereafter, he claimed, she had broken every promise she had made relating to the freedom of the church, and also 'had not only had designs on his dignity, but even on his life'. He therefore commanded that everyone should now assist King Stephen, who had been chosen by the will of the people and approved by the pope, and he threatened with excommunication all members of the party of the empress, with the sole exception of Matilda herself.

'I do not say,' says Malmesbury, 'that this speech was kindly received by all the clergy, though certainly no one opposed it.' There was one present who did, however, a 'layman sent from the empress', who flatly contradicted much of what the bishop had said. Further, he accused him of actually inviting Matilda to England by 'frequent letters', and even of conniving at the captivity of the king. Despite the harshness of his language, 'by no means sparing the legate', he seems to have made little impression on the bishop himself, who was thus allowed to escape with a cloak of respectability covering his year of double-dealing.

If Bishop Henry needed to re-establish his authority, so too did the king. He was, after all, God's anointed, and the ignominy of capture and captivity needed to be erased by some glorious assertion of his majesty. This was achieved at his Christmas court, held not at Westminster but at Canterbury. We have a full description of the ceremony from Gervase of Canterbury, though the re-crowning he was recalling was in fact that of Richard I some half a century later. Like Stephen, Richard needed to wipe away the stain of captivity and, says Gervase, his ritual followed exactly that of his predecessor Stephen. Thus we know that Stephen was invested anew with all the potent symbols of monarchy – sword, spurs, rod, sceptre and crown – each accompanied by a separate prayer, before solemnly processing into the cathedral for a celebration of the Holy Mass. Afterwards, when the coronation robes and crown had been exchanged for something a little lighter, the king and queen entertained bishops and magnates at a splendid feast.

It was a full court. Almost all the earls and barons had hurried back to declare their loyalty to Stephen. The earls of Surrey, Pembroke, Hertford, York, Northampton, Arundel, Richmond and Derby were present, while notable among the barons were William of Ypres, William Martel, Baldwin fitz Gilbert de Clare and Robert de Vere. We have the list of names from a charter issued at the time to Geoffrey de Mandeville, confirming all he had acquired from the empress, so Geoffrey himself, Earl of Essex, would also have been there; but conspicuously absent were the Beaumont brothers. Waleran, still nominally Earl of Worcester, was now firmly supporting the Angevins, and Robert, Earl of Leicester, was apparently keeping well out of the way.

After Christmas there was something of a lull during which, says Malmesbury, 'the respective parties of the empress and the king conducted themselves with quiet forbearance.' In truth the two principals were probably exhausted. The *Gesta* declares that Matilda 'had been much shaken and almost worn to death by the retreat from Winchester,' while Stephen, too, would later show alarming after-effects of his time in captivity. Several months apparently passed quietly, and it is the middle of Lent, March 1142, before we hear of any further activity. Then the *Gesta* tells us that Matilda, now fully recovered, moved her court back to Oxford. With Wallingford, this now formed the most easterly point of Angevin territory, and measures were quickly taken to secure it from royal attack. While the town defences themselves were strengthened, fortifications were also improved at Woodstock to the north, and castles and other fortifications rapidly thrown up at Bampton, the Thames crossing at Radcot, and at Cirencester to the west, securing the Thames Valley as a corridor to lands firmly held for the empress.

On the way to Oxford Matilda met with her supporters in a council at Devizes, where, says Malmesbury, 'her secret designs were debated.' The outcome of this was a decision to send to Count Geoffrey of Anjou, inviting him to come to England to support his wife's cause. Suitable envoys were dispatched, but the response received many weeks later was not at all what had been hoped for. Mediated through the pen of Malmesbury, it was to the effect that while he was somewhat in favour of what they wanted from him, he was only prepared to deal with Robert of Gloucester, whom he knew personally to be wise and loyal. If Robert would come to him he would do what he could, but no one else need bother making the journey.

This has often been interpreted as a refusal by Geoffrey to help his wife, and an indication that he was solely interested in Normandy. There is, however, rather more to it than that. This was not the first communication between the two, though it may have been the first direct plea for help. Members of Geoffrey's household had been with Matilda the year before. They had witnessed charters for her and carried some back to be countersigned by Geoffrey and their son Henry. Geoffrey would have been well aware how close Matilda had come to the crown, and how far away that now seemed to be once more. In the past year he had made significant gains in Normandy, which was also, we must remember, his wife's inheritance, so it is unfair to accuse him of doing nothing to help.

At the very least he was drawing away considerable support that would otherwise have gone to Stephen. His answer, in fact, reveals him to have become both a shrewd and a cautious man. If he had left Normandy at that time with an army of the size required to put his wife on the throne of England, there was a strong chance he might have failed in both England and in Normandy. He was unknown in England and hated in the duchy, and even his own county of Anjou was subject to frequent rebellions. If, on the other hand, he remained in Normandy, particularly if he could entice over a man of Robert of Gloucester's standing, who was known and respected there, the tide was flowing sufficiently in his favour for him to be able to take complete control of the entire duchy. Then, even if Matilda should ultimately fail in England, there would be a part of her inheritance secured for her and for their son.

It may also have been in his mind that at the time the messengers came to him, Stephen was seriously ill. The royal party had enjoyed success during Lent, when the important castle at Nottingham was retaken from the empress by William Peverel. Then after Easter, the king and queen had travelled north to York. They might have been simply showing their faces and asserting control of the north of England, but John of Hexham declares that they 'put an end to the passages of arms which were being carried on between William, Earl of York, and Alan, Earl of Richmond.' This has been interpreted as everything from a friendly tournament to a local war, but whatever it was, the king disapproved. The same source tells us that Stephen had then gathered an army 'to go and avenge his former injuries', possibly intending to retake Lincoln or Oxford or both, but being 'seized with illness' was forced to abandon this idea. He had got as far as Northampton before he fell ill, according to Malmesbury, and whatever the illness was, it was 'so severe ... that he was reported almost throughout England as being at the point of death.'

No doubt this news was also carried to Normandy, and would have given Geoffrey a further reason to delay. If Stephen were to die, there may be no need for Geoffrey to take any action at all. This is a more generous interpretation of the count's thinking than that allowed by William of Malmesbury. He was more concerned with the risks to the cause of the empress in England which would be involved in the count's proposal, particularly as, by the time Geoffrey's reply was received, it was clear Stephen was not going to die. These risks were also apparent to Earl Robert himself. He pointed out the perils of the journey, and the increased danger his sister might face, while 'in his absence those persons would hardly be able to defend her, who distrusting even the strength of their own party, had nearly deserted her in his captivity.' Nevertheless, in the end he was persuaded to go, possibly gambling on a swift return for himself and a slow recovery for the king.

He took with him a number of young men, the sons of 'chief persons', whom Malmesbury describes as hostages to ensure the loyalty of their parents in his absence. Robert of Torigny, however, declares that it was the parents who asked him to take the young persons and 'place them under the charge of Count Geoffrey,' suggesting this was akin to placing a son in the household of a magnate for purposes of education. He too, though, uses the word 'hostages', and adds the expectation that Geoffrey 'would arrive in England and prepare himself for the subjugation of that kingdom.'

Robert's fears for the perils of the journey were very nearly realised. Setting sail from Wareham towards the end of June with a number of ships, he was about half-way across the Channel when a storm blew up and scattered his little fleet. Only two reached the intended port, one of which held Robert himself. He met Count Geoffrey at Caen, the count coming reluctantly, according to Malmesbury, and explaining the difficulties – 'and those not a few' – which prevented him from immediately agreeing to accompany Robert to England. He was, in fact, so persuasive that, far from making a swift return, the earl found himself drawn into Geoffrey's summer campaign.

Pushing westward from a line between Caen and Falaise, together they took castle after castle, four of them in Stephen's own county of Mortain, including Mortain itself, and Tinchebrai, where Henry had had his greatest victory. Robert of Torigny adds the capitulation of Avranches and Coutances to the successes of this year, though other sources place this in 1143. Pontorson on the border with Brittany may also have been taken, advancing Geoffrey's control to the Bay of Mont St Michel in the south-west.

The military skill of Robert of Gloucester, along with his name and reputation, certainly helped the Angevin cause in Normandy this year, yet Malmesbury notes in disgust, 'even by this activity, he furthered the end of his mission but little.' As each excuse for remaining in Normandy was swept away, Geoffrey managed to find another, until the campaigning season came to an end in September and Robert was forced by circumstances to return to England.

In fairness to Geoffrey it should be noted that his single-mindedness in pursuing the conquest of Normandy brought him success within the next two years. A determined campaign in 1143 in the Cotentin Peninsula culminated in the surrender of Cherbourg, leaving all of western Normandy in his hands.

Meanwhile, further east, the conquest of Verneuil and Vaudreuil, with the submission of Walter Giffard, Earl of Buckingham, to preserve his lands in the Pay de Caux north of Rouen, meant that that the traditional capital of the duchy was now surrounded by Angevin supporters. By the end of the year all that was left to Stephen was Rouen itself, and some lands to the north-east held by William of Aumale, Earl of York; by the Count of Eu; and by William of Warenne, Earl of Surrey.

The latter, still in his mid-twenties, seems to have been Stephen's sole commander in the area, a position that put him in direct conflict with his half-brother, Waleran de Meulan, when that convert to Anjou was sent at the end of 1143 to soften up Rouen ready for the final attack. When this came, early in January 1144, the city was surrendered almost at once, but the tower, garrisoned by William's men, held out for another three months, through constant bombardment, until starved into submission. At around this time Geoffrey was formally recognised as Duke of Normandy by his overlord, Louis VII of France.

Geoffrey's success in Normandy was aided by a number of factors, not the least of which was the apparent indifference of Stephen to its loss. At no point did the English king appear to value the duchy, or to make appropriate efforts to secure it for himself. It always seemed to come a poor second in his mind to the glittering prize of the crown of England. Nor did he seem to appreciate its strategic importance in cementing the loyalty of those magnates with large estates on each side of the Channel. Possibly he felt they would be loyal to his cause in any eventuality, and by the time he had learned differently in 1141, it was too late to do anything about it. By then Stephen had barely the resources needed to carry on a fight in one land, never mind two, but the loss of Normandy also severely damaged his chances of complete success in England.

Another factor favouring Geoffrey was Louis of France's change of policy at about this time. Originally established with Theobald of Blois and Ralph of Vermandois as his chief advisors, he soon fell out with the former in order to support the latter. The cause of the problem was Petronilla of Aquitaine, also known as Alix, younger sister of Queen Eleanor. Despite being married to Count

Theobald's sister Eleanor, Ralph determined to marry Petronilla. The match was encouraged by the queen and permitted by King Louis, but Theobald was horrified that his sister's marriage should be so casually set aside. War followed, lasting from 1142 to 1144, and involving the occupation of Theobald's county of Champagne by royal forces. The House of Blois thus became the enemies of the French king, who naturally began to favour Theobald's enemies, the Angevins. Furthermore, this war with Louis prevented Theobald from playing any part at all in a possible defence of Normandy against the advances of Geoffrey of Anjou.

Geoffrey was still some way short of his ultimate triumph when Robert of Gloucester left him in October 1142, but he was determined he would not give up his gains in the duchy to chase a possibly forlorn chance of a throne in England. Instead he sent his young son. 'The youth is named Henry, after his grandfather,' writes Malmesbury very shortly afterwards, 'may he hereafter resemble him in happiness and power.' Henry was, at the time, nine years old, not a soldier but a rallying point and a possible promise of an alternative to Matilda for those who acknowledged her dynastic claims but would not support the empress herself. It is likely the count also sent some troops, since Earl Robert returned with fifty-two ships and between 300 and 400 horsemen. They would be needed, too, for the situation in England had changed dramatically in the months he had been away.

Stephen's recovery, already underway when the earl left, had progressed rapidly, and by August he was, says the *Gesta*, 'as it were, roused from sleep and waking to life and new activity.' He seemed, too, to find a new resolution to end the troubles in his kingdom once and for all.

Wareham was his first target, the key Angevin port from which Robert had sailed and to which he would likely return. The town and castle were held by Robert's son William, but he was no match for Stephen's unexpected strike. The town was plundered and burned, the castle quickly taken, and Stephen moved rapidly on to the newly established fortifications in the upper Thames

Valley. These too fell easily, Cirencester, according to the *Gesta*, being set on fire and razed. Then having disposed of the outlying protective shield, on 26 September the king suddenly appeared before Oxford itself.

Matilda was caught completely by surprise. Though much work had been done on the outer defences of the town, it appears she had only a regular garrison to protect her, and by some accounts the castellan, Robert D'Oilly, had died two weeks before and not yet been replaced. It seems odd that the empress should have been left so ill-guarded in a fortress so far into Stephen's territory, but clearly neither Miles of Gloucester nor Brian fitz Count were close enough to render any effective assistance. It was, in fact, the realisation of Robert of Gloucester's worst fears.

The *Gesta* gives a detailed account of the arrival of the king, from an unexpected direction, on the west bank of the River Thames that wound around the city. He had with him 'a numerous body of veteran soldiers', and as soon as he approached the ford that gave the place its name, the garrison came out to oppose his crossing. Presumably they felt securely able to do so. The *Gesta* reports them 'assailing him and his people with abuse across the river, and others, shaking their arrows out of their quivers, sharply annoying them over the water'.

There was, however, another way across, 'an ancient and very deep ford', which was now pointed out to the king. 'He plunged boldly into the stream himself, at the head of his troops,' says the *Gesta*, 'and swimming rather than wading across, they charged the enemy with impetuosity.' Delightful though the image is of King Stephen in his armour swimming the River Thames, presumably with his sword clenched between his teeth, it is far more likely that it was the horses that did the swimming, a safer and considerably more comfortable way of crossing. Stephen's force certainly fell upon the garrison with speed enough to drive them back through the city gates, following so closely that 'the royalists, being mingled with them, found themselves within the walls without opposition.' In this completely unforeseen eventuality, some of the garrison escaped to the castle with the Empress Matilda, while others were captured or killed as the king and his men took complete possession of the town.

The siege of the castle began on 26 September, and was pursued with the greatest vigour and vigilance for three months. It was abundantly clear to Stephen that 'the civil wars would be brought to a close, if he were able to subdue her with whom they originated.' According to Malmesbury, the supporters of the empress began to gather in great numbers at nearby Wallingford, ready and willing to attack the king if he came out to offer battle, but the city had been so well fortified by Robert of Gloucester before his departure, that they could see no way to overcome him while he remained inside the defences. Stephen, meanwhile, 'declared no hope of advantage or fear of loss should induce him to depart till the castle was delivered up, and the empress surrendered to his power.'

This was how matters stood when Earl Robert finally returned from Normandy. He landed at Wareham, and despite Stephen's precautions had little trouble in retaking the town and port, though the castle had to be put under siege. According to Malmesbury he then waited patiently while, according to custom, the garrison sent to see if the king would come to relieve them before surrendering. Malmesbury declares that Robert hoped in this way to draw Stephen away from Oxford, and praises his courage in preparing to face the king's army with his few horsemen. Stephen, however, was not to be moved. Even when Robert set about securing the Dorset coast – Portland, the Isle of Purbeck and Lulworth – the king remained doggedly at the Oxford siege.

By the end of November matters were becoming desperate. Having deposited his young nephew in Bristol where he would remain for the next year or so, Robert set about collecting an army in Cirencester, intending to march on Oxford and 'courageously determining to give the king battle, unless he retreated'. Before they could do so, however, Matilda took matters into her own hands.

Shortly before Christmas, 'despairing of any relief coming from without,' says the *Gesta*, 'she issued forth one night, attended only by three knights chosen for their wary prudence.' How was this done? According to the Anglo-Saxon Chronicle, 'they let her down from the tower by night with ropes, and she stole away.' Sadly, Malmesbury declares he doesn't know how it was achieved, though rumour suggests the guards were less vigilant than before, looking over their shoulders for the approach of the earl's army. No doubt had Malmesbury ever learnt the truth he would have filled his pages with dramatic detail, and he promises to do so 'in the following volume'. Unfortunately, that volume was never written, and here we say goodbye to another of our faithful chroniclers, who died shortly after the events he had just recorded.

Other writers, however, do provide details of Matilda's progress once outside the tower. It was apparently a freezing night with deep snow all around. Henry of Huntingdon declares that 'the empress escaped across the Thames which was then frozen over, and, wrapped in a white cloak, deceived the eyes of the besiegers, dazzled by the reflection of the snow.' The *Gesta* adds that she passed through the royal guard posts 'while the silence of the night was broken all around by the clang of trumpets and the cries of the guard.' One man, it claims, did see her escape, but he was bribed to silence. Then, passing clear out of the town, she and her companions had a 6-mile walk through the snow and ice to the safety of Wallingford.

'I have never heard,' declares the *Gesta* writer, 'of any woman having such marvellous escapes from so many enemies threatening her life, and from such exceeding perils.' Presumably writing very close to the time, he speculates whether God was indeed sparing her in order that she might rise to the highest honour in the land, or if it was simply that He felt England deserved further punishment by way of civil war. The chronicler would soon have his answer.

With Matilda safely away, the garrison at Oxford surrendered on terms to the king and with Christmas shortly following there was a seasonal pause in campaigning. No doubt they spent the time taking stock of their respective positions and considering what might be the next move in the game. If anything, the lines between the parties were by now more firmly drawn on the map than they had been before. For Stephen, the south-east – London, Kent, Surrey and Sussex – was the heartland of his cause. In the north Yorkshire was firmly held, and the Scots king and his son were causing no problems in their respective territories. In the Midlands Robert, Earl of Leicester, and Ranulf, Earl of Chester, were at least theoretically loyal to Stephen, Ranulf having become reconciled with the king the previous year. He and Robert, however, were more concerned with vying with each other for control of lands from Staffordshire to the Vale of Belvoir, and neither was much inclined to become involved in the king's affairs. Lincoln, Derby and Nottingham were Stephen's, held respectively by Ranulf, by Robert de Ferrers and by William Peverel, while further south, Warwick, Northampton and East Anglia were all held for the king.

With Oxford now secured under William de Chesney, Stephen could rightly claim to hold, at least nominally, the larger portion of the country. On the other hand, the far west and south-west, from Worcester to the south coast south of Salisbury, was fairly solidly held for the empress, with Henry de Tracey in Somerset the only active supporter of Stephen in the area.

Within these areas of influence each party had outlying and isolated castles, vulnerable to attack by the other; Wallingford and Newbury, for example, for the empress, and Bath, Malmesbury and Sherborne for Stephen. As William of Newburgh was later to lament, 'Perpetual discord still existed between the king and the empress; sometimes parties were equal, at another time one had the ascendancy; but this in turn was subject to the uncertainty of fortune.'

In 1143 Stephen was to discover once more just how uncertain that could be. His major military aim for that year was to attack the party of the empress in Dorset and Wiltshire. From there, via his strong castle at Sherborne, he could cut a corridor through to his own adherents in Somerset and divide the empress from her supporters in Devon and Cornwall. The initial target was Wareham, but this was to prove a tougher proposition than the year before. Robert of Gloucester had improved its fortifications to such an extent that it was not long before the king abandoned his attempt to retake it. Instead, by the end of June, Stephen had moved on towards Salisbury. He was accompanied by his brother

Bishop Henry, and, according to the *Gesta*, 'a strong body of military to support his enterprise'. He had also, by that account, summoned barons from all parts of England to join him. This was clearly to be a serious attempt to retake the town and castle of Salisbury, at that time high on a hill to the north-east of the present town, on the site now known as Old Sarum. Considerable forces would be needed to storm or besiege the place, and it may be that afterwards the king intended to move against the headquarters of the empress herself at Devizes.

While he waited for these forces to assemble, Stephen based himself at Wilton a few miles to the west, fortifying an area around the abbey. There, on 1 July, he was surprised by a sudden attack led by Robert of Gloucester. There are two very different accounts of this Battle of Wilton. Gervase of Canterbury, writing some years later, claims the attack was made at sunset, just as the royal household was settling for the night, and that Stephen and Bishop Henry were able to slip away unnoticed in the confusion. The *Gesta*, on the other hand, describes a real set-piece battle like that at Lincoln, with both armies using cavalry and infantry, and drawn up in full battle order. It claims that Robert of Gloucester's men attacked 'with spirit', forcing the king to retreat, 'and unless he had fled precipitately in company with the Bishop of Winchester, he would have been subjected to the disgrace of being again captured.' Stephen had clearly learnt his lesson. Reckless bravery was one thing, but there was a limit to how many times even a king could recover from ignominious captivity.

That he was able to escape at all seems largely due to the actions of William Martel, described as the king's steward. While the *Gesta* says that most of the king's army had dispersed and fled with the king, Martel fought a rearguard action until, surrounded and overwhelmed by the enemy, he was forced to surrender. Nor was that the end of the matter. Clearly intent on seizing the king at all costs, the fugitive troops were pursued by the earl's men into the town where they tried to hide in houses and churches, 'but setting the place on fire, he filled it with tears and blood, sparing neither the citizens nor the remnant of the royal troops, but pillaging and killing, insulting and burning in every quarter.' The greatest crime, according to the *Gesta*, was breaking into the convent itself, 'without regard to the sanctity of the place ... and dragging from the altar with naked swords ... those who fled for safety to the church.' It was acceptable to deal harshly with enemies, and 'with what measure they mete, to measure to them again', but it was recognised at the time that sanctuary could be claimed in a church, and Robert had clearly broken the rules in violating that sanctuary. He did not find his quarry, however. The king was gone, and the *Gesta* claims that God had his vengeance on Robert with a series of misfortunes that befell him and his party soon after.

The king had escaped but the cost was to be very high, both in ignominy and in practical terms. 'All the king's friends were at this time reduced to great humiliation,' says the *Gesta*. Like his father before him, Stephen had not only run from a battle but he had left his friends behind to be captured by the enemy. By far the most important of these was William Martel.

After the departure of Waleran de Meulan, Stephen had come to rely more and more on an intimate group of court officials. Of these William of Ypres was earl in all but name, but William Martel was close behind in terms of importance to the king. Clearly he could not be left to languish in an enemy dungeon, and Stephen regained a certain amount of respectability by agreeing to ransom him. The price, though, was his castle at Sherborne, effectively the gateway to the west, and by giving it up, the king gave up any chance of penetrating that region and re-asserting his authority there. Indeed, shortly afterwards Henry de Tracey finally recognised he would get no further help from the royalists and surrendered to the empress, triggering the submission of a whole string of minor castles across Somerset. The *Gesta* claims de Tracey's truce was to last 'until such time as the king should be more powerful in that quarter,' but he would be waiting a long time for that to happen, and when it did the war would already be over.

Now, says the *Gesta*, the party of the empress was in high spirits, ruling 'one half of all England from sea to sea'. This seems to be something of an exaggeration. Even if the rather dubious loyalty of Ranulf of Chester is included, the total comes to considerably less than half. Nor were all those offering allegiance to be fully relied on. In Wiltshire, for example, Patrick of Salisbury and John Marshal, both supporters of the empress, were not averse to fighting each other to increase their holdings.

Soon after Wilton, an opportunity arose for Matilda to extend her reach along the south coast. William de Pont de l'Arche, former treasurer to King Henry and a leading figure in Winchester, fell out, not for the first time, with Bishop Henry, and retired to his castle at Portchester. He sent to Matilda, offering her the castle if she would dispatch a military force to defend it against the bishop. A Flemish mercenary captain, Robert fitz Hildebrand, was duly sent. Unfortunately, the Fleming had other plans. After obtaining possession of William's castle and his treasure, and seducing his wife, Robert had the unfortunate William bound in fetters and thrown into a dungeon, and handed the castle over to Stephen. Soon afterwards, the *Gesta* notes, the 'base seducer' came to a grisly end by means of 'a worm (which) grew in his vitals,' so that he died in agony. The description sounds a great deal like cancer.

If Stephen was already out of favour with his earls, he was about to make matters a great deal worse. In September 1143, at his court at St Albans, he suddenly arrested Geoffrey de Mandeville, Earl of Essex. Why he did this is a matter of dispute, and since the different writers have different explanations, the real reason is necessarily obscure. The *Gesta* talks of the great wealth and power of Geoffrey, a man it describes as 'remarkable for his great prudence, his inflexible spirit in adversity and his military skill.' It suggests that jealousy on the part of those 'familiarly and intimately connected with the king' might have been a motive for false accusations of treachery. Indeed, the king himself may have been jealous, since it also declares that 'in public affairs he was more attended to than the king himself, and the royal commands were less obeyed than his own.' It could well have been that Geoffrey possessed the commanding presence which the affable, easy-going king so clearly lacked, and that, at a time of personal failure, Stephen just snapped.

The description in the *Gesta* is strikingly similar to that preceding the arrest of the bishops some years before. Again there are the whispers that Geoffrey secretly favoured the empress and the king must arrest him for the security of the kingdom. These whispers clearly reached as far as Henry of Huntingdon who, while deploring the manner of the arrest, declares that if Stephen 'had not taken this step (he) would have been driven from the throne.' Similar, too, to the arrest of the bishops was Geoffrey's arrest at court, to which he had apparently come all unsuspectingly, with again a story of a sudden fracas between Geoffrey and the barons which required the interference of the king.

On the other hand, William of Newburgh has a completely different reason for the earl's arrest, based on a longstanding grudge held by the king. This story is based on Geoffrey's position as custodian of the Tower of London at the time of the Battle of Lincoln. Newburgh declares that Queen Matilda and her daughter-in-law Constance were resident in the Tower at that point, but the queen wanted to move both of them away to a safer area. Geoffrey, however, 'took the daughter from the protection of the mother; and though she resisted with all her might, yet he detained her, and suffered the queen to depart in ignominy.' This insult, he claimed, had rankled with Stephen for more than two years, and when Geoffrey, described as 'a desperate character' and 'an object of terror to the king,' appeared at St Albans, he seized the opportunity to be avenged.

This clearly gives Stephen a more robust motive for taking action against the earl, but the story is significantly absent from the more contemporary writings, while the character given to Geoffrey seems to have been drawn from his later actions, rather than the prudent, generally loyal behaviour of the man to that date. True he had deserted the king at Lincoln but so had everyone else, and he had been quick to return to him, unlike some, such as Waleran de Meulan, who had gone for good.

Geoffrey's own reaction to the accusations brought against him did nothing, however, to reassure the king. 'Instead of taking the least pains to clear himself of the charge,' says the *Gesta*, 'he treated it with ridicule, as an infamous falsehood.' The result was that he was dragged to London, and threatened with hanging if he didn't give up the Tower and two other castles he had fortified at Saffron Walden and at Pleshey.

Again the parallels with the bishops' arrest are startling. As soon as the castles were handed over Geoffrey was released, but the earl did not take his punishment like a bishop. Instead he assembled 'all his dependants ... and a formidable host of mercenary soldiers' and took himself off to the fenland in the north of Norfolk, to defy the king and take his revenge on him wherever he could. The fact that he went first to Ely may be the cause of the *Gesta*'s claim that now all the king's enemies rose up in rebellion against him.

Bishop Nigel, however, was in Rome at the time, and the only backing for the earl outside his own network of relations, seems to have been the rather tacit support of Hugh Bigod, and the neutrality of the Clares and de Veres with their extensive East Anglian estates. In fact nothing in Geoffrey's subsequent reign of terror suggests that he was allying himself with the empress. He was simply living like an outlaw because the king had made him an outlaw, and he intended to have his revenge.

His most notorious action was the taking over of Ramsey Abbey in the heart of the fens, and turning it into his own military headquarters. In this, recent events had given him some assistance. Abbot Walter of Ramsey had been forced to resign by a 'scheming monk' named Daniel – the same Daniel who had, some years before, guided King Stephen across the marshes to oust Bishop Nigel from Ely. Daniel had been confirmed as the abbot of Ramsey by Stephen, but the monks were still in some confusion when, at daybreak on a December morning, Geoffrey and his men burst in to take over the abbey. The men of God, Daniel among them, were unceremoniously expelled to make way for the men of war. Horses were stabled in the cloisters, and the impressive gateway was turned into a fortified barbican. From there, for much of the next year, men would ride out to plunder and ravage the countryside, and to seize prisoners who would be tortured into paying a ransom for their release. Geoffrey, says William of Newburgh, had 'converted the sanctuary of God into the habitation of the devil.'

He was a devil, moreover, that was exceedingly hard to get at. With the watery protection of the fens and the River Ouse, and with castles thrown up, particularly by his illegitimate son Arnulf, at Woodwalton, Fordham, Mildenhall, Chatteris and Benwick, there seemed no way he could dislodge the earl from his new 'kingdom'. Stephen certainly tried, particularly after his own town of Cambridge was sacked and burned, but by the summer of 1144, with his castles in the west under attack, he resorted to building fortifications of his own around Geoffrey to try to contain the menace.

Abbot Walter did rather better. Returning from Rome, where he had appealed to the pope and been reinstated as abbot, he marched into Geoffrey's camp and seizing brands from the fire set alight the tents of the men and the gate of the barbican. Under violent threats from the soldiers, he was busy excommunicating everyone in sight when he was rescued by Geoffrey. The earl listened to his complaints about robbery and famine, but he claimed he was only doing what he must, having lost his own lands to the king. He did, though, permit the abbot and monks to return to part of the abbey.

So notorious did Ramsey become that it was said the walls of the church there sweated blood. We might put this down as a romantic flight of fancy, except that Henry of Huntingdon, a near neighbour, declares, 'This was seen by many persons, and I observed it with my own eyes.' The reign of terror, though, was relatively brief. Stephen's castles were a threat to Geoffrey's activities, and it was while attacking one of these at Burwell on a hot August day that the earl unluckily removed his helmet and was targeted by an archer. A slight wound to the head seemed not to be serious, but, as with many another before and since, it turned out to be fatal. Geoffrey, having retired to Mildenhall, died there towards the end of September, filling his last hours with attempts to make restitution for all he had taken, including directing the return of Ramsey to the monks.

There is a very medieval postscript to this, in that, following the edict of a church council the previous year, anyone like Geoffrey dying excommunicated from the church could not be buried. The

Knights Templar, from their London base, claimed his body, and for the next twenty years it remained encased in a lead coffin, some said suspended from a tree, so as not to contaminate the ground. Eventually, in 1163, his son succeeded in obtaining a posthumous absolution for him from Pope Alexander, and he was finally buried at Temple Church, where his memorial can still be seen.

In 1143 both the king and the empress suffered the loss of a significant supporter. For the empress it was Miles, Earl of Hereford, accidentally killed while hunting on Christmas Eve. His son Roger inherited both title and lands, but was a less forceful, less committed upholder of Matilda's cause. Like many at this time, he was probably beginning to realise that there would be no outright winner of this long-drawn-out war.

For Stephen the death of Pope Innocent on 23 September 1143 would, in the long term, prove a serious setback. While Innocent had been committed from the start to Stephen's cause, his immediate successor, Celestine II, was inclined to the opposite party. Bishop Henry now found his office of legate at an end and the more neutral authority of Archbishop Theobald on the rise, while church matters, which had already proved difficult, now became more complicated than ever. The arrest of the bishops had been defended by the Archbishop of Rouen with the tacit approval of Pope Innocent, but Nigel, Bishop of Ely, and Walter, Abbot of Ramsey, both hounded out of office in 1143, received a far more sympathetic hearing from Celestine. More importantly, the tangled affair of the Archbishop of York would turn into a showdown between king and pope.

Following the death of Thurstan in 1140, it had taken three elections to produce a candidate with any prospect of taking up the appointment. The first election named Waltheof, a step-son of David of Scotland, who was rejected by Stephen. The second named Henry Sully, nephew of Stephen, who had already been rejected as Bishop of Salisbury. He was turned down by the pope, as he had since been appointed Abbot of Fécamp and wanted to combine the two posts. At the third election William fitz Herbert, the treasurer of York, was chosen, but against considerable opposition, particularly from the Cistercian monasteries of the diocese.

The Cistercians were a relatively new order, founded, like the Cluniacs before them, to return to a simpler, purer form of monastic life, closer to the rule laid down by Benedict. They possessed the most influential churchman of the day in Bernard of Clairvaux. Holy, austere and very persuasive, Bernard had founded Rievaulx Abbey in Yorkshire some ten years before, on land given by Walter Espec. He intended Rievaulx to be the first of many Cistercian houses in the north of England, and he was particularly keen to see a Cistercian abbot become the new Archbishop of York.

Following the election of William, the Cistercians claimed he had achieved his result because of interference from the king. It was said the Earl of York had ordered the cathedral chapter to elect him because he was Stephen's choice. Archbishop Theobald refused to consecrate him and there was an appeal to Pope Innocent who, in 1143, ruled that William could be consecrated if there was sworn evidence there had been no such interference. He was duly consecrated by Bishop Henry, acting as papal legate, on 26 September 1143 – three days after the death of Pope Innocent, and therefore after the expiry of his papal authority. By the time William journeyed to Rome for his pallium in 1145, two more popes had come and gone, and the new man, Pope Eugenius III, was a Cistercian and a friend of Bernard, having been a monk at Clairvaux. Instead of receiving his pallium, William found himself violently opposed by Bernard and, after a long delay, was removed from office early in 1147.

Nor was it only church appointments that were causing friction between Stephen and the church. By this time plundering and ravaging the country had become so much the practice of both sides that churches and church property were by no means exempt. 'Tenserie', which could be viewed either as a tax or as protection money, was demanded from the clergy as from others and, says Henry of Huntingdon, 'no respect was paid to them or to God's holy church by marauders, and the clergy were made prisoners and submitted to ransom just as if they were laymen.' As a result, a church council in 1143 decreed that anyone laying violent hands on any cleric should be excommunicated, and that this penalty could only be lifted face to face by the pope himself. Not only was such a person denied the sacraments in life, but he would be refused burial when he died. There was a proviso that a person repenting on his deathbed could be absolved, but this didn't help Geoffrey de Mandeville, who was already unconscious before a priest could reach him to grant the absolution. Strangely, though, the decree seems to have been ignored completely in relation to Miles of Gloucester, who was similarly excommunicated for violence against the church at Hereford, but who was quickly buried at Llanthony Priory.

In fairness, it should be mentioned that the *Gesta* accuses bishops, too – 'not all, indeed, but several of them' – of joining in with the ravagers of the land. The bishops of Winchester, Lincoln and Chester are named as shamefully 'girt with the sword and sheathed in bright armour', riding mettlesome horses, and receiving their share of the booty.

For the war by this time had moved beyond battles and become a matter of skirmishes, sudden attacks, sieges and waste. While most of the great magnates managed to hold off from engagement, neither side had power to inflict a knockout blow on the other. All they could do was nibble away piecemeal at the borders of their territories and cause what damage they could, until forced to withdraw when threatened with a larger force. By the mid-1140s, most of this niggling action was taking place in the area between Oxford and Gloucester.

In 1144 Robert of Gloucester attempted to take Stephen's outlying castle at Malmesbury, initially sending William Peverel of Dover to build a new castle at Cricklade, cutting off access along the Thames Valley from Oxford. Stephen, hurrying back from tackling Geoffrey de Mandeville in Norfolk, managed to resupply the besieged castle and send in a new commander, Walter de Pinkney, before himself attacking Robert's nearby castle at Tetbury. Stephen had already penetrated the outer defences and was bringing up his siege engines when he found Robert had assembled a great army and was marching towards him. According to the *Gesta*, the army consisted not only of his own men and those of Roger, Earl of Hereford, but others from nearby loyal castles, a contingent of 'fierce and undisciplined' Welshmen, and foot soldiers (presumably militia) from Bristol and other towns.

Clearly he was intending to give battle – he had, after all, been successful in two battles with Stephen already – but Stephen's barons were having none of it. They advised the king to raise the siege, and 'for a while draw off his army on some other enterprise,' so as not to 'expose his small band of men-at-arms among such a crowd of butchers.' Stephen agreed and, wisely avoiding the advancing horde, marched off to storm and take a castle at Winchcombe, which belonged to the new Earl of Hereford and almost overlooked that earl's chief city of Gloucester. Without the means to attack so great a city, however, Stephen in turn withdrew and turned his attention back to East Anglia.

It was Hugh Bigod he was concerned with there, 'the most turbulent of his enemies', as the *Gesta* calls him. Presumably in support of Geoffrey de Mandeville, Hugh had taken advantage of Stephen's absence to engage in 'predatory excursions' against royal castles. There is some evidence that Stephen's administration in the area had broken down some time before, and though Hugh was one of those who, after Winchester, had apparently taken little action for one side or the other, it may well have been that he was the one interfering with royal rights. For whatever reason, Stephen seemed determined to wrest back control, though Hugh appears to have got off lightly. The *Gesta* records that he was attacked with great energy and his troops either taken prisoner or dispersed, but his castles were not confiscated, and he seems thereafter to have been left in peace. Hugh was apparently a nuisance rather than a threat, and only needed putting in his place.

The *Gesta*, however, says Stephen spent a considerable time in the area, and taking that broadly we may be able to tie in certain other recorded events to around the end of 1144 and the beginning of 1145. At some point in the earlier year the king had begun a siege of Lincoln Castle, but then abandoned it when 'eighty of his workmen were suffocated in the trenches.' Presumably this was an attempt to undermine the walls that went badly wrong.

'About this time,' too claims the *Gesta*, Turgis of Avranches rebelled against the king, 'a thing so absurd that it was hardly credited.' Turgis had long been a most loyal household officer, 'the most trusty of all his courtiers', and probably for this reason had been entrusted with Geoffrey de Mandeville's confiscated castle at Saffron Walden. Either he completely mistook the king's grant, or the promotion went to his head, for he began to act as though the castle and its surrounding land was his own. When Stephen went to pay a visit he was refused admittance, but retaliation was not far behind.

Turgis was out hunting one day when the king suddenly appeared with a troop of horse. The unfortunate would-be baron was seized, bound in fetters and threatened with immediate hanging unless he surrendered the castle at once, which he was forced to do. Thereafter he is found as a humble household knight in the service of Simon of Senlis.

In the early part of 1145 Stephen is found at Ipswich in company with a new papal legate, Imar of Tusculum, who, incidentally, had brought with him a pallium for William of York, which was never collected and thus was returned to Rome. This is likely to have been the time when the king became reconciled with Bishop Nigel of Ely, who may have travelled with the legate. It was not the most joyful of reconciliations, however. Nigel had to pay 300 marks and hand over his son Richard as hostage for his future good behaviour.

Once again, though, the year 1145 continued to be dominated by events in the upper Thames Valley. Robert of Gloucester was again before Malmesbury, and William Peverel was on the rampage between Cricklade and Oxford, not at all afraid to engage the troops Stephen had left to guard the area. At some point William managed, by an unexplained 'stratagem', to capture Walter de Pinkney, commander of Malmesbury, and to deliver him up to the empress at Devizes. There, says the *Gesta*, she 'strove both by her blandishments, and by threats of torture and death, to induce him to surrender Malmesbury Castle,' but he steadfastly refused, even when loaded with chains and 'thrown into a loathsome dungeon'. The siege went on.

William Peverel was now replaced at Cricklade by Philip, a younger son of Robert of Gloucester, whose character reference in the admittedly biased *Gesta* seems rather extreme. He was, it says, 'a quarrelsome man, of great cruelty, ready for the most desperate enterprises and consummately malignant'. He was also full of drive and energy, thrusting forward in the name of the empress along the way towards Oxford. It was at his suggestion that a castle was built at Faringdon and garrisoned with 'the flower of his troops'. This carried the attack dangerously close to Stephen's city, and close enough, too, to Wallingford to allow some mutual support.

Stephen's response was immediate. Raising a powerful force, he marched to Faringdon and put the castle under siege. Remaining there for a period of time, however, would make him a target for others, and he was clearly nervous about this, surrounding his own camp with a trench and outworks before attempting to bludgeon into submission this most daring outpost of the empress. A fierce campaign is described with archers and great siege engines employed on a daily basis, so that 'at one time missiles of every description poised on high were hurled through the air,' thinning the ranks of defenders within. Flower of the army they might have been, but it was the leaders of the garrison who eventually made terms for their surrender, handing over to Stephen 'the crown of his fortune and the height of his glory'.

This seems a high claim for the winning of one small castle, but it is seen by many as the turning point of the whole war. It may well be that the empress and her brother had poured all their dwindling resources into this one push forward into enemy territory. Had they succeeded in taking Oxford the balance might once again have tilted in their favour and encouraged others, particularly those with lands in Normandy, to return to their side. As it was, they had lost, and when Philip decided to defect to the king, in return for castles and land and 'many magnificent gifts', it was an especially hurtful blow. Stephen's prestige was clearly rising once more, and their own falling.

This defection meant that Bristol and Gloucester, the heart of the Angevin territory in the west, were now ringed by enemy garrisons at Bath, Malmesbury, Cricklade, Cirencester and Winchcombe. Soon after, the activity of Philip added Miserden, only 6 miles from Gloucester, to that list. This may well have been the reason for Roger of Hereford suddenly seizing by violent means the castles at Berkeley and Dursley belonging to his own ally Roger of Berkeley, thereby keeping open the road between Gloucester and Bristol. It may also have been the reason why peace talks are recorded in the following year. 'And now the king and his adherents and the countess (Matilda, countess of Anjou) and hers, had a meeting to treat of peace,' says the *Gesta*. We don't know where it was held, but we do know that safe-conducts were issued so that interested parties could attend. We know this because young Philip, in an excess of zeal, ambushed and held captive his own uncle, Reginald de Dunstanville, on the way to the meeting, and earned the king's anger for doing so.

These were the first peace talks for five years, but they seemed doomed from the start. Stephen, feeling he was gaining the upper hand, was giving nothing away; while far from setting out grounds for negotiation, Matilda simply restated that the throne was hers by right and demanded he should abdicate. The meeting was ineffectual, declares the *Gesta*, because 'the demands of both parties were arrogant.'

Perhaps the most surprising events of 1146, however, centred around the figure of Ranulf of Chester. This earl of ambiguous loyalty had spent the previous five years consolidating his possession of all he could get his hands on in the midland shires. Though he had submitted to Stephen at Winchester, his actions against royalist barons had persuaded many that he was still on the side of the empress. As recently as 1144 he had fought both Robert Marmion, Lord of Tamworth, and William of Aumale, Earl of York, and perhaps the king's attack on Lincoln Castle, which he still held, was intended as either retaliation or a warning. At the beginning of 1146, however, he came to the king at Stamford and humbly submitting to him was restored to favour.

It has been suggested that his brother-in-law Philip, newly converted to the king's cause, may have eased this reconciliation, and if he did he should have been well rewarded by Ranulf, for the pact now made with the king seems extremely generous. Ranulf was granted the castle and city of Lincoln, to hold until he regained the lands he had lost in Normandy – a forlorn hope –with substantial lands across the Midlands and north, including parts of the Honour of Lancaster between the Ribble and Mersey. In fact he seems to have granted him virtually all that Ranulf had earlier taken for himself.

When we look for reasons as to why Ranulf should come to Stephen at this time, and why he received such a warm welcome, they are fairly easy to find. If Ranulf had been fence-sitting for years, he now seems to have decided which was the winning side. Added to that there was trouble brewing on his Welsh border, and he still had an ongoing dispute with Matilda's uncle, David of Scotland, concerning the lands around Carlisle. The *Gesta*, however, sees a more sinister motive. Ranulf, it says, was 'secretly devising means how best, without open shame, he could betray the king to his enemies.' On Stephen's side, he badly needed the additional resources the earl could provide. His recent successes may have led him to believe that one final push would rid him of his enemies for ever. The backing of the man who was probably at that time the most powerful in the country might just enable him to complete that final push. In any case, in propaganda terms, the open alliance of the earl with the royalist cause would be another severe blow to the party of the empress.

By the terms of the agreement Ranulf was to remain with the king – a common requirement for the newly reconciled – and he quickly made himself useful. Bedford was retaken from Miles de Beauchamp and, as 'a faithful and attached friend' of Stephen's, William of Newburgh records that he 'rendered him powerful aid at Wallingford', though again the siege was unsuccessful. After this Ranulf was permitted to take his men home to deal with the increasing Welsh action whereby the city of Mold had already been lost.

It is not quite clear when he broached the subject of Stephen mounting a campaign against the Welsh. It may have been at

Wallingford, or later when he discovered the extent of the danger. If the king joined him, he declared, the Welsh would be alarmed at his very name, while his presence would be worth more than a thousand soldiers.

At first Stephen seemed amenable to the idea. The *Gesta* said he had even begun preparations when his inner circle of counsellors began to make the claims of treachery later set out by that writer. They pointed to Ranulf's past record, and the dangers and opportunities for ambush in the distant mountains and woods of Wales. It was, they said, 'too rash and daring a scheme for the king to commit himself so carelessly in the territories of the earl, who had before raised the better part of the kingdom against him.' A compromise was agreed. Stephen would go with the earl, but only if he first restored 'all he had unjustly usurped', if he performed fealty in public and left hostages for keeping this fealty.

At the end of August Stephen held his court at Northampton. All unsuspecting, Ranulf arrived and was presented with this list of demands. The earl protested, 'they quarrelled, and words of defiance were used on both sides.' Accused of treason, says the *Gesta*, the earl reddened with confusion, 'as though he felt himself guilty.' It was enough to confirm their suspicions and he was fettered and led away to prison. It has a familiar ring to it – the innocent approach to court, the whispers of treachery, the manufactured quarrel. Twice before Stephen had seized opponents in this way and you might almost think the earl should have been expecting it. Yet again the demand was the same. Give up the castles you have wrongly taken, particularly Lincoln and Coventry, and you can go free. Again the earl was forced to comply, at which point, says William of Newburgh, he was liberated and 'became the king's irreconcilable enemy ever after'.

It sounds particularly smug or perhaps complacent that Stephen held his Christmas court and crown-wearing at Lincoln Castle that year, apparently defying an old superstition that said English kings should not do so. Robert of Torigny praises his courage and 'how little he feared these imaginary dangers,' but Stephen was probably fearing little at that time. He was clearly in the ascendancy, and was not even much affected when early in the following year numbers of men from both sides answered the call from Bernard of Clairvaux to join an ill-fated Second Crusade to the Holy Land, following the fall of Edessa in 1144.

When his chief adversary, Robert of Gloucester, died of a fever at Bristol Castle on 31 October 1147, Stephen must have felt the war was over. There was no one now who could put Matilda on the throne he had occupied for nearly a dozen years. Matilda thought so too. In February 1148 she finally left England, returning to the duchy secured by her husband, now fully acknowledged as Duke of Normandy. She would spend most of the rest of her life in semi-retirement at the Priory of Notre-Dame-du-Pré near Rouen, but she was not giving up on her claim to the English throne. It was simply time for the younger generation to take over the struggle.

10

The Young Generation

(1147 – May 1153)

Henry Plantagenet, as he came to be known, was approaching his fifteenth birthday when his mother, the empress Matilda, returned from England. He had already visited the country twice. First, as a nine-year-old, he had spent probably something over fifteen months at Bristol being tutored with Robert of Gloucester's second son Roger, under the guidance of Master Matthew and the canons of St Augustine's Priory. The experience seems to have left a happy impression on the boy, while his presence there was the first tangible evidence presented to the supporters of the empress that there was a promise for the future, even if currently the road was hard. It was not the most successful year for that party, however, and may have exposed the child to the reality of the situation. The year before, young Henry had exuberantly confirmed one of his mother's charters as, 'Henry, son of the daughter of King Henry, rightful heir to England and Normandy'. Before he returned to Normandy he was signing simply as 'son of the Count of Anjou'.

By the beginning of 1144 Geoffrey of Anjou had almost completed his conquest of Normandy and it is likely he wanted his son to return so he could begin to train him for his future role as duke. There was no fierce rivalry such as that shown between William the Conqueror and his sons. As early as 1145, Geoffrey was writing to Henry, 'who by the grace of God will surpass me and all my predecessors in power and dignity.' Not only was the Angevin tradition markedly different, but Geoffrey may well have realised from the start that he was never going to be the most popular duke in Normandy, and that associating his son with the government of the duchy would help appease his new subjects.

Henry seems to have been a diligent pupil, and for the next couple of years, in Anjou and in Normandy, he did all that was expected of him. Though he had his share of the self-confidence of youth, and maybe more than his share of daring; in early 1147, without the approval, or probably knowledge, of either parent, he decided to launch his own expedition to England. The spur for this may well have been the defection of Robert's son Philip, whom he must have known as a boy in Bristol, and whose blatant disloyalty he could not forgive.

The *Gesta*, for the first time calling Henry 'the rightful heir and pretender to the crown of England', makes his arrival a great event. 'The kingdom was struck with perturbation,' it says. His supporters 'rejoiced as if a new light had burst upon them,' while those of the king 'were for a time depressed as if a thunderbolt had crushed them.' The reason for this, however, was simply wild rumour advancing before the teenage Henry. It said he had brought many thousands of men with him, was backed by unlimited resources of money, and was overrunning one district after another.

The truth was far less impressive. In fact he had brought a small band of mercenaries recruited with no ready pay but a promise of riches to come in England. What kind of mercenaries they were we don't know, but their reputations would not be advanced on this campaign. Only two actions are recorded, one an attack on Cricklade, and the other probably at nearby Purton. According to the *Gesta*, Henry's troops 'were driven in disgrace from the one, and, taken with panic, precipitously fled from the other.' As a bid for glory it was an utter failure. Worse than that, the men were demanding money and Henry had none. If he was expecting to be backed by his mother or her wealthier supporters, he was disappointed again. Appeals to Matilda and to Robert of Gloucester drew a blank. He was a distraction and an embarrassment, and was not to be rewarded for his failure. Young Henry, however, was nothing if not resourceful. A secret approach was made to King Stephen, 'to implore him humbly, that of his goodness, he would make provision for his pressing wants, and remembering their near relationship, listen kindly to his request.' Amazingly, Stephen did just that, paying off the mercenary band and allowing Henry to return safely to Normandy, where, no doubt, he suffered the wrath of his father.

Was this just another example of Stephen's reckless generosity, helping the man 'from whom, of all others, he ought to have withheld assistance'? Many thought so, but not the *Gesta* writer. Stephen, he says, did it 'from wise and noble views; for the more kindly and humanely a man treats his adversary, the more he humbles him and lessens his power.' It is likely he also wanted to make sure this band of potential troublemakers left his kingdom, and possibly he also wanted to point a contrast between Henry's neediness and the strength of his own son Eustace.

Eustace was probably now in his late teens, a handful of years older than Henry, and the *Gesta* gives him a glowing testimonial. He was 'a young man of high character … his manners were grave; he excelled in warlike exercises and had great natural courage … he was courteous and affable … and possessed much of his father's spirit … ever ready to draw close the bonds of peace' but 'never shrank from presenting a resolute and indomitable front to his enemies.' It should be mentioned that neither Henry of Huntingdon nor the Anglo-Saxon Chronicle saw Eustace in the same light. The latter called him 'an evil man who did more harm than good wherever he went,' and, sympathising with his wife Constance, declared that 'she was a good woman, but she had little bliss with him.'

In 1147 Stephen may also have been feeling generous, having settled his own sons so well. Eustace, of course, had been married for some time to the sister of Louis VII of France, though there were as yet no children of the marriage. Then, in the spring of the year, a splendid marriage was arranged between Stephen's second son William and the daughter and heiress of William of Warenne, Earl of Surrey, neither of whom had yet reached their teens. Her father was about to embark on the Second Crusade and no doubt wanted matters settled at home before he went. It gave William the promise of great wealth and power, a promise to be quickly realised when the earl was killed less than a year later at the Battle of Mount Cadmus.

In 1147, too, Stephen knighted his son Eustace, and there is authority for claiming that both sons were made earls, though without any specific territorial designation. The *Gesta* clearly states that Eustace was given 'the high rank of an earl' and at least one charter refers to his brother as 'Earl William, the king's son' before the death of his father-in-law was known. The awards are clearly meant as honours rather than responsibilities, though Eustace is now to be found assisting his father in conflicts around the country.

Stephen may well have felt in need of some new earls, since he was falling out with those he already had on a regular basis. Ranulf of Chester had been liberated the year before on terms that he would remain at peace with the king, though if Stephen ever thought that would be the case, he seriously underestimated the man he was dealing with. As was usual with such deals, hostages were nominated to ensure good behaviour, and one of these was Ranulf's nephew, Gilbert fitz Richard de Clare, Earl of Hertford. When Ranulf immediately went off to attack Lincoln, Stephen seized the younger earl and demanded he hand over his castles. There is also some suggestion that Gilbert was imprisoned for too long, or otherwise unfairly treated. The *Gesta* says he was 'committed to close custody and strictly guarded' until he surrendered his castles, whereupon he hurried to join Ranulf in his attacks on the king's lands.

This brought into play another uncle, Gilbert de Clare, Earl of Pembroke, who declared that as senior family representative, he, rather than the king, should have custody of young Gilbert's castles and lands. Stephen refused, having according to the *Gesta* some suspicions of Gilbert's own loyalty. These suspicions seemed confirmed when the earl immediately withdrew from court with, claims the *Gesta*, the intention of fortifying his castles in Kent and Sussex against the king. Stephen, however, was too quick for him. When Gilbert reached his nearest castle, possibly Leeds Castle in Kent, he found the king already there and only escaped 'by disguising his person and concealing his face'. That castle and two others were taken by Stephen in quick succession, and Earl Gilbert was besieged at Pevensey until forced to surrender. There was a reconciliation of sorts with the king, but the earl died soon after, and the Clare family, who had never previously supported the empress, would in future be distinctly cool towards King Stephen.

Pevensey Castle was, in fact, given to Eustace, who, although the king's eldest son and heir, held rather less land in the country than might have been expected. He had almost certainly received his mother's Honour of Boulogne, centred on Essex, when he was knighted, but his marriage, although prestigious, had not increased his wealth at all. He had given sterling service to his father in actions against Ranulf of Chester at Lincoln, and later at Coventry where the king himself was wounded, and it may be that it was that wound which now turned Stephen's mind towards securing the succession for his son. The young man had probably already been accepted as the rightful heir to the County of Boulogne, but Stephen had some experience of the effectiveness of sworn oaths in England. As a result, he wanted his son actually crowned, French-style, before his own death. To achieve that, however, he would need the co-operation of the church; and his relations with the church were about to hit an all-time low.

Pope Eugenius was already at loggerheads with Stephen over the Archbishop of York, having deposed William fitz Herbert early in 1147. He had ordered a new election to be held, but in June of that year the result was fairly evenly divided between the king's candidate, Hilary, who in the past had been clerk to Bishop Henry, and Henry Murdac, the abbot of the Cistercian Fountains Abbey in Yorkshire. Unsurprisingly the pope appointed Henry Murdac, whom he had known well when they were both monks at Clairvaux. There was no consultation with the king about this, no formal seeking of royal consent or even the agreement of the cathedral chapter, as was traditional, and though the pope himself consecrated Murdac on 7 December 1147, when he finally travelled to Yorkshire he was refused entry both to York and to his own cathedral. The new archbishop was forced to take up residence in Ripon instead, and he was there for some time.

In the middle of this, in October 1147 the pope summoned a church council to meet at Rheims the following March, and directed that those he called must attend or be suspended from office. Only a small number of English bishops had attended the last church council and Stephen decided that only three would be sent this time. These were Robert of Hereford, William of Norwich and Hilary, who had been compensated by the pope for losing out to Henry Murdac by being appointed Bishop of Chichester. Whether Stephen's decision was in deliberate defiance of the pope we cannot be sure, but faced with disobeying either his pope or his king, Archbishop Theobald chose the latter. With the ports apparently being watched to prevent him leaving, he hired a small fishing boat and accompanied by Gilbert Foliot, Abbot of Gloucester, made the crossing 'like a survivor from a shipwreck'. He was warmly welcomed by the pope, who decided that all the English bishops who did not attend at Rheims should be suspended. They could be reinstated by Theobald, he said, if the archbishop chose to do so, with the exception of Bishop Henry of Winchester, who, suspected of assisting Stephen's defiance, would have to come and explain himself to the pope in order to secure his reinstatement.

Stephen was, of course, furious. When Theobald returned at the end of April he was met with a demand that he should answer to the king for defying him. Instead, like several of his predecessors, he chose to go into exile, first in France, then later at the request of Queen Matilda at St Omer in Boulogne.

Theobald's defiance was not the only issue between king and pope, however. Bishop Robert of Hereford had passed away while at the council in Rheims and, probably on Theobald's advice, Pope Eugenius had immediately filled the vacancy by appointing Gilbert Foliot as the new bishop. Hereford, of course, was out of Stephen's territory, and Gilbert, as a relative of Miles of Gloucester, was believed to have Angevin sympathies. He remained with the archbishop at St Omer and was consecrated by him on 5 September 1148, despite the refusal of three English bishops who had been invited to assist in the ceremony. They declared it was against English tradition to consecrate a bishop abroad, and anyway the king had not yet consented to the appointment.

While the archbishop was away Stephen took into his own treasury the revenues of Canterbury, thereby causing yet more friction. An appeal was made to the pope, who authorised Theobald to place the entire country under an interdict, effectively depriving it of all the services of the church, unless by Michaelmas the king had changed his mind and reinstated the archbishop and his revenues. When Theobald did this, however, it proved to be a step too far. According to John of Salisbury, at that time a clerk in the papal chancery, letters were sent to all the bishops instructing them to abide by the interdict, but the instructions were largely ignored. In the Canterbury diocese there were no services, but elsewhere the bishops stood by the king rather than the archbishop.

It was time for Archbishop Theobald to move from confrontation to negotiation. Messages were exchanged, and soon afterwards he returned to England, not to Canterbury but to the Suffolk castle of Framlingham, under the protection of Hugh Bigod. More talking followed, to the king's intermediaries and to his fellow bishops, and by the beginning of November the matter had been smoothed over. Gilbert Foliot swore fealty to the king – much to the disappointment of the Angevins – and Theobald returned to Canterbury where one of his first actions was to consecrate an abbot for the new monastery at Faversham in Kent. This was a significant mark of reconciliation since the monastery was founded by Stephen, and more especially by his queen, Matilda, and built on a grand scale. It was intended as the final resting place of both of them, and of the members of the dynasty that they hoped would follow them on the throne of England. It was probably also the place where they intended Eustace should be crowned in his father's lifetime.

No doubt it was part of the deal with Theobald that he should use his influence with the pope to bring about this coronation, but if he tried, he failed. Nor would he crown the young man without the consent of the pope, since the earlier Pope Celestine had forbidden such an 'innovation' in English affairs. It is possible that in the course of the two visits Bishop Henry paid to Rome in the autumn of 1148 and 1149, he may also have requested permission for such a crowning, but if so, he too failed. On the first visit he was in disgrace, not only for failing to attend the pope's council, but also for trying to prevent the archbishop from attending. In fact he only narrowly escaped excommunication. On the second occasion, while the atmosphere was a little sweeter, he was still so out of favour with Bernard of Clairvaux – who called him a 'son of perdition', and a 'man who walks with Satan' – that there was no chance of any request being granted. By then Stephen may have been more than ever anxious to secure the coronation of his son, for in 1149 young Henry Plantagenet was back in England.

He arrived at the end of March, possibly as a result of a family conference in Rouen the previous autumn when father, mother and all the brothers are known to have been together. The aim this time was not invasion but the knighting of the young man on whom all the Angevin hopes were now fixed. He was sixteen years old and, according to John of Hexham, a 'man of powerful frame ... possessing somewhat of the gravity of age'. It was high time he was knighted for he could make no claim to rule anything until this essential rite of passage to manhood had been achieved.

Henry would receive his knighthood from his great-uncle, King David of Scotland, at Carlisle. Before that, however, he needed to make himself known to major supporters of his cause in England, not only the long-time warriors such as Reginald de Dunstanville and John Marshal but the second-generation inheritors of the struggle like himself. Accordingly he landed, most likely at Wareham, and made his way to Devizes. There he was joined by, among others, his cousin William, the new Earl of Gloucester, and Roger, the new Earl of Hereford. There may have been other young supporters present as well, as the *Gesta* records that a number of the sons of nobles accompanied Henry to Carlisle and were knighted at the same time. One name conspicuously absent from the gathering is that of Brian fitz Count. He many have been detained at Wallingford, but he fades out of the picture at this point and he may already have died. Within a year or so we find William Boterel, a possible kinsman, being named as constable of Wallingford Castle.

Before Henry could set off for Carlisle some skilled diplomacy was needed. One of the reasons for Matilda's departure from Devizes was the fact that the castle was still technically the property of the Bishop of Salisbury. That individual had been striving to recover it by legal means for some time, even appealing to the pope for backing, and Matilda had been threatened with excommunication if she did not give it up. The same threat hung over Henry as he continued to occupy the place. With presumably some show of maturity and eloquence, however, he managed to placate the bishop by handing back the surrounding manor and promising to give up the castle when he no longer needed it and 'God has shown me that I may give it back to him.'

Henry may have entered the country very quietly this time and was able to travel to Carlisle through lands that were favourable to him, with no alarms being recorded on the way. At Carlisle, says John of Hexham, 'King David entertained him with great respect and sumptuous provision of costly munificence.' Then, at Pentecost, which fell that year on 22 May, David knighted him, 'assisted by his son Henry, and Ranulf, Earl of Chester'.

This is a most surprising pairing, given Ranulf's long dispute with the Scots over the lands of Carlisle. His animosity to Stephen, however, had led him to take the necessary steps to patch up this quarrel. David was Stephen's enemy, albeit for a long time an inactive one, therefore David was to be accepted as Ranulf's friend. Thus, says John of Hexham, he 'laid aside the animosity with which he had been wont to claim Carlisle as of hereditary right, and did homage to King David.' In return he was given the lordship of Lancaster, lands conveniently bordering on his own, and it was arranged that his son should marry one of the daughters of David's son Henry. It seems doubtful that this marriage ever took place, though a grand-daughter of Ranulf did marry Prince Henry's youngest son.

David seems to have been extending a welcome to all manner of outcasts at the time, since Henry Murdac was welcomed to his court and may even have been present at the knighting ceremony. The good archbishop, banished from York, had been busily putting the city under an interdict and excommunicating his enemies. The chief of these were William of Aumale, Earl of York, and Hugh Puiset, archdeacon and treasurer of York and nephew of Bishop Henry. The archdeacon retaliated by excommunicating Henry Murdac, then either by himself, or with the added force of William of York and Stephen's son Eustace, ensured that the church services continued at York in spite of the interdict.

It may have been this mutual animosity that drew Stephen to York at this time. John of Hexham, in fact, says the citizens 'induced the king to come thither by promises of a large sum of money'. On the other hand, he may have become aware of the gathering of his foes at Carlisle, and come north to protect his own interests. Henry of Huntingdon claims he was 'alarmed lest they should proceed to attack York' and therefore 'established himself in the city with a large army'.

There was indeed some such plan. John of Hexham declares that King David, Henry and Ranulf of Chester 'formed a joint design to act with their united forces against King Stephen', though he does not specify a particular target. This must have taken some organising, and Ranulf seems to have gone back to Chester to gather his forces. Then, says Hexham, King David and Henry marched south to Lancaster expecting to meet the earl there, 'but retracting all that he had undertaken he abandoned this project.' In a slightly different version of the same story, the *Gesta* has them almost at the gates of York before they found Stephen and his army in battle array and turned back. This is echoed by Henry of Huntingdon, though he places the kings as far apart as Carlisle and York, when 'fearing a rupture (they) mutually avoided meeting, and thus separated peaceably, each to his home.'

Stephen remained for some time around York, possibly still fearing an attack that didn't come. While he was there, he destroyed a castle outside the city, possibly at Wheldrake, which had been causing annoyance, and he proposed building one of his own at Beverley until, according to John of Hexham, he was dissuaded by an apparition of the local saint, John of Beverley, who threatened him. He also seems to have taken the opportunity of refilling his treasury by fining the citizens of Beverley for allowing Henry Murdac to reside there, and then levying a heavy tax on the chief men of York, 'according to the station of each and his amount of wealth'.

Meanwhile Henry was having an adventurous time on his journey south. The *Gesta* says men were sent from Stephen to try to intercept him on his way down to Hereford. Thereafter Eustace, who had been attacking the lands of Henry's supporters, set out to trap him himself. No less than three ambushes were laid on the last stage of his journey between Dursley and Bristol, but he avoided them all by travelling before he was expected, through the middle of the night. There was, says John of Hexham, 'a rivalry in excellence' between Henry and Eustace, 'for they both aimed at the sovereignty of the same kingdom.'

It was Eustace who now led attacks in Wiltshire, but when his father joined him, probably around high summer, a new policy was adopted. It was a scorched earth policy, according to the *Gesta*. Goods were plundered, houses and churches set ablaze, and even the newly harvested crops destroyed so as to leave nothing edible to support the enemy through the coming months. Special attention was given to the area around Marlborough and Devizes. It may be that attacks made at about this time on Lincoln by Ranulf of Chester, and on Bedford and in East Anglia by Payn de Beauchamp and Hugh Bigod, were intended to stop this wanton destruction. If so they were successful, drawing away, at least for a while, Stephen to Lincoln and Eustace to East Anglia.

Henry managed to regroup at Devizes and even launched an attack on one part of the West Country that was not already supporting him. Bridport in Dorset was captured, but then a sudden assault by Eustace on Devizes drew him quickly back to defend that essential stronghold, and Eustace was forced to withdraw. If the aim of all this brutality was to drive Henry away, it eventually succeeded. Probably reasoning that he could do nothing positive in the circumstances, and that the attacks would only stop when he was gone, Henry followed the advice of his supporters and early in January 1150 he withdrew to Normandy.

He had been away less than a year, but in that time a number of circumstances had changed. Although still short of his seventeenth birthday, he was clearly a man now, a challenger for the throne of England and heir to all that Geoffrey of Anjou had patiently built up across the Channel. Geoffrey himself was suffering increasing bouts of ill health. He had always seen himself as something of a caretaker duke in Normandy, claiming the land through his wife and son rather than as a conqueror, and it was at this point that he decided to hand over the duchy to Henry.

It was a decisive moment. Henry the upstart, Henry the son of an empress without a kingdom, was now duke of Normandy. He had acquired status, in rather the same way that William Clito had acquired status when he became Count of Flanders, and he now well outranked his rival Eustace both in that and in the resources available to him. There were bound to be consequences and they were not long in coming.

King Louis of France had returned from the Second Crusade barely two months before, and he had not returned in a good mood. The crusade had been an utter disaster from start to finish. He had set out, with Eleanor his queen, against the advice of his counsellors, and although the aim of the campaign had been to retake Edessa from the Turks, he had insisted instead on going to Jerusalem, and then beginning a fruitless siege of Damascus that lasted less than a week before the besiegers were driven away. In the course of his travels his army, and the larger one led by the German emperor Conrad, acquired a reputation for robbery and pillage. Then both were almost completely annihilated, together with with multitudes of camp followers. 'First,' says Henry of Huntingdon, 'they were wasted by famine ... and afterwards they were destroyed by the enemy's sword.' Robert of Torigny adds, 'since that enterprise had its commencement, for the most part, in pillaging the poor and robbing churches – the perpetrators of which disgraceful disorders escaped unpunished – nothing worthy of being remembered occurred in this expedition.'

There was something to be remembered, however, and that was the complete breakdown of the marriage between Louis and Eleanor. They had been married for a dozen years and had only one daughter, and the high-spirited Eleanor was clearly mismatched to a man she once referred to as 'a monk'. Her uncle Raymond was Prince of Antioch, and when the crusade reached that place, rumours began to fly about a far too close relationship between uncle and niece. When Louis spoke of continuing to Jerusalem, Eleanor asked to remain at Antioch but was forced against her will to leave with her husband. After the debacle at Damascus they sailed for home on separate ships and were apart for more than two months as a result of storms at sea and pirate attacks. Eventually reaching Italy, they visited the pope at Tusculum and it is believed Eleanor raised the possibility of an annulment of her marriage. The grounds for this would be the ones most conveniently used at the time to get rid of an unwanted spouse, consanguinity. The degrees of relationship within which one was forbidden to marry went far beyond those recognised today, and far beyond those likely to be in living memory of the family of the husband and wife concerned. Indeed, since the upper levels of society were restricted to marrying each other, most marriages involving treaties or land settlements, it was possible to find such a forbidden link in almost any marriage if one looked hard enough. In the present case both parties were descended from Robert II of France, who had lived more than 100 years before, but that still placed them within the prohibited degrees. The pope, however, was having none of it. He encouraged the pair to reconcile, and insisted they slept in the same 'marriage bed', which he blessed. The result was another pregnancy – and another daughter – but very little reconciliation.

Having, therefore, suffered extensive damage to his reputation, his treasury and his private life, Louis was unlikely to look kindly on any further challenges, such as those he identified in Normandy in January 1150. Not only was Geoffrey of Anjou besieging the castle of Louis's seneschal in Poitou, a man who had recently led an uprising in Anjou, but a new Duke of Normandy had apparently been invested without any consultation or the consent of the French king as the overlord of the duchy. This new duke, moreover, had a substantial claim to the throne of England. Louis had managed to stomach the uniting of Anjou and Normandy under Duke Geoffrey in 1144, but the thought that England might also fall into the same hands filled him with horror. Such a scenario would also mean that his sister was no longer in line to be Queen of England. From being vaguely neutral in the struggle going on for the English throne, Louis moved abruptly to the side of Stephen and his own brother-in-law, Eustace.

In this, of course, he would only be encouraged by envoys sent from Stephen about this time. If it seems surprising that Henry's short and fairly inconsequential visit to England should have inspired such sudden panic, it must be remembered that the whole basis of Stephen's seizure of England had now disappeared. He had based his claim on hereditary right, on the avoidance of a female ruler and on the backing of the church. He had now lost that wholehearted backing, and his opponent was a young and apparently capable male, whose hereditary claim was a long way superior to Stephen's own. No wonder then that having driven Henry back to Normandy, the English king was keen to carry on the fight in a duchy that he may still have harboured hopes of recovering.

The fact that nothing much happened in Normandy in 1150 is probably due to two things. Firstly, the church, particularly those clerics advising the French king, Arnulf, Bishop of Lisieux, and Suger, the abbot of St Denis, consistently urged all parties to seek peace. Secondly, the winter of 1149/50 was one of the hardest recorded. 'For three successive months,' says Robert of Torigny, 'the winter was so exceedingly severe, that the extremity of the cold injured the limbs of many persons.' This harsh weather continued through the spring, 'when agricultural operations are carried on' and resulted in widespread famine.

This was true both in Normandy and in England, where 1150 was also a quiet year. The only recorded action was Stephen's unsuccessful attempt to take the castle at Worcester from Waleran de Meulan's constable, William de Beauchamp. In England, though, there may have been another quite different reason for the inaction. There Stephen was finding his nobility less and less inclined to fight. Even William of Ypres had become old and blind, while others, though still supporting one side or the other, were actively making agreements with each other to limit the potential damage to their lands.

It would be reasonable to expect those on the same side to agree to support each other in time of war. Robert of Gloucester, for example, had such a treaty with Miles, Earl of Hereford, which was later renewed by their respective sons, while a serious dispute between Patrick of Salisbury and John Marshal was settled in the usual way, by a marriage, in this case of John to Patrick's sister. By 1150, however, agreements were being made for advantage across party lines. William, the new Earl of Gloucester, for instance, whom the *Gesta* dismisses as 'a chamber knight, not a brave soldier', handed back to the Bishop of Salisbury all the bishop's lands around Sherborne, in return for being allowed to continue his occupation of the castle itself.

A prime mover in making these agreements seems to have been Robert, Earl of Leicester. Not only did he form an alliance with William of Gloucester by marrying his daughter to the young earl, but his later agreement with Ranulf of Chester is an even more surprising 'non-aggression pact' between two who had spent years trying to get the better of each other. They now laid down a considerable number of rules to regulate their future relations. To foster peace between them there would be no more castle building in what had previously been the most fiercely contested area. Each would help the other against anyone except his liege lord and one other named person, in the Earl of Leicester's case, Simon of Senlis, Earl of Northampton. Furthermore, they would not fight each other unless giving a fifteen-day notice of 'defiance' first, or unless required to do so by their liege lord, and if they were so required, only twenty knights, the minimum possible, should be committed to the struggle. Any goods captured in such a fight would be returned later. It is notable that nowhere in the agreement is the 'liege lord' named, nor the fact that each was committed to a different lord. This was an agreement between themselves, guaranteed by the new Bishop of Lincoln, and part of a network that meant most of the major magnates of England would do much to avoid confronting each other in furtherance of a struggle which they no longer fully believed in.

By 1150 Stephen had fallen out with the church to such an extent that he refused a papal legate safe conduct to travel through England to Ireland. He was still trying to get his son crowned, however, and this desire so overruled everything else that at the very end of the year he finally agreed to accept Henry Murdac as Archbishop of York, this despite the fact that William fitz Herbert was at the time residing with Bishop Henry of Winchester. It was apparently a major part of the deal that Murdac would then travel to Rome on the king's behalf. Almost immediately after his installation at York on 25 January 1151, therefore, the archbishop set off, his mission, according to John of Hexham, 'that the king's son Eustace, might be established by papal authority as heir to the throne.' Stephen's logic was impeccable. Murdac was a Cistercian, a friend of fellow Cistercians Pope Eugenius and Bernard of Clairvaux. Surely this time...? But the answer was still 'no'. There was some sign of recognition as the heir, but no movement at all on the issue of a coronation. Now more than ever, both father and son needed to bring about the downfall of the only realistic rival, Henry, Duke of Normandy. In the summer of 1151 the alliance of Louis VII and his brother-in-law Eustace, mooted the year before, finally sprang into action. Eustace himself attacked Normandy from the north-east, initially taking the fortress of Neufchâtel, then moving to Arques to threaten Rouen from the north. Louis meanwhile, with his brother Robert, Count of Dreux, moved up from the south through lands belonging to Waleran de Meulan, who had grown closer to the French court during the rigours of the crusade. Robert initially penetrated the duchy far enough to burn the town of Sées. Then, in the month of August, Robert Torigny describes the build-up to what should have been a major battle. 'King Louis marched, with all his power, to the banks of the Seine between Meulan and Mantes. Equally energetically, Geoffrey, Count of Anjou, and Henry his son, Duke of Normandy, marshalled their forces, and sat down on the borders of Normandy to defend their own.'

The battle never came. Louis fell ill – 'as I believe by God's disposal,' says Torigny – and 'some wise and religious men mediated between them,' arranging a truce to last until the king had recovered. The truce turned into a peace agreement and as quickly as the war had begun it was ended. Geoffrey and Henry travelled to Paris, where Henry obtained recognition of his status as Duke of Normandy at the cost of doing homage to Louis and handing over part of the Norman Vexin, which had, in fact, already been promised on an earlier occasion. Deserted by his ally, Eustace had to hand back all he had taken and return home. If he had finished with Henry in Normandy, however, at least temporarily, Henry had by no means finished with him. He hurried to Lisieux, calling a council of his Norman magnates to begin planning an invasion of England. Once more, however, fate would intervene between the two.

While Henry was hurrying to Lisieux, Geoffrey had returned to Anjou and there he was suddenly stricken with a severe fever. A story tells how he went swimming in a cold river and, presumably, caught a chill. Whatever the cause, it rapidly worsened, and in the poetic words of Robert of Torigny, it 'carried him off upon the road appointed for all living'; on 7 September, at Chateau-du-Loir, Geoffrey of Anjou died. 'He was a man of great worth,' adds Torigny, 'and was universally lamented,' but his untimely death just after his thirty-eighth birthday was to cause some unexpected problems for his son Henry.

William of Newburgh, writing some time later and a long way away from the action, carries a story not found elsewhere of detailed dispositions made by Geoffrey on his deathbed. 'In his last hours,' he says, 'he bequeathed by will the county of Anjou to his second son,' that is to say, to Geoffrey. This was because he was unwilling that provision for his younger sons 'should be wholly dependent on their brother's good-will, not knowing how he might be disposed towards them.'

Once again this sounds like a less than united family, but then they had probably been scattered by circumstances since they were barely old enough to leave their mother's household. There was a proviso, however, to this gift. Geoffrey was only to come into possession of Anjou when Henry had 'obtained the fullness of his mother's right, that is, Normandy together with England'. In the meantime, Geoffrey was to be contented with three substantial castles, at Chinon, Loudon and Mirabeau.

Henry was not present at his father's deathbed so, again according to Newburgh, the nobles and churchmen who were present were bound by an oath that they would not allow Geoffrey's body to be buried until Henry had sworn to abide by this last will. When the duke did arrive, he was apparently very reluctant to swear this oath, particularly as he was not given access to the will. Eventually he gave in to pleas not to let his father's body putrefy unburied and took the required oath, though later he was freed from the obligation by the pope as it had not been sworn freely.

None of this appears in Torigny, who was closer in both time and geography. According to him, Henry got Anjou, and Geoffrey got four castles, and there is some suspicion that the story was later planted by Geoffrey to justify his dissatisfaction with his brother's good fortune. At the time Henry was so little concerned about his prospects in Anjou that he did not hold his first council there and require fealty from his vassals until several months after his father's funeral. In the meantime, he had returned to Normandy to ensure there would be no sudden rush on the part of his outside enemies to take advantage of his father's death.

It must be remembered that Henry was still only eighteen years old, and now fully in charge of an extensive and potentially troublesome territory. Nor had he abandoned his ambitions to extend that territory. The council at Lisieux had, of course, come to nothing. There would be no assault on England that year, but Henry had time on his side and through the appalling weather of the autumn of 1151, was almost certainly already planning the next year's campaign. When he had left England, he had probably intended to be away only long enough to raise sufficient resources for a determined attempt on the throne. He had already been away for two years, however, and although the uneasy balance of power in that land had not shifted, there was always a chance that it might, particularly if Stephen could prevail on the pope to authorise the coronation of his son.

In the spring of 1152 Reginald de Dunstanville was sent from England to urge Henry to hurry up with his intended invasion but, in fact, the year was to be one dominated by deaths and by one spectacular marriage. The first of the deaths was that of Count Theobald of Blois, brother of King Stephen and Bishop Henry, who died at the end of January. He left a number of territories to be divided up among his numerous children, and his eldest son, Henry, chose to become Count of Champagne, considered to be a lesser county at the time, though he would go on to make it great. Theobald, the second son, therefore became Count of Blois, and a third son, Stephen, Count of Sancerre.

It may have been this hint of mortality that inspired the English king to try again to secure the throne for his own son. At his Easter court in London at the end of March, Eustace was acknowledged as heir by 'a good number of nobles', who may even have sworn fealty to him. Then, says Henry of Huntingdon, Stephen 'required Theobald, Archbishop of Canterbury, and the other bishops whom he had assembled with that design, to anoint him king, and give him their solemn benediction.' Theobald, by now papal legate in England, refused to do so, and was firmly backed by the other bishops. Again the decree of Pope Celestine was quoted, and this time, boldly, the reason for it, that Stephen had wrongfully obtained the throne of England by breaking his oath to King Henry.

'Upon this,' says Huntingdon, 'both father and son, greatly disappointed and incensed, ordered the bishops to be shut up together, and by threats and hardships endeavoured to compel them to comply with their demand.' The churchmen were alarmed, he says, 'for Stephen never much liked the bishops,' but still they stood firm. By one account Theobald escaped and went briefly into exile in Flanders, but the king quickly realised he had gone too far this time. The bishops were released and their possessions returned to them. What little chance had ever existed of getting Eustace crowned, however, was clearly gone for ever. The only alternative now for Stephen to secure his dynasty was to get rid of the hated rival in Normandy.

For a time it seemed as though fate was playing into the hands of the English king, as Henry appeared to be going out of his way to pile up enemies. On 21 March 1152 a council of the church at Beaugency in France finally accepted that the marriage of Louis VII and Eleanor of Aquitaine was prohibited by reason of consanguinity. It was duly annulled, though without affecting the legitimacy of their two daughters, one of whom was only about eighteen months old, and Eleanor immediately departed for her own lands in Poitou. She was now once again a very eligible lady, and one person who appreciated this fact was Henry's brother Geoffrey, who apparently lay in ambush to abduct her and marry her himself. According to William of Newburgh, however, Eleanor already had plans to marry someone else. Even during her marriage to Louis, he claims, 'she aspired to a marriage with the Duke of Normandy, as more congenial to her feelings.'

She can only have met Henry for the first time the previous August when he and his father were in Paris, but that was enough to make her determined to secure a divorce from Louis in order to marry a man some nine years her junior. Nor did they wait very long to do so. Having evaded Geoffrey's trap, of which she was forewarned, Newburgh claims that she and the duke, 'having met at an appointed place, were then united by the conjugal tie.' The wedding took place on 18 May at Poitiers, and was carried out 'not very splendidly ... but with guarded prudence, lest any pompous preparation for their nuptials should allow any obstacle to arise.' No doubt many obstacles might have arisen to prevent such a scandalous marriage, apparently arranged by the parties themselves, without the permission of an overlord, and within two months of the divorce of the bride from the overlord himself. Not only was Louis personally insulted, but the territorial implications were huge.

'Soon afterwards,' says Newburgh, 'The Duchy of Aquitaine, which extends from the borders of Anjou and Brittany to the Pyrenees ... gradually withdrawing itself from the power of France, yielded to the dominion of the Duke of Normandy, in right of his wife.' By his marriage Henry had acquired not only a wife, but mastery over roughly a third of the entire area of France.

11

'A Very Good Peace'

(May 1152 – December 1154)

The marriage of his former wife Eleanor to Henry Plantagenet, and Henry's subsequent absorption of the Duchy of Aquitaine into what was rapidly becoming an Angevin empire, was a situation Louis of France could not allow to go unchallenged. He did not have to look far, however, for allies to take action against the upstart. His brother Robert of Dreux had scores to settle with Anjou. The new counts of Champagne and Blois, the sons of Count Theobald, would step into their father's shoes as supporters of Stephen and opponents of the Angevin faction, and had an additional motive in that they themselves felt threatened by this sudden expansion of Henry's power. A more unexpected ally, but therefore doubly welcome, was Henry's brother Geoffrey. Not only was he angry that Henry had inherited *all* their father's possessions, but the duke had now also acquired the wife Geoffrey had himself meant to take by force, a wife who would have made him his brother's equal in power and wealth.

The most obvious allies for Louis were, of course, Stephen, King of England, and his son Eustace. They would certainly be keen to resume the fight against Henry, but were a little delayed in joining the alliance owing to a personal tragedy of their own. On 3 May, at Hedingham Castle in Essex, Queen Matilda died. We don't know the exact cause of her death, but she had been present at the Easter court, and had been visiting a great friend, the Countess of Essex, wife of Earl Aubrey de Vere, when she was taken ill. There was certainly time enough for her husband and son to reach her deathbed, and there is no doubt that her passing was a great shock to both of them. It is no exaggeration to say that Matilda was an equal partner in her marriage, and her death deprived Stephen of a firm support and a wise and steadfast counsellor. Her body was initially taken to London and then into Kent, to Faversham Abbey, the new foundation whose building she herself had carefully overseen in recent years. Far sooner than they had intended, her burial there would be the first in Stephen's new dynastic church.

It is probable that Eustace was now formally installed as the new Count of Boulogne, and soon after that he was ready to join the concerted attack on Henry in Normandy. Torigny, in his list of Henry's enemies, omits the name of Theobald, the new Count of Blois, but all the others are there. The alliance, he says, had the aim of 'depriving Henry of the lordships of Normandy and Anjou, and of the Duchy of Aquitaine ... and indeed of stripping him of all his possessions,' which would then be divided up among the allies.

It seems impossible that Henry could not have had some suspicions as to their intentions, but at the end of June when they were finalising their plans he was at Barfleur, again engaged in preparing for an invasion of England. He had an army, but it was in the wrong place when the alliance finally moved against him on a number of fronts at once. Torigny describes how Geoffrey 'had undertaken to harass (Henry) to the uttermost in Anjou', while the main force attacked and besieged a key castle of Neuf-Marché on the border of Normandy. We can believe Torigny's account of a mighty thunderstorm over the castle and its surrender due to the treachery of the garrison, but the tale of 'an immense dragon' flying over can surely be discounted.

'Nearly all the Normans now thought that Duke Henry would speedily lose the whole of his possessions,' he writes, but the young duke would not go down so easily, and 'conducted himself with the greatest prudence, manfully defending himself on all sides.' Nowhere did he directly engage Louis, his overlord, though it came close when the French king crossed the Seine at Meulan and attempted to outflank the Norman defences. Henry's rapid appearance at Pacy-sur-Eure forced a sudden retreat, however, and his forces contained and beat back their attackers to such good effect that by the end of August the duke himself felt free to go into Anjou and take the war to his brother. Geoffrey crumbled under the onslaught and quickly came to terms, and by the autumn King Louis himself was also prepared to agree a truce. In the north-east Eustace was still besieging the castle of Neufchâtel, but bereft of allies he had got no further when Henry made up his mind to draw him off by taking the war to England.

In that country, too, there was a pressing need for vigorous leadership as Stephen was again attempting to drive the followers of the empress back into their heartland of Bristol and Gloucester. To this end he had attacked John Marshal's outpost at Newbury, and we have some surprising details of this action from a biography of John's son, the famous William Marshal. As a boy of some five years of age, he was left as a hostage with the king as part of a truce, while John apparently went to consult about surrendering the castle. It may well be that, by this time, there was some confidence that Stephen did not make war on women and children. In any event, rather than surrender the castle, John took the opportunity to restock and re-garrison it, before departing to Marlborough, leaving his son to his fate. The biography declares that the child was paraded before the garrison and it was threatened, among other things, that he would be hanged or hurled from a siege engine if they did not surrender, but to no avail. Apparently oblivious of these threats, the boy chatted happily to his captors, even asking the Earl of Arundel if he would let him hold the 'fine javelin' he had, and so melted the king's heart that he took him in his arms and declared: 'You will not die today.' There is even a touching scene describing the two of them playing in the king's tent with straw soldiers, and apparently William remained safely with Stephen for some time.

If the king's heart had softened towards John's son, it had hardened towards John and his fellows. Newbury was duly taken, and Wallingford was soon under a more determined siege than it had seen for some time. A counter-castle was built just across the river at Crowmarsh, and a large force was camped about the place, defeating all attempts to relieve or resupply the fortress. According to Henry of Huntingdon, after some months of this the traditional petition was sent to Duke Henry, that he must 'either send them relief, or that they might have licence to surrender the castle into the king's hands.'

The loss of Wallingford after all this time would have been a huge blow, and it may well have been this petition that decided Henry to make his long-awaited reappearance in England. Matters in Normandy were still finely balanced and he could not afford to strip the duchy of its armed men. Consequently, he left most of his forces behind under the command of his newly reconciled brother Geoffrey, and travelled to England in a flotilla of thirty-six ships, with only 140 knights and 3,000 men. He came at a most unexpected time of year, in early January 1153, an occasion causing Henry of Huntingdon to break into poetry as he imagined a ruined, exhausted England calling for a saviour. 'She turns to thee her dim and feeble eye, But scarce can raise the suppliant's plaintive cry; "Save me, oh save me! Henry, or I die."' And the answer, '"I come to cause the tyrant's rule to cease," And o'er the gasping land spread smiling peace; ... Or lifeless on thy bloodstained soil to lie, For thee to conquer, or for thee to die.'

Dramatic stuff! No doubt it should be followed by a mighty battle where the tiny force of the liberator overcomes the power of the tyrant – but not in this case. Henry had taken in his father's hard-learned lessons. Be cautious, be careful, and if you are overmatched, avoid the greater risks involved in open battle. In any case, the majority of the magnates were by now in no mood to fight. Among themselves they had achieved a sort of peace, and the wiser heads might even have been looking for an opportunity to extend it to the whole country. It is a small but interesting point that none of the chronicles, even the most contemporary, refer to Stephen's son as 'Prince Eustace'. He is always 'the son of King Stephen.' Compromise was becoming the order of the day.

Henry probably landed at Wareham and moved quickly to Devizes where he gathered around him his chief supporters.

These included the earls of Cornwall, Chester, Lincoln, Gloucester and Hereford, who, according to Huntingdon, were somewhat disappointed at the numbers he had brought with him. While the loyalty of most of these had already stood the test of time, that of Ranulf of Chester was rapidly cemented by promises of the county of Stafford to add to his English territories, together with a return of Norman lands and powers, particularly in the area of Avranches where there were family roots.

Instead of rushing to attack the strong force that Stephen had planted around Wallingford, Henry's first target was the castle at Malmesbury, an equally important outlier of the king's territories. The town was stormed, but the castle, under the command of a man known only as Jordan, held out, while Jordan himself escaped to inform the king of the siege. By this time Eustace had returned to England and he accompanied his father to Malmesbury with 'many thousands of armed men', apparently ready and willing to settle with Henry there and then. If the duke's aim had been to take the pressure off Wallingford, he had succeeded, but it is not clear whether he had really meant to provoke a straight fight with the king so soon. William of Newburgh says when Stephen arrived, Henry simply remained in his camp and refused battle, but Henry of Huntingdon has a more interesting version of events.

'The day after his arrival,' he says, Stephen 'drew up his army in battle array,' and marched in good order to where Henry had drawn up his own more limited forces, on the bank of a river near the town walls. However, says Huntingdon, God was not with the king, 'For the floodgates of heaven were opened, and heavy rain drove in their faces, with violent gusts of wind and severe cold.' Not only rain, but snow and sleet poured down – it was January, after all – so that the river between them became impossible to cross. Huntingdon is clear that God is on Henry's side, since he and his men had the rain and wind on their backs, 'while it drove in the faces of the king and his army, so that they could hardly support their armour and handle their spears, dripping with wet.' Then, he says, 'the king could no longer endure the severity of the weather,' and withdrew to London.

It may have been more than the weather, though, that made Stephen turn back. For one thing there was probably little food available for his men in the area. For another, the *Gesta* suggests that even those of the king's followers who had been most trustworthy in the past now showed signs of making conciliatory approaches to Henry. It is possible that, even this early in the year, the seeds of peace were being quietly sown. Some sort of truce was apparently agreed, with a condition that the castle at Malmesbury be pulled down. Instead, as soon as the king had departed, it was handed over to Henry, who then allowed his men some respite from their struggles in the depths of the winter. We are not told how Eustace reacted to this outcome, though even he may have realised a cold, wet January was no time for a battle.

In the course of his account of events at Malmesbury, Huntingdon declares: 'It was the Almighty's design that his child' (meaning Henry) 'should gain possession of the kingdom without the effusion of blood.' This, of course, was written with the benefit of hindsight, but certainly from that point on there seems to have been a steady tide running Henry's way, not for a total and devastating triumph, but for the achievement of his ends by means of slow and peaceful compromises. This may not have been the intention of either the duke or the king – and along the way there were flashpoints that might have ended the whole process – but both seem to have been carried along by outside influences, until the end became almost inevitable.

Sometime in February or March the town of Southampton was surrendered to Henry. While he was there, we find witnessing a charter for him the most surprising name of Joscelin de Louvain, younger brother of Queen Adeliza who had died in 1151. Joscelin had been provided with an estate in Sussex where he was a tenant of his brother-in-law, William, Earl of Arundel, who had been at Stephen's side throughout his reign. Since the death of Adeliza, however, both held their lands only by the goodwill of Stephen, and it has been suggested that this first contact with the duke was made, probably on behalf of both of them, with the aim of being on the right side of whatever settlement the year might throw up.

Such a settlement seemed to come a step closer a few weeks later, when we find Henry and his chief supporters meeting at Stockbridge with the senior clerics of England. Stockbridge was the place where the party of the empress had suffered its most serious setback in 1141, with the capture of Earl Robert on the retreat from Winchester. Whether that was in anyone's mind at the time we don't know. It may simply have been a conveniently neutral place to meet, with a river between the rival parties. It does seem, however, that the meeting was a significant one.

Ostensibly it was about Henry's continued occupation of the castle at Devizes, and an agreement was made with the Bishop of Salisbury that he should have it for a further three years. The witnesses to this agreement, however, included the earls of Cornwall and Gloucester, John Marshal, the Archbishop of Canterbury, Bishop Henry of Winchester and the bishops of Bath and Chichester, which suggests there was far more to the meeting than that.

Since the death of his wife, Stephen seems to have drawn closer to his brother once more, but in recent years the agenda of the church had moved well away from outright support for the king. Without knowing the detail of what was discussed at the meeting, then, it is probably reasonable to suppose that there might have been some exploration of each side's position, and that at least tentative suggestions might have been made as to what sort of settlement they might eventually find acceptable.

Further, it seems likely that some kind of extended truce may have been agreed, since, for the next few months, Stephen and Henry stayed well away from each other and did nothing to provoke an immediate confrontation.

While Stephen continued his blockade of Wallingford, Henry withdrew to his own side of the country, spending Easter in mid-April at his 'royal' castle of Gloucester. There, not only did he formally assume the title 'Duke of Aquitaine', but he welcomed another sign that England was warming to him. For a long time, Robert, Earl of Leicester, had done his best to stay out of the wider struggles for the kingdom, acting only to protect his own holdings (against Ranulf of Chester) and those of his brother (against all comers), for example when destroying the siege castles the king had erected at Worcester a year or so before. Now it was his son, also Robert, who appeared at Henry's side, first at Bristol and then at Gloucester, and who was immediately rewarded with the Norman honours of Breteuil, conveniently left available by the death of William de Pacy. This was done, says Torigny, 'because he was the lawful heir on his mother's side', but it also indicated to his father that an approach would be welcomed, and, sure enough, the earl himself duly appeared at Gloucester.

He was the last major defector to Henry's side, and the last substantial source of support, for King David of Scotland, who might at this stage have ventured forth again, died on 24 May at Carlisle. 'There has been no prince like him in our days,' laments John of Hexham, but David had had his own worries in the last year. His son Henry, Earl of Northumberland and Huntingdon and heir to the Scottish throne, had died unexpectedly in June 1152, leaving an eleven-year-old son, Malcolm, and David had spent the interim period introducing him to the people of Scotland as his heir. Henry's earldom of Huntingdon passed to Simon of Senlis, whom, it seems, alone of Stephen's followers, would not be tempted from his side, so Duke Henry could look for no help from that quarter.

From Gloucester the duke moved to Leicester with his new friend Earl Robert, and was there in time for Pentecost at the beginning of June. By this stage he was not only confirming the earl in his Norman lands but also confirming the territorial adjustments he had made in England with his cousin, Earl Roger of Warwick, another sign that his star was rising while Stephen's was on the wane. The castle at Warwick had for some time been garrisoned by the king's men, and the earl himself was in the south with Stephen. Now, however, his wife Gundreda, who was half-sister to Robert of Leicester, tricked the garrison into handing over the castle to Henry. When the news was taken to Earl Roger on 12 June he collapsed and died, though whether from shock or shame is hard to tell.

At this time Henry seems to have confined his actions to the Midlands, possibly at the request of the earls of Chester and Leicester, picking off a castle here and there and burning the town of Bedford. It was only at the beginning of August that he turned south again, to attempt to relieve the Siege of Wallingford. It has been suggested that whatever informal truce had existed with Stephen ran out at this time, or possibly it was simply that the besieged were hard pressed and appealed for help. Huntingdon declares they were 'now almost exhausted by famine'. It is Huntingdon, too, who claims Henry was able to resupply the castle, but his main aim was to destroy Stephen's counter-castle at Crowmarsh. Unable to take it by storm, he established his own camp outside, blockading the blockaders, and thereby causing Stephen to strike back. Torigny reports an attack by William de Chesney from Oxford, which was beaten off. Then Henry, in what might be seen as a major statement of intent, ordered his own men to return any plunder that had been taken to its rightful owners. 'He had come,' he said, 'for the purpose of delivering the poor from the pillaging hands of their powerful oppressors, and not that he should plunder them himself.' His aim may well have been to distance himself from earlier methods employed in the conduct of the war, and to this end one chronicler at least declares he used no mercenary soldiers in his actions at Crowmarsh.

By sitting down outside Wallingford, however, Henry had made himself a target. Stephen was not slow to appreciate the fact, and, says Huntingdon, 'assembling the whole force he could muster throughout his territories, seriously threatened the duke's position.' Henry, in turn, 'raising the siege, marched out in good order against the enemy.' There was no rain, snow or wild river between them this time, and it seemed inevitable the final battle was about to take place. 'Then,' says Huntingdon, 'the traitorous nobles interfered.'

Torigny puts it a little differently. 'Certain religious persons,' he says, 'moderated between them.' Whichever way it happened the result was the same. The armies simply refused to fight. They 'proposed among themselves terms of peace,' including a five-day truce, the removal of the castle at Crowmarsh and the requirement that Henry and Stephen meet face to face to arrange future negotiations. Huntingdon imputes, probably unjustly, that the magnates arranged this because they wanted to prolong the war rather than achieve a final peace. 'They felt no desire to exalt either the one or the other of the pretenders to the throne' because, by humbling one, 'they might be entirely subject to the other.' They preferred that 'the two being in mutual fear, the royal authority should ... be kept in abeyance.' This seems an unfair reading of the situation, and not at all borne out by the subsequent behaviour of those involved.

That the king and duke were not enthusiastic participants in this turn of events is clearly shown by the comments of the chroniclers. For Huntingdon, they were 'reluctantly compelled to make a truce between themselves,' while Torigny puts it rather higher, at least on the part of the duke. When he was told of the terms agreed, which Torigny thought were most honourable ones, 'he took the matter very ill,' and complained about the actions of his friends, 'who had accepted such terms as those, and pledged his word for their performance.'

The duke did, however, agree to them, and they were duly carried out. Some prisoners were returned to Stephen, the Crowmarsh castle was dismantled, and king and duke 'had a conference together, without witnesses, across a rivulet, on the terms of a lasting accommodation between themselves', each apparently grumbling about the faithlessness of their followers.

This was not a peace. It may not even have been the beginning of the peace, which likely dated back to the meeting at Stockbridge earlier. It was, however, the first time the rivals had been brought face to face to admit that there should be a peace, and probably to authorise others to continue negotiations on their behalf. The one person notably absent from this conference, either overlooked or excluded by the assembled magnates, though he was present at Wallingford, was Eustace.

It would have been completely obvious to him that any lasting peace settlement between his father and Duke Henry would involve himself as the sacrificial lamb. Henry would settle for nothing less than the crown, even if a little postponed. Stephen was, at the very least, approaching his sixties and might be expected to die within the next handful of years, but there was never any likelihood of power-sharing between Henry and Eustace. As a result, Eustace took himself off to his base at Cambridge, attempting to extort money from the abbey at Bury St Edmunds, presumably to fund his own private war with Henry. Being refused, he vented his fury on the lands of the abbey, returned with his plunder to Cambridge, sat down to a meal of his ill-gotten gains and promptly died. Food poisoning, deliberate poison and the wrath of God have all been suggested as the cause, but to misuse a quote from Shakespeare, 'Nothing in his life became him like the leaving of it.'

The chroniclers are almost ecstatic. Says William of Newburgh, his death afforded 'an admirable opportunity for laying the basis of a reconciliation between the princes,' which, had he lived, his 'youthful impetuosity' and 'lofty pretensions' would surely have prevented. Huntingdon adds that, in consequence of his death, and that of Simon of Senlis who died in the same week, 'the hopes and courage of all who were opposed to the duke vanished at once.' It certainly reduced the problems facing the peacemakers, chief among them Archbishop Theobald and Henry of Winchester, who now set to work to hammer out an acceptable agreement. In particular, John of Hexham says, Bishop Henry 'strenuously exerted himself to promote the interests of Duke Henry,' which Huntingdon puts down to a bad conscience over giving the crown to Stephen in the first place.

In the meantime, almost to keep their hand in, as it were, Henry and Stephen besieged and took castles far apart, Stamford, in the case of Henry, and Ipswich in the case of Stephen. An attack was also made by Henry on William Peverel's castle at Nottingham, at the request of Ranulf of Chester, who believed William had tried to poison him.

Several months passed before, on 6 November 1153, the king and the duke met again, this time at Winchester, not to debate the terms of a settlement but to ratify the terms that had now been threshed out. There in the cathedral, before magnates and clergy from both sides, Stephen formally established Henry as his heir to the kingdom of England 'by hereditary right'. In return, Henry did homage to the king and swore to accept him as his liege man, and to honour and protect him in accordance with the terms of their agreement. Many of these terms related to settlements made on Stephen's second son, William, who had no pretensions to the crown and was happy to accept all that was given him and do homage to Henry in his turn. Stephen also undertook to govern, with the advice of Henry, in all parts of the kingdom, and Henry, at least according to John of Hexham, undertook to be guided by Bishop Henry. There were oaths to be sworn and homage paid by the supporters of each to the other side, and the terms included the destruction of all castles built without permission during the time of trouble, and the return of all land to those who held it 'on the day when King Henry was alive and dead,' that is, on 1 December 1135.

'What boundless joy,' says Henry of Huntingdon, 'what a day of rejoicing, when the king himself led the illustrious young prince through the streets of Winchester.' The joy followed them to London in December, where the agreement was formally written down and sealed. There was a joint Christmas court at Westminster, and another joint court at Oxford when, on 13 January 1154, many of the magnates formally performed the homage and swore the oaths required of them. One who had missed out on all of this, however, was Ranulf of Chester, who had been taken ill on the road to Derby and had died on 16 December 1153. His death would enable Henry to fulfil one of the promises he had made, by stripping away all the lands Ranulf had acquired over a period of a dozen or more years, leaving his young heir with only those estates held in 1135.

In the following months the agreement seemed to be working well. There was, says John of Hexham, an edict issued 'for the suppression of outrages, the prohibition of spoliation, the dismissal from the kingdom of mercenary soldiers and archers of foreign nations, and the destruction of the fortresses which ... everyone had built on his own property.' Except for a mild falling out in January when Henry declared that, 'by the indulgence or the policy of the king,' Stephen was not being firm enough in the demolition of castles, the relationship between the two seemed to be good. From Oxford to Dunstable and back to the south again, their joint progress appeared to be entirely amicable. Says Henry of Huntingdon: 'Thus, through God's mercy, after a night of misery, peace dawned on the ruined realm of England.'

In March 1154 Henry returned to Normandy, his confidence in his position in England shown by his taking with him the earls of Cornwall and Leicester, two of his most formidable supporters. Torigny reports a number of attempted incursions by Louis of France while the duke had been away, but these had all been dealt with by the men he had left behind, with Geoffrey, no doubt, being advised by his mother Matilda who was still active in affairs despite her retirement at Notre Dame du Pré. Peace was eventually made with Louis in the following August.

'During this time,' says William of Newburgh, 'King Stephen, making a progress through England with royal pomp, and exhibiting himself as a new monarch, was received and regarded by all with becoming respect.' He was, says Huntingdon, 'for the first time reigning in peace'. How long could it last? Even now Huntingdon suggests that certain persons 'made zealous attempts to sow the seeds of discord between the king who was present and the duke at a distance.' He names no names, however, and nor does anyone else suggest any falling away from the agreement so solemnly made.

If Stephen was enjoying himself in the summer of 1154, perhaps we could forgive him, and he had not long to enjoy the kingship he had so earnestly desired back in 1135. In October he was meeting with Thierry of Flanders at Dover when he suddenly fell ill, possibly with dysentery. A few days later, on 25 October, he breathed his last at Dover Priory, and was laid to rest with his wife and son in Faversham Abbey.

Urgent messages were sent to Normandy by Archbishop Theobald, urging Henry to hurry to his new kingdom, but in fact he was held up by the weather and 'other circumstances' for some time. Since the other circumstances including besieging and taking a castle at Torigny, we might conclude that Henry was supremely confident in his succession and felt no need of haste. His judgement was confirmed by both Huntingdon and

Robert of Torigny who report that in the interval England was 'perfectly tranquil,' while his accession to the throne was never called in question.

Finally, just before Christmas, Henry arrived in England with his wife and brothers, and he was consecrated and crowned king of England in Westminster Abbey on 19 December 1154. There was, says Huntingdon, 'becoming pomp and splendour, amidst universal rejoicings, which many mingled with tears of joy.' The nineteen years of winter recorded in the Anglo-Saxon Chronicle was finally over. England had a new and undisputed king and, so it says, 'all the people loved him, because he did good justice and made peace.'

12

Anarchy?

'The beginning and course of (Stephen's) reign was overwhelmed with so many and so violent discordant commotions, that how to describe them, or what may be their termination, no one can yet know.' So wrote Richard of Hexham, who experienced first-hand the upheavals in the north of England in the early years of the reign.

In his entry for 1140 Henry of Huntingdon breaks into verse.

> Oh! for a font of tears to flow
> And weep my country's bitter woe ...
> Fated intestine wars to see
> Fire, fury, blood and cruelty...
> A castle's wall are no defence
> Against the sons of violence ...
> Churches in vain and holy ground
> Which erst religion fenced around,
> Open their gates to shelter those
> Who refuge seek from bloody foes...
> Gaunt famine, following, wastes away
> Whom murder spares, with slow decay.

He finishes, despairing for England,

> The cup of mingled woe she drains.
> All hell's let loose and chaos reigns.'

'At this period,' says the *Gesta*, covering the events of the following year, 'England was in a very disturbed state: on the one hand, the king and those who took his part grievously oppressed the people, on the other frequent turmoils were raised by the Earl of Gloucester; and what with the tyranny of the one, and the turbulence of the other, there was universal turmoil and desolation.'

'Then was corn dear, and flesh and cheese and butter, for there was none in the land.' Thus says the monk at Peterborough continuing the Anglo-Saxon Chronicle. 'Wretched men starved with hunger – some lived on alms who had been erstwhile rich; some fled the country – never was there more misery, and never acted heathens worse than these … well mightest thou walk a whole day's journey nor ever shouldst thou find a man seated in a town or its lands tilled.' He concludes in one of the most famous passages from the Chronicle, 'The earth bare no corn, you might as well have tilled the sea, for the land was all ruined by such deeds, and it was said openly that Christ and his saints slept. These things, and more than we can say, did we suffer during nineteen years because of our sins.'

There is a striking unanimity in the accounts of robbery, bloodshed and devastation, but it was the Victorian historian John Horace Round who first labelled the period as 'The Anarchy', a term that has been challenged by later writers. If we take a dictionary definition of the word – 'a state of lawlessness due to the absence or inefficiency of the supreme power' – we can see why Round felt it an appropriate description for the period. It is worth considering, however, whether the 'lawlessness' was quite as long-lasting and widespread as the label implies, and, indeed, if it was really 'law-less', or perhaps simply playing to a different set of rules for much of the reign.

It is certainly true that there was a great deal of violence, and that most of the country suffered at some point in the nearly nineteen years of Stephen's reign. The exception to this is the extreme south-east – London, Kent, Surrey, Middlesex and Essex. This heartland of support for the king escaped almost entirely the bitter struggles found in other areas. Even in 1141, Empress Matilda entered London only by invitation, and was chased away by a singularly bloodless revolution. Other areas were not so lucky, though in the majority of cases the violence was short and sharp before order of a kind was restored, though not necessarily the king's order. In the far north, for example, which suffered extremes of barbarity, the major conflict was virtually over by 1139 when King David and his son were granted lawful possession of Northumbria and Carlisle. Similarly, in the south-west, at least from 1143 onwards, the king's writ had ceased to run, and the area was fully controlled by Robert of Gloucester and his adherents. Even the *Gesta* admits that they then set about 'restoring peace and tranquillity', albeit demanding the labour of the people in the construction of castles. Bristol was besieged only once, and Gloucester and Hereford, after it had been taken for the empress, not at all. East Anglia, too, apart from the brief rampage of Geoffrey de Mandeville, by and large escaped the turmoil of some other regions.

By far the worst and most prolonged violence was mainly suffered in two areas. The first, reflecting the struggle between king and empress, was the wide strip of land in central southern England between Cirencester and Oxford in the north and Devizes and Reading in the south. Here warfare of a kind flowed back and forth for well over a decade. In the north Midlands, too, in Staffordshire and the north and east of Leicestershire, the violence between Ranulf of Chester and Robert of Leicester dragged on for a number of years. Those living in or near these areas may well have perceived the chaos to be total and long-lasting, and, as refugees fled to other parts and monks travelled between monasteries, their stories may well have convinced the writers of the *Gesta*, the Anglo-Saxon Chronicle and other chronicles of the time of the truth of their claims.

Contributing to the idea that 'all hell's broke loose' would be the methods of warfare used at the time. The work of a late fourth century Roman writer usually referred to as Vegetius was seen as the classic text for such affairs. In *De Re Militari* – 'Concerning Military Matters' – he wrote of the type and training of a soldier, the organisation of an army and some basic tenets for carrying on a campaign, though these last have been dismissed by some as statements of the obvious. One such declares that a commander should only engage in battle when he has no choice or when he is certain of victory. A long campaign of ravaging an enemy's land was to be preferred, and this was a tactic widely used by all parties during Stephen's reign.

Such a policy not only weakened the enemy physically, but it was also demoralising and pointed up a lord's failure in his primary duty of protecting his own people. It might involve driving off all livestock, and not only taking stored provisions but burning crops in the fields, hayricks, houses and even churches. In the first assessment of the land for revenue due to the new king, Henry II, a large proportion is written off as 'waste', that is to say, the land was useless or derelict. Again, this is not evenly spread. In some counties such as Kent and Sussex it was as little as five per cent, while in others such as Leicestershire it was in excess of fifty per cent. Historians warn against reading too much into this, but a large allowance for restocking estates in some twenty-one counties can surely be taken as a measure of widespread losses.

As protection from such activity, castles were built. By this time many of the earlier examples were being rebuilt in stone, at least as far as the central keep was concerned, but the various chroniclers record large numbers of new castles – so-called 'adulterine castles', that were built without the king's permission. These would almost all have been of the more primitive motte and bailey type, with a wooden keep perched atop a large earth mound, and probably surrounded by an outer wooden palisade. It was to build this type of castle that Robert of Gloucester commandeered the local people, and many others did likewise. 'For every rich man built his castles,' says the Anglo-Saxon Chronicle, 'and they filled the land with castles.' Robert of Torigny at one point claims some 1,115 such castles were built, though in another place he modifies this number to 126. Many of these castles could be stormed and burnt down. Where they or their more durable predecessors could not, however, a siege was necessary, and a besieging army settled in one place for some time would need to be fed.

There were no organised supply trains in this age. Armies expected to live off the land wherever they went, and in many cases small groups of cavalry would be sent to take what they wanted from the surrounding district. Livestock and crops would be taken as of right, and the longer the siege lasted the wider was the area to suffer in this way. Even without a siege, a castle garrison would expect to be supported by the neighbourhood they 'protected', with greater or lesser damage done depending on whether the castle was in friendly or unfriendly territory. Both Brian fitz Count and Geoffrey de Mandeville justified taking what they needed from surrounding lands and from travellers on the basis that their own lands and rights had been taken from them by the king, and this was the only way left for them to support themselves and their adherents.

The result of all this, of course, was famine, as reported in the chronicles. The *Gesta*, for example, speaks of people who 'disgustingly devoured the flesh of dogs and horses', while others 'appeased their insatiable hunger with the garbage of uncooked herbs and roots'. So severe was this that towns and cities were depopulated, and later harvests left un-gathered, since all who could have gathered them had been 'struck down by the famine'.

While it was the poor who suffered the worst of the hunger, those even higher up the social scale were not immune and had themselves to suffer hardships and losses. For a lucky few there might be some protection for themselves and their goods in the castles. Others turned to the churches and monasteries in the hope of safety on holy ground. Even there, however, there was no security, not in the cathedral at Worcester sacked in 1139, nor in the many churches and churchyards around the country repeatedly plundered by armed men against whom there was no defence. The threat of excommunication, once a terrible and rare punishment, now became so common as to be, for the most part, ignored. 'The bishops and clergy were ever cursing them,' says the Anglo-Saxon Chronicle, 'but this to them was nothing, for they were all accursed and forsworn and reprobate.'

To a considerable extent the excesses of the time were put down to the numbers of mercenaries, particularly foreign mercenaries, who had been recruited by both sides to carry on the conflict between king and empress. William of Malmesbury refers to 'numbers of freebooters from Flanders and Brittany (who) flocked to England in expectation of rich pillage.' The *Gesta*, too, records 'a crowd of fierce strangers, who had flocked to England in bands to take service in the wars, and who were devoid of all bowels of mercy and feelings of humanity.' 'They enlist themselves,' says John of Worcester, 'They accept the terms, they array themselves in arms, and the conqueror seizes all that belongs to the vanquished.' Many of the castles would have been garrisoned by such as these and, says the *Gesta*, 'their sole business was to contrive the most villainous outrages ... to watch every opportunity of plundering the weak, to foment troubles and cause bloodshed in every direction.' Several of the chronicles declare that not the king, nor the empress, nor Robert of Gloucester acting on her behalf, was able to control the numbers of mercenaries they had enlisted. Says the *Gesta*, those who had hired them 'were neither able to discharge their pay out of their own revenues, nor to satisfy their insatiable thirst for plunder and remunerate them by pillage ... because there was nothing left anywhere whole and undamaged.' These men of war therefore took matters into their own hands.

Some, such as Robert fitz Hubert and Robert fitz Hildebrand, were bold enough to seize castles for themselves. Others resorted to kidnap, torture and extortion, attacking the possessions of monasteries, neighbouring towns and anywhere else that they could easily overcome with troops of armed men. Many of the chronicles describe gruesome tortures devised for the purpose of extracting money, the mildest of which seems to have been hanging the victim upside down by the feet over 'foul smoke'.

Malmesbury describes how they seized anyone reported to have money and 'compelled them by extreme torture' to pay whatever they demanded. 'Plundering the houses of the wretched husbandmen even to their beds, they cast them into prisons; nor did they liberate them but on their giving everything they possessed, or could by any means scrape together for their release.'

This was indeed lawlessness, and of its very nature hard to estimate how widespread or long-lasting it was. Perhaps some clue is given in the fact that one of the first consequences of the peace treaty between Stephen and Henry, as recorded by John of Hexham, was that an edict was issued 'for the suppression of outrages, the prohibition of spoliations (and) the dismissal from the kingdom of mercenary soldiers and archers of foreign nations'. It may well be, too, that Stephen's meeting with Thierry of Flanders immediately prior to his death was at least partly concerned with the repatriation of the notorious Flemish mercenaries.

It is clear, then, that for at least large parts of the country and for some period of time there existed what could well be described as 'anarchy'. Nor do we have to look far for further evidence of failure on the part of Stephen's 'government'. By the end of Henry's reign his exchequer was a smooth-running piece of administrative machinery, producing large sums of money for the king on an annual basis, as well as keeping a careful check on what was owing and what had been remitted. Within a few years, Stephen had run through all his uncle's treasure and from then on was continually hard pressed for money. A number of factors account for this. First would be his hiring of expensive mercenaries instead of using the English militia, who, apart from the London militias, were rarely called upon. Second, he developed a habit of giving away royal estates, and even the royal rights and privileges that accrued from the various shires. Several of his earls were thus enriched at the king's expense. A further point is that he lost control of the currency. Previously, kings had jealously guarded their right to issue coins, and only a certain number of mints were licensed to do so, paying well for the privilege. In Stephen's reign, however, we find coins issued in a wide number of places, some clearly by or on behalf of the king, though not always using the official dies, but others bearing the name of the empress or of a local earl, or even some non-specific name such as William. Malmesbury, indeed, accuses the king himself of tampering with the coinage by issuing silver pennies of less than the standard weight, and thus devaluing the very coins that bore his own name. Finally, it is clear that while in a few areas, particularly in the south-east, Stephen may have been able to gather in his taxes as usual, over a large part of the country and for a considerable number of years, this simply did not happen. In some parts similar taxes may have been collected on behalf of the empress, who herself was perennially short of money. In other areas they may not have been collected at all, or may have been replaced by the 'tenserie' exactions of whatever lord or band of mercenaries was dominant at the time.

Perhaps surprisingly, given the battering the church received at the highest levels and at the lowest, it seemed to come out of Stephen's reign fairly well. Certainly by 1154 Archbishop Theobald's authority had significantly improved from the time when he was subordinate to Henry of Winchester as the papal legate, and the two had clearly acted together for the good of church and country in negotiating the treaty that finally brought peace to the land. At ground level too there were many more churches and monasteries in England at the end of Stephen's reign than there had been at the start. One reason for this, of course, was that founding a church or monastery was a recognised form of penance for sins, and there were many during this time that needed to have their sins forgiven.

Stephen himself had been involved in spreading the Savignac monastic order to England, the founding monastery of that order being at Savigny, within his own county of Mortain. He founded Savignac monasteries at Furness in Lancashire, and at Buckfast in Devon, but his falling out with the church in the late 1140s was reflected in difficulties within the order itself, and in 1147 it became affiliated to the Cistercian order led by Bernard of Clairvaux, who was no friend to the English king. Thereafter Stephen cut his ties with the Savignacs, and it is notable that the 'family' abbey, founded at Faversham in 1148, was a Cluniac monastery, the order in which his brother Henry had been raised.

All chronicles agree that Stephen was a genuinely pious man, performing with great sincerity the rituals of the church. He was a good family man, too, faithful to his wife after marriage and caring towards his children. Unlike his uncle Henry, only one pre-marriage mistress is recorded, the mysterious Damette, or Little Lady, who bore him at least one and probably three sons. One of these, Gervase, became the abbot of Westminster soon after his father's accession to the throne, and certainly through his influence.

Stephen was a 'king of peace', says John of Worcester. He was 'a person of the greatest energy and boldness', says Robert of Torigny. 'Mild and compassionate to his enemies, and affable to all', says William of Malmesbury, while the *Gesta* talks of his 'kind and gentle demeanour' and adds, 'in him, what is rare in our times, wealth was joined with humility, munificence with courtesy.' How was it, then, that such a man became embroiled in a struggle that devastated a large part of his kingdom? Malmesbury gives a clue. 'This easy man,' he says, 'must pardon me for speaking the truth; who, had he entered on the sovereignty lawfully, and not given a ready ear to the insinuations of the malevolent ... would have wanted little in any princely quality.'

In good times, then, Stephen might have been lauded as a good king – but it was his own rash act that set in train all that followed. 'He was a man of activity, but imprudent,' says Malmesbury again, 'kind as far as promise went; but sure to disappoint in its truth and execution.' Nor was he wise in dealing with those who rebelled against him, for 'he always concluded matters more to his own disadvantage than to theirs.' A man, then, who did not foresee consequences, who promised more than he could fulfil; brave, but maybe lacking in intelligence, and not the greatest judge of his fellow man. He had lived at the court of the mighty Henry I. He had seen his pomp and how he was obeyed and even feared by those around him. Perhaps the young Stephen had thought that these things came automatically with the crown. He soon discovered that they did not. Even at the time of his election there may have been some reservations about the ability of the new king. The *Gesta* in particular emphasises that the vigour of Stephen would be supported by 'the power of his adherents and the wisdom of his brothers' and that therefore, 'whatever was wanting in himself would be fully supplied by their aid.' Malmesbury, too, attributes his troubles to the fact that he 'soon afterwards neglected the advice of his brother ... by whose assistance he had ... obtained the kingdom.'

There is a concept in business management known as the 'Peter Principle', which states that, in a hierarchy, people will rise to the level of their incompetence. What thsi suggests is that a person showing ability gets promoted until he reaches a level where his abilities are no longer adequate, and he will not then be promoted any further. King Henry had seen Stephen's abilities and promoted him to the appropriate level as Count of Boulogne. In effect, though,

Stephen had promoted himself again, and he soon discovered that the skills needed to be a good king were greatly in advance of those needed to govern a relatively small and peaceful county. He was soon floundering with no effective policy of his own, and listening to all the wrong people in trying to cope with a situation he himself had created.

He was seen as a fine military leader – the *Gesta* describes him as 'bold and valiant, cautious and persevering' – but he lost every battle he was engaged in, the only notable triumph of the reign being the Battle of the Standard, led by others with the king far away. Nor, with some notable exceptions, did he persevere with sieges, often rushing from one to another, or abandoning them due to lack of resources. His attempt to create earls as regional governors impoverished himself and was largely a failure, but at least he abandoned it later, perhaps by force of circumstances. It is notable that in the latter part of his reign, those household officials upon whom he chiefly relied were given none of the honours so lavishly scattered in earlier years.

According to Malmesbury, many of the bad policies adopted in Stephen's reign, especially those relating to the church, 'are not so much to be ascribed to him as to his advisors'. A shame then, that in the early years at least, he chose his advisors so poorly. Waleran de Meulan in particular had never been the steadiest of characters, and his record of choosing the wrong side in any dispute would lead to his losing almost all of his lands and power in Normandy before his death in 1165.

Two other possible advisors, both of them close to Stephen, would have been a far better choice for a king with apparently few ideas of his own. Bishop Henry has been much derided, not only as a churchman more interested in wealth than religion, but as a man who turned his coat so many times it was hard to establish just who, other than himself, he was really supporting. Brian Fitz Count at one point declared sarcastically that the bishop had a great gift for discovering that duty lay in the same direction as expediency. If we take a more charitable view of his actions, however, we can find some consistency in his approach to the problems of the kingdom. He must take a good deal of responsibility for obtaining the kingdom for Stephen in the first place, but thereafter seems to have made at least some attempt to work for a peaceable settlement between the two sides. He was apparently in touch with the Angevins from the start, and may have attempted negotiations as early as 1139, meeting Robert of Gloucester soon after his arrival in England. Thereafter, on several occasions, peace talks were established, while Bishop Henry's support for Matilda in 1141 may have been intended to bring peace by accepting the supposed dominance of her party. Only when that dominance proved illusory did he revert to what might be seen as his 'default' support for his brother. He does at least seem to have had a wider vision and more statesmanlike approach than Stephen, and certainly accepted long before the king the necessity of coming to a compromise with Duke Henry.

There is another, though, even closer to the king, whose contribution is rarely acknowledged. Matilda of Boulogne seems by far the more capable of the two marriage partners, co-ruler of the County of Boulogne and behind most of the more decisive actions of Stephen's reign. She took and held Dover Castle for the king in 1138, negotiated the treaty of Durham with David of Scotland in 1139, arranged the marriage of Eustace to the French king's sister, and rallied Stephen's supporters and arranged for his release after his disastrous captivity at Lincoln in 1140. Nor did she dissipate her landholdings as the king did, handing over to Eustace the Honour of Boulogne intact on her death in 1152. We don't know how much Stephen consulted his wife or relied on her advice, but it has been rightly pointed out that her level-headed and determined actions during the time he was held captive in Bristol were the means of saving the kingdom for her husband. Her death certainly deprived the king not only of a much-loved wife but also a most capable and steadfast partner. However, had she lived, it is difficult to imagine her accepting the deposition of her son in favour of Duke Henry.

If we accept, therefore, that Stephen was a king with definite limitations and often poorly advised, can we say that the alternative would have been any better? 'Great by birth, greater by marriage, greatest in her offspring' was the inscription on the Empress Matilda's tomb, and while we can agree that the latter is certainly true, it is almost impossible to say whether or not she would have made a great Queen of England. The odds were stacked against her from the moment of her father's death, if not before. She was a woman and no female had ever ruled in England. She was in the wrong place with the wrong husband and little substantial backing in a land to which she was a virtual stranger from the age of eight onwards. Once Stephen made his move, her chances of regaining the crown shrank almost to nothing – and yet she almost made it!

Had she faced a less intelligent and committed opponent than Stephen's queen in 1140, she could very well have found herself in the position her father had intended for her. It could have been his teaching, too, that led to accusations of arrogance and wilfulness – suitable for a king, maybe, but less acceptable in a potential queen facing misogynist prejudices. Even those who opposed her, though, showed grudging admiration for her courage and resourcefulness when she later had repeatedly to escape from hopeless situations in order to continue to assert her own claims and the entitlement of her son to the crown. Those who chose to serve her, served faithfully through all the difficult years, so there again it is hard to see in her the cold aloofness claimed by others, or to reconcile it with the 'Good Queen Matilda' acclaimed by the Germans during her time as Empress in Germany.

It is an interesting point that the stumbling block for many in England in 1135 was her husband, Geoffrey of Anjou. Yet, once he had overcome his youthful excesses in attacking Normandy in the late 1130s, once he had been offered a genuine chance to take over the duchy, he did so slowly and cautiously, and then ruled it well. Furthermore, it is clear he saw himself as acting on behalf of his wife and son in doing so, and he handed over to Henry as soon as the boy was capable of ruling for himself. It is tempting to think that had the English accepted him in 1135, he might have been an equally effective steward in England and spared the country all the destruction of Stephen's nineteen long years.

As it was, the result was the same in the end, with the crown that was taken from the daughter of Henry I restored to his grandson. As for Matilda herself, she had the last laugh, outliving her rivals and remaining contentedly in palatial quarters attached to the priory of Notre Dame du Pré, while her son ruled unopposed in England, Normandy, Anjou and Aquitaine. Although in theory retired from any active role in government, she is known to have acted on behalf of her son during his absences from Normandy, and she remained well in touch with events in the outside world. Early in Henry II's reign, in particular, she was always there to give advice. Some of this he accepted – not to invade Ireland on behalf of his brother William for example – and some he did not. It is known that later she advised him not to appoint Thomas Beckett as Archbishop of Canterbury and he rejected that advice with unhappy results.

She died on 10 September 1167 and was buried before the high altar at the abbey of Bec. Her epitaph, quoted above, concludes: 'Here lies the daughter, wife and mother of Henry.' She may never have had the crown of England on her own head, but it was her legacy, rather than Stephen's, that would shape the destiny of England for all the centuries to come.

A Note on Sources

We have many excellent contemporary and near contemporary sources for the time of the Anarchy. In particular we can get some kind of balance of opinions from two sources, the *Gesta Stephani*, which for most of its length is strongly biased towards Stephen, and the chronicle of William of Malmesbury, equally biased towards Matilda, and especially her champion, Robert of Gloucester, to whom he dedicated the work. With views from around the country and beyond, we have a variety of witness statements. While, as witnesses do, they often contradict each other, they give us a good picture of how events were seen by those living at the time. The following are the main sources referred to in this book.

Anglo-Saxon Chronicle
Written in the English language, by the time of the Anarchy this long-running account of English history was being continued by a monk at Peterborough Abbey. It gives fewer day-to-day details than the other chronicles, but its brutal assessment of the nineteen long years when 'Christ and his saints slept' is a clear-eyed overview of the feelings of most ordinary people at the time.

Gesta Stephani
Written anonymously, very close in time to the events it covers, this 'Deeds of King Stephen' aimed to give a full account of the king's reign. As such it reflects the stories current at the time, in particular

accepting the claim that Stephen came to rescue England from chaos after the death of Henry I. There has been much speculation about the author. A west-country bias has been detected, though details of other places make it clear the writer travelled around at least the southern part of England. The name of Robert of Lewes has been put forward as a likely candidate. This protégé of Henry of Blois became Bishop of Bath in 1136, and the author certainly knows a great deal about the area around Bath and that bishop's involvement in the events of the time. It has been suggested that after 1147 a different writer may have taken over, since there is a fairly dramatic change of view, from fully supporting King Stephen to calling Henry Plantagenet the 'right heir' to the kingdom. It may simply be that this part was written later, when it was clear Henry would succeed to the throne, and therefore reflects that change of circumstance.

Chronicle of the Kings of England – William of Malmesbury

Born around 1095, William had a Norman father and an English mother and spent his adult life as a monk at Malmesbury Abbey in his native Wiltshire. He was a great scholar and lover of books, with an extensive library, and he aimed to follow Bede in writing objective, factual history. At Malmesbury he would have been in the thick of the action in southern England and he clearly favours Matilda and her cause throughout. Allowing for that bias, however, he gives a fully detailed description of the events and personalities of the time. In several places he corrects himself and adds details he has learnt later, declaring that he does not want to commit to posterity anything he has not been able to check for himself. He is, indeed, an eye witness to some of the events he relates, and in other cases would have received the details direct from other eye witnesses. Fully determined that Matilda was in the right, his death, probably in 1143, deprived him of the vindication of seeing her son crowned as king.

The Acts of King Stephen and the Battle of the Standard – Richard of Hexham

Richard of Hexham was a canon at Hexham Priory in Yorkshire, and in 1141 was elected prior. His detailed account of the early years of Stephen's reign is not only contemporary but written by one living in the midst of the action in northern England. He gives much local detail concerning the multiple invasions from Scotland and the Battle of the Standard, but he is also the only chronicler to include the full text of the letter of Pope Innocent confirming Stephen as King of England.

The History of the Church of Hexham – John of Hexham

John of Hexham was a local man who became the prior of Hexham following the death of Richard. His chronicle is a continuation of the chronicle of Simeon of Durham, and whereas Richard of Hexham's work stops at 1139, John's continues to 1153, encompassing all the years of the Anarchy and the peace settlement of that year. While a slightly later work and unreliable as to dates, the chronicle gives useful local insight into matters that were within living memory when he wrote, in particular the disputed elections of the Archbishop of York and the Bishop of Durham.

An Account of the Battle of the Standard – Ailred of Rievaulx

Ailred was born at Hexham in 1110, and spent some years at the court of King David of Scotland before becoming a monk at Rievaulx Abbey in Yorkshire in 1134. In 1147 he became the abbot of Rievaulx. His account of the Battle of the Standard was probably written around 1153, but the author would have had close local knowledge of the conflict, and almost certainly contact with some who were present.

History of the English – Henry of Huntingdon

Henry of Huntingdon was born around 1088. His father was an archdeacon in the Diocese of Lincoln and Henry grew up in the household of Bishop Robert Bloet, succeeding his father as archdeacon in 1110. Henry's *History of the English* was requested by Bishop Alexander of Lincoln, the son of Roger of Salisbury, and covering the period from before the Romans to 1154, detailed events right up to the time of writing. Henry is especially outraged, therefore, by the arrest of the bishops, and claimed it was the cause of the fall of the House of Stephen. His disillusionment with the world becomes increasingly apparent towards the end, but he welcomes Henry Plantagenet as a saviour of England and promises to write about his reign. Presumably only his death prevented him from doing so.

Chronicle of John of Worcester

John was a monk of Worcester Priory who was asked by Bishop Wulfstan of Worcester to copy and extend the *Chronicle of Chronicles* begun by an Irish monk, Marianus Scotus. John added a great deal, particularly about events within his own lifetime, and gives a detailed eyewitness account of the sack of Worcester in 1139. His chronicle ends in 1140 and it is thought he must have died soon after.

The History of William of Newburgh

William was born at Bridlington, Yorkshire, around 1135, and became an Augustinian canon at Newburgh Priory. He was asked by the abbot of Rievaulx to write a history of England, and declared that he did so in order to overturn the lies and inventions of Geoffrey of Monmouth whose work was fashionable at the time. Though written some time later than the other chronicles, it covers the period from 1066 to 1197, aiming at a serious and precise narrative showing causes and effects of actions.

Ecclesiastical History of England and Normandy – Orderic Vitalis

Orderic was born of a Norman father and an English mother in 1075, and at the age of five was sent to Shrewsbury Abbey School. Six years later he was sent away to the Abbey of Saint Evroult in Normandy, where he spent the rest of his life. It was in Normandy that he acquired the name Vitalis as they claimed they could not manage his English name. His *Ecclesiastical History* has a rather eccentric approach to chronology, but the later books, written between 1133 and 1141, reflect the events he himself lived through in a monastery in the middle of Normandy during the troubles of the late eleventh and early twelfth century. He acknowledges his debt to other writers, but much of what he writes is original, containing stories (and speeches) not found elsewhere.

Chronicles of Robert de Monte – Robert of Torigny

Robert was born at Torigni in Normandy, probably of a noble family, and entered the monastery at Bec when he was in his teens. He rose to become the prior of Bec and later Abbot of Mont-St-Michel – hence he is known as both Robert of Torigni and Robert de Monte. In his time Mont-St-Michel became a centre of learning, while Robert himself was both a pious monk and a diplomat. His chronicle copied and added to earlier material. He incorporated much of Henry of Huntingdon's chronicle, having been visited by Henry at Bec, but like Orderic Vitalis, he himself witnessed much of the turmoil in Normandy at the time of Stephen and Matilda, and in particular the takeover of the duchy by Geoffrey of Anjou.

Life of King Louis the Fat – Abbot Suger

Suger was given to the monastery of St Denis as a child oblate around 1090. He first met Louis VI of France when he was young, and then became closely involved with the king and his court, as both a friend and a counsellor. This closeness continued into the reign of Louis VII, and his work contains, incidentally, much that is relevant to the story of the rulers of Normandy and England.

Bibliography

Primary Printed Sources

An Account of the Battle of the Standard, Ailred of Rievaulx, in Alan O. Anderson (ed.) *Scottish Annals from English Chroniclers AD 500 to 1286* (London: David Nutt, 1908)

Acts of King Stephen and the Battle of the Standard, Richard of Hexham, trans. Rev. Joseph Stevenson (London: Seeleys, 1856)

Anglo-Saxon Chronicle, ed. and trans. J.A. Giles (London: G. Bell & Sons, 1914)

Chronicle of Henry of Huntingdon, ed. and trans. Thomas Forester (London: Henry G. Bohn, 1853)

Chronicle of John of Worcester, trans. Thomas Forester (London: Henry G. Bohn, 1854)

Chronicle of the Kings of England, William of Malmesbury, ed. and trans. J.A. Giles (London: Henry G. Bohn, 1847)

Chronicles of Robert de Monte, trans. Rev. Joseph Stevenson (London: Seeleys, 1856)

Ecclesiastical History of England and Normandy, Vols. 3 and 4, Orderic Vitalis, ed. and trans. Thomas Forester (London: Henry G. Bohn, 1854 and 1856)

Gesta Stephani, The Acts of King Stephen, ed. and trans. Thomas Forester (London: Henry G. Bohn, 1853)

History of the Archbishops of Canterbury, Gervase of Canterbury, trans. Rev. Joseph Stevenson (London: Seeleys, 1858)

History of the Church of Hexham, John of Hexham, trans. Rev. Joseph Stevenson (London: Seeleys, 1856)

History of William of Newburgh, trans. Rev. Joseph Stevenson (London: Seeleys, 1856)

Journey Through Wales, Gerald of Wales, trans. L. Thorpe (Harmondsworth: Penguin Books, 1978)

Life of King Louis the Fat, Suger, trans. Jean Dunbabin (Internet Medieval Sourcebook)

Secondary Sources

Ackroyd, Peter, *London, the Biography* (London: Chatto & Windus, 2000)

Appleby, John T., *The Troubled Reign of King Steven 1135–1154* (London: Bell, 1969)

Ashley, M., *Mammoth Book of British Kings and Queens,* (London: Robinson Publishing, 1999)

Barlow, F., *Feudal Kingdom of England 1042–1216* (London: Longman, 1972)

Bradbury, Jim, *Stephen and Matilda, The Civil War of 1139–53* (Stroud: Sutton Publishing, 2005)

Carpenter, David, *The Struggle for Mastery* (London: Penguin, 2004)

Castor, Helen, *She-Wolves, The Women Who Ruled England Before Elizabeth* (London: Faber & Faber, 2010)

Chibnall, Marjorie, *The Empress Matilda, Queen Consort, Queen Mother and Lady of the English* (Oxford: Blackwell, 1992)

Cronne, Henry Alfred, *The Reign of King Stephen 1135–54: Anarchy in England* (London: Weidenfeld & Nicholson, 1970)

Crouch, David, *The Normans, History of a Dynasty* (London: Hambledon & London, 2002)

Crouch, David, *The Reign of King Stephen 1135–1154* (Harlow: Pearson Educational, 2000)

Davis, H.W.C., *England Under the Normans and Angevins* (London: Methuen, 1921)

Davis, R.H.C., *History of Medieval Europe, From Constantine to Saint Louis,* ed. R.I. Moore (Harlow: Pearson Education, 2006)

Davis, R.H.C., *King Stephen* (London: Longmans, 1967)

Given-Wilson, C. and Curteis, A., *Royal Bastards of Medieval England* (London: Routledge & Keegan Paul, 1984)

Hollister, C. Warren, *Henry I* (New Haven and London: Yale University Press, 2003)

King, Edmund, *King Stephen* (Newhaven and London: Yale University Press 2010)

Poole, A.L., *Domesday Book to Magna Carta, 1087–1216* (Oxford: Oxford University Press, 1955)

Round, J.H., *Geoffrey de Mandeville; A Study of the Anarchy* (London: Longmans, Green & Co., 1892)

Soar, Hugh, *The Crooked Stick, A History of the Longbow* (Yardley: Westholme, 2004)

Index